GANDHI AS WE HAVE KNOWN HIM

GANDHI
AS WE HAVE KNOWN HIM

by

Lavanam Gora and Mark Lindley

assisted by

Vijayam Gora

with a preface by

C. N. Patel

NATIONAL GANDHI MUSEUM
RAJGHAT, NEW DELHI - 110002

In Association with:

GYAN PUBLISHING HOUSE
NEW DELHI - 110002

GANDHI as we have known him

First Edition : 2007

ISBN : 81-212-0863-7

Price : Rs. 690 (Hard bound)
Rs. 150 (Paper back)

Published by:
National Gandhi Museum
Rajghat, New Delhi-110002
Phones: 23311793, 23310168, 23328310
Fax: 91-011-23311793
E-mail: gandhimk@nda.vsnl.net.in
Web-site: www.gandhimuseum.org

In association with:
Gyan Publishing House
Publishers-Exporters
5, Ansari Road, Daryaganj,
New Delhi-110002
Phones: 23261060, 23282060
Fax: 91-011-23282060
Email: gyanbook@vsnl.com
Web-site: http://www.gyanbooks.com

Laser Type Setting by:
Tact Computer Graphics, Delhi

Printed at:
Salasar Imaging System, Delhi

CONTENTS

PREFACE

Gandhi Seen Through Secular Humanists' Eyes

This refreshingly, or startlingly (according to one's point of view) original study of Gandhi's views on several of the many topics on which he expressed himself can be read with profit by both Gandhiphiles and Gandhiphobes, as it is likely to correct the biases of the former and the prejudices of the latter.

In regard to some inconsistencies such as those with which the authors seem to me to have charged Gandhi, the Mahatma explained, in 1933:

> "...I would say to this diligent reader [a correspondent who had charged him with inconsistency on the question of varnadharma] of my writings and to others who are interested in them that I am not at all concerned with appearing to be consistent. In my search after Truth I have discarded many ideas and learnt many new things. Old as I am in age, I have no feeling that I have ceased to grow inwardly or that my growth will stop at the dissolution of the flesh. What I am concerned with is my readiness to obey the call of Truth, my God, from moment to moment, and, therefore, when anybody finds any inconsistency between any two writings of mine, if he has still faith in my sanity [note the utter humility implied in this qualification], he would do well to choose the later of the two on the same subject." [*Collected Works of Mahatma Gandhi*, LV, 61]

The dictum in this last sentence may properly be applied, I believe, to his remarks on every subject. If so, then even the most advanced progressive should not ask for anything more.

C. N. Patel

4 Neelkanth Park, Navrangpura
Ahmedabad - 380009 (India)

March 16, 1998

ACKNOWLEDGEMENTS

We were very generously helped by Prof. Patel, who was a great scholar and served as Deputy Chief Editor of the *Collected Works of Mahatma Gandhi*; by Dr. Hari Dev Sharma, Director of the Nehru Memorial Museum and Library; by Dr. Y. P. Anand, Director of the Gandhi National Museum; by Sri K. K. Bhavsar, Acting Chief Librarian at Gujarat Vidyapith; by Professors Raman Modi, S. K. De and Ranjit Chaudhuri of the Institute of Gandhian Studies (Gopuri), and Sri Ravindra Varma, the Director of that institute and Chairman of the Gandhi Peace Foundation; by Dr. B. N. Pande and Dr. N. Radhakrishnan, Chairman and Executive Director (respectively) of the Gandhi Darshan Samiti; by Dr. Jacob Pulickan, Coördinator of the Centre for Gandhian Studies at the University of Kerala; and by Rukun Advani, R. K. Lee, and Azra Razzack. None of them should have to answer for our treatment of the material, however.

We are grateful for the vital material support given to this project by the Harvard University Humanist Chaplaincy, the Humanist Association of Massachusetts, Dr. Joseph Gerstein and Prof. Lisa Kuhmerker.

CHAPTER 1

INTRODUCTION

This is a work of loving reminiscence and analysis. Some personal reminiscences of Gandhi are recounted in Chapter 2. For the analysis in Chapters 3-6 of how he changed in certain ways over the years, we will cite excerpts from his writings and from his talks of which transcriptions are available.[1] Those chapters have two purposes: to show (in Chapter 3) how Gandhi's basic outlook seems to have changed throughout his life and especially during the last part of it (long after he had won the title *mahatma*, meaning "great soul"), and to trace in detail (in Chapters 4-6) some changes in his attitudes toward religion and caste which one of the authors may be uniquely well qualified to describe because of the direct observations made by him and by some of his family members who were likewise particularly alert to those changes at the time.

The main changes traced in Chapters 4-6 were from praising the alleged beauty of the caste system ("difficult to imagine a better harmonious human adjustment") and advocating prohibition against intermarriage ("essential to a rapid evolution of the soul") to yearning for the day when there would be only one caste and Brahmins would marry Harijans, and from "Truth is

1. Each excerpt is extracted to illustrate something efficiently and hence without showing more than necessary of the original context. We have thus inevitably misrepresented Gandhi's rhetoric, but have of course avoided, to the best of our ability, any substantial distortions of the content. Modern American spellings are used (such as "Moslem" instead of "Musselman" and "Ganges" instead of "Ganga").

God" to "In the name of God we have indulged in lies [and] massacres. I am not aware if anybody has done these things in the name of Truth. With the same name on my lips I have broken the fast."

No one cherishes Gandhi more than we; but we abjure the idolatry that he himself often disparaged:[2]

[1] *1920*: "I think it very dangerous, in this age, for anyone to accept another as a guru or be another's guru." (*C*, XIX, 180)

[2] *1928*: "If you feel at any time that my conclusions are based on inadequate data or incorrect reasoning, draw my attention to the fact.... Faith has no place in a matter which can be grasped by reason." (*C*, XXXVIII, 217)

[3] *1937*: "There is another and graver risk:... [that] whenever there is any difficulty you will turn to my writings... and swear by them." (*C*, LXV, 89)

[4] *1940*: "Let Gandhism be destroyed if it stands for error. ...You are no followers, but fellow students, fellow pilgrims, fellow seekers, fellow workers."[3] (*H*, 2/iii, 23)

[5] *1946*: "I ask nobody to follow me. Everyone should follow his or her own inner voice. If he or she has no ears to listen to it, he or she should do the best he or she can... [and] in no case imitate others sheeplike."[4] (*C*, LXXXVIII, 160)

2. For some other pertinent passages, see *C*, XXIV, 232 (praising an opponent who refused to call him "Mahatma"); *C*, XXXIII, 246; and *C*, LXIX, 401.

3. The absence of "fellow travelers" is significant.

4. See also *C*, LV, 61; *H*, 28/iii/1936, 49; and *C*, LXX, 203.

He often said his ideas were liable to change (although he was often slow to change them):[5]

[6] *1927*: "I am a humble but very earnest seeker after truth. And in my search I take all fellow seekers in uttermost confidence so that I may know my mistakes and correct them. I confess that I have often erred in my estimates and judgements." (*C*, XXXIII, 246)

[7] *1928*: "We would be utterly lost if we tried to... show that there was no contradiction in our lives.... In trying to preserve such forced harmony, we would have to resort to untruth." (*C*, XXXVII, 264)

[8] *1945*: "We ...seekers after truth... change whenever we find ourselves in the wrong. I changed like that many times in my life." (*G*, 44)

In assessing the teachings of the greatest religious figures of history — among whom he could reasonably expect himself to be counted — he distinguished between teachings of permanent value and those dependent on circumstance:

[9] *1934*: "In the teachings of each prophet like Mohammed, Buddha or Jesus, there was a permanent portion and there was another which was suited to the needs and requirements of the times. It is only because we try to keep up the... impermanent aspects of their teachings that there

5. Romain Rolland remarked in 1931: "He was very slow to change. He is a patient man, tenacious in his ideas; when he believes they are right, he needs repeated and decisive experiments before he will give them up." (*R*, 535)

is so much distortion in religious practice today." (*C*, LIX, 319f)

His greatness was due to his striving constantly to improve his ideas, as well as to his self-discipline, moral depth, and masterful use of language and symbolic action.

Because of these latter qualities, he is an uncomfortable figure and it can be difficult to examine his ideas dispassionately. Yet some of them are so valuable that humanity has much to gain by adapting them to current conditions. Some great political leaders of the last fifty years have done this — people like Willy Brandt, Martin Luther King, Jimmy Carter in his diplomatic work as ex-president, Julius Nyerere, Oscar Arias Sanchez, Nelson Mandela and Aung San Suu Kyi. While other books may seek to explain the secrets of Gandhi's political method, ours will show something of what they were *not*, by showing how in his last years he reconsidered certain cherished beliefs — some of which had even helped him develop his great invention of non-violent *satyagraha* — because he had meanwhile seen them become destructive of his deepest longings.

The appendix gives some background information about his life so that the chapters needn't explain too many biographical details. The glossary on pages 294-95 explains briefly a few indispensable terms that may be new to some of our readers.

CHAPTER 2

REMINISCENCES

(TOLD BY LAVANAM)

Foreigners may not realize how high Gandhi's status has remained in India — much higher than that of George Washington or Abraham Lincoln in the USA. Many Indians still feel the way General MacArthur did when he attributed to Gandhi a vital role "in the [future] evolution of civilization, if it is to survive,"[6] or Albert Einstein when he said that "generations to come" might "scarce believe that such a man ever in flesh and blood walked on this earth,"[7] or Nehru when he said, "The light has gone out of our lives... and yet... a thousand years later that light will still be seen."[8] So it is only natural for those of us who knew Gandhi personally to write down our recollections of him.

From the hour of my birth I was linked to Gandhi, in a curious way. I was born in 1930, the year when he initiated, as part of India's national liberation movement, the civil-disobedience campaign against the British salt-tax. With 78 carefully chosen companions he marched nearly 250 miles to the sea, picked up a handful of natural salt from the shore, and thereby called upon all Indians to use salt obtained without paying the tax imposed by colonial law. My father, who was a college biology teacher, had been active in the national libera-

6. Fischer 1950, 11.

7. Einstein 1944.

8. *H*, 15/ii/1948, 37.

tion movement ever since Gandhi in 1920 had called upon the people of India to boycott British goods and the colonial educational and judicial systems; in the mid-1920s he had become a thorough-going Gandhian; and now, in his excitement for the first really nationwide civil-disobedience movement, he gave me a radically new name: "Salt," or rather, in Sanskrit, "Lavanam."[9] No last name, just the one word.

Back in 1921, my grandfather, who was a colonial government official and secretary of the local government employees' association, had donated two bags of rice to the independence movement by giving them to Gandhi at a public meeting in Kakinada. The next day he was suspended from his job. He was a deeply religious man, so he immediately took to meditating and composing devotional songs. This was soon interrupted when some local leaders of the Indian National Congress (which under Gandhi was leading the anti-colonial movement) came to his house and urged him to join. He said he would consider it, and this was enough to frighten his boss into inviting him to return to work, which he did.

When Gandhi next visited our district, which was in December 1933, he auctioned off a hand-woven garment that someone had donated for the purpose. It was a splendid piece of cloth, with a festive Sanskrit verse from the *Ramayana* embroidered around the border. Gandhi had already put it up for auction somewhere else, but it had not fetched as high a bid as

---

9. This rhymes with "rob a Tom."

he was hoping for; so this time he said the bidding must start at 50 rupees. Someone obligingly cried out "50!", and my grandfather, impulsively, "116!", which was, because of a popular superstition, a traditional amount for a rich man's charitable donation, but was a lot more than he could really afford. There were some rich men in the crowd, from whom Gandhi had every right to expect a higher bid, but they all sat in silence. Gandhi asked them why and they explained that no one wished to outbid such a deeply religious and honest fellow as my grandfather. So, he had to pay, and the cloth became our family heirloom.

At that same meeting, my aunt impulsively donated her ring to be auctioned off somewhere else. My mother recalls her own joy at seeing Gandhi's devotion to national independence and the eradication of untouchability.

I should mention that apart from Gandhi, there was another, very different reason why my parents gave me an unorthodox name. In 1928 they had declared themselves atheists,[10] and now they were determined to resist family pressures to name me after one of my grandfathers, because *their* names were evocations of Hindu gods. So my name was implicitly associated with atheism as well as with Gandhi.

---

10. My grandfather was distressed by this and banished Gora from his home. But in the fullness of time they were reconciled, and around 1940 my grandfather even told him, "You are an atheist, you have gone too far; but stick to your principles: if you back down now, you are not my son!"

A few months before I was born, my father had sent Gandhi a succinct and perhaps rather too articulate letter: "You use the word *god*. May I know its meaning and how far the meaning is consistent with the practice of life?"; and Gandhi had sent a very brief reply: "God is beyond human comprehension."[11] That was how their acquaintance began.

When I was five years old and went to school, my classmates made great fun of my name on the first day. I suffered like Falstaff as they pinched and licked me and shouted with glee, "You're not really so salty!" (In my frustration I slapped one of my classmates. She later became a good friend; she was the daughter of a magistrate and had the unique privilege of coming to school in a bullock-cart instead of by foot.) That night at home I asked my father to give me an ordinary name, and he explained about the one I had. The next day I proudly explained all about it at school, and became a celebrity.

After that I always listened with rapt attention when Gandhi was the topic of conversation — which was quite often — and, as soon as I learned to read, would devour everything about him in the newspapers, no matter how little I understood of it.

In 1936 and '39 my father visited Gandhi's experimental commune or "ashram" at Segaon and was struck by the simplicity of his way of life there, which could readily be seen even by a visitor who did not meet Gandhi personally.[12]

11. *G*, 26.

12. The G. Ramachandra Rao referred to in *C*, LII-LIV is Guduru R. Rao, not Gora (whose Hindu name was Goparaju R. Rao).

In 1939 the principal of my father's college dismissed him because he was an atheist. The board of trustees reinstated him, and he accepted this in good grace; but a year later he decided to leave and establish an atheist social-work center in a remote village, Mudunúr (this rhymes with "to be sure"), where he had given one of his talks and the local people had invited him to live. My mother went along whole-heartedly with this decision; she saw in it the challenge of emulating Gandhi's example when he had, already in South Africa, embraced non-possession in order to serve moral truth and humanity.

My parents let me choose now whether to go on attending school (I was ten years old), and I decided not to, since Gandhi had called for his followers to boycott the British educational system and since academia seemed to have become such an uncomfortable place for my father.

Our way of life at Mudunúr was based in many ways on the model of Gandhi's ashram. We cultivated simplicity, hygiene, girls' and women's education, integration of "untouchables," political activism, and general consciousness-raising. Perhaps the main differences were that we had no prayer meetings, nor any requirement of chastity among the married adults, and our consciousness-raising was science-oriented. There was also another difference of nuance, however. Gandhi's central theme in India in the early 1940s was, perforce, national independence[13] (somewhat as his chief aim in South Africa had been to fight against the color bar against Indians), so he was to some extent obliged to treat social reform as a secondary theme even though he was personally very concerned about many of the humiliations endured by the "untouchables." But for us it was the other way around: more of our time was given to social work than to politics. And as it happened, our social policies were well in advance of Gandhi's, since he was still upholding the main lineaments, such as *varnashrama* and inherited vocation, of the caste system. (See Chapter 4.)

Because of this, I am fond of saying that while Gora's character would certainly have been incomplete without Gandhi's influence, Gandhi's career was in fact incomplete because he was assassinated shortly after national independence was achieved and at a time when the fruits of Gora's growing influence on him years had only begun to ripen.

This aspect of Gandhi's unceasing growth in his last years — which is the theme of this book — began as follows.

Dasu Ramaswamy was an "untouchable" who had managed to attend Madras University where he graduated in 1941 with high honors in chemistry. Already for some years he had known of Gora's social work, and now when Gora began to devote himself entirely to it, Ramaswamy would make himself useful whenever Gora had occasion to visit Madras. They became dear friends. Upon graduating from university, Rama-

13. For an extreme instance, see Reading 64 (on page 70).

swamy had to decide whether to pursue graduate studies or else live and work with Gandhi or Gora or Ambedkar, the political leader of the "untouchables." At Gora's suggestion he decided to visit Gandhi, who persuaded him to stay in his ashram. (The name of the village had now been changed from "Segaon" to "Sevagram," which means "service village.") Before very long, however, Ramaswamy had occasion to tell Gandhi that he would rather work with Gora after all, because *he* was serving the "untouchables" better.[14] Gandhi was surprised to hear this — and because of his devotion to truth, asked Ramaswamy to keep him well informed about Gora's work. This encouraged Gora to write again to Gandhi; and in due time (after their respective internments by the British during the war), some further conversations with Ramaswamy led Gandhi to invite Gora to visit Sevagram. Of course our whole family was thrilled.

It was my father's habit, when he attended a meeting or went walking from village to village, to take along one of his children. Up to now he had usually taken me, but this time he chose my younger sister, who had recently turned 12 and was showing interest in his social work. She had long had a great affection for Gandhi — partly for a reason like my own: she was born at the time of the 1931 Gandhi-Irwin Pact and so was named, hopefully, "Mythri," meaning "Friendship." My

14. Ramaswamy reported this to Gora and later confirmed it to me. I often asked Ramaswamy to write an account of his conversations with Gandhi, but it was never a pressing concern to him. He died in 1992.

parents had of course told her about Gandhi's championing of peace and non-violence, and she liked this because she thought quarrels were stupid. She was also devoted to Gandhi as the leader of the freedom struggle, in which she had participated indirectly by helping Ramaswamy and me care for the next three younger children (Vidya, Vijayam and Samaram) for six months when my parents and my elder sister, Manorama, had been sent to jail for marching in the road with a big Indian National Congress flag. So of course Mythri was glad to go with my father and see Gandhi.

In those days the railway went only as far as Wardha. Gora and Mythri walked the five miles to Sevagram, carrying their luggage. The next day Gandhi arranged to meet them during his evening walk and, after greeting them, asked them how they had come from Wardha. Then, after expressing his appreciation of their having walked — he was himself a great walker and a great champion of self-sufficiency — he asked my sister her name. She told him; Gora explained why she had it; and Gandhi beamed with pleasure and said, "Oh, Mythri, since you have that name, come here to me!" (But she was shy and stayed by her father.)

Everyone at the ashram — rich, poor, intellectuals, the lot — had to do some physical "bread labor" each day.[15] Gora's and Mythri's early-morning labor during this visit was to help take care of the latrines. A team of designated workers would get

15. See the fourth paragraph (on page 125) of Reading 140.

up before dawn to do this. There were some ten out-houses, of bamboo lattice-work, each with buckets inside for urine and "night soil."[16] The task was to carry the buckets to the fields, empty them in a trench (there were no septic tanks), cover the material with a layer of earth, wash the buckets and put them back. (When we all came on the next visit, the whole team consisted of men and women from Mudunúr. My uncle told me he was glad to do this work; it taught him the dignity of labor and a sense of respect for "scavengers.")

Mythri was struck by the ways in which daily life at Gandhi's compound resembled that at Mudunúr. The compound was neat, people did their work punctually, and all the adults were supportive of all the children, girls as well as boys and with no regard for caste.

Gora had an interview with Gandhi the day after arriving, and another three days later. For that second visit he took Mythri along and instructed her not to intervene in the adults' discussion. The meeting began as follows: "You are half a minute too soon." — "I am sorry [stepping back], it is four o'clock by my watch." — "No, no, come in! Watches may disagree, but let *us* not!" Then they sat on the floor and Gora and Gandhi got on with their discussion. After a while there

16. Gora promoted the building of out-houses in every village he visited. They were particularly useful to women, who would otherwise have to wait until dark in order to avoid exposing themselves to improper gazing. (For an account of Mirabehn's work in making latrines in a village in 1936, see *H*, 1/ii/36.)

was a pause while Gandhi was served some honey-flavored water. He turned now to Mythri and said in Hindi, which she understood just enough to get by, "I've been having a meeting with your father; now I'll have one with you. If you stay with me at the ashram, I will teach you Gujarati and Hindi, and Abha will teach you Bengali, and since Prabhakar [a Christian, formerly "untouchable," who was in charge of organizing the prayer meetings] speaks Telugu, you won't have any problems, so you can live here. And wherever I travel, I'll take you with me." — "Please no, I cannot leave my parents." — "All right then, better stay with them. Now and then you can come and visit me."

Gandhi's secretary heard this and soon everyone at the ashram was urging Gora to make Mythri stay — it would be such an honor! — but he respected her natural wish to remain with her parents.

Gandhi encouraged her to learn how to ride a bicycle. This was forward-looking, since at that time in India it was customary only for boys to be so active. Prabhakar taught her for two days, until she was cruising about on her own and enjoying it tremendously. (But in Mudunúr there was no bicycle and we couldn't afford to buy one. Sometimes in those days we couldn't buy vegetables to accompany our daily rice.)

Gora and Mythri took their leave of Gandhi on the last evening of the visit. On their way to Wardha the next morning they saw him with his entourage approaching from a distance in the dark. It was about 6:00, soon after the first prayer-meeting of the day, and Gandhi was heading back to the ashram at the end of his morning walk. Gora said to Mythri, "Let's not disturb Bapuji; you can see how he's talking seriously with his colleagues. If he notices us, let's just wave good-bye." When Gandhi did notice them, however, he came over, patted Mythri on the back and told her, with his face beaming in the way she had come to love,[17] "Mythri, you are doing very well! You are carrying your own luggage and learning the dignity of work. I do the same. When will you return to Sevagram?" She answered, delighted but still a bit shy, "I'll come again!"

Gandhi had actually invited the whole family to live at Sevagram, and to bring along some colleagues from Mudunúr to visit for a few weeks. They would come and go in batches while the family stayed for longer; and thereafter Gora and/or I (his eldest son) would periodically visit for a few weeks.

Mythri was with me when I first met Gandhi. He asked us if we were familiar with any handicrafts, and we were ready for that question. Mythri had noticed that he normally sat on the floor, and she had also seen how people in the village of Sevagram wove mats with date-palm leaves, rather like the mats we made at Mudunúr. She thought a mat like that would make a nice gift for Gandhiji; so we told him we knew how

---

17. A sympathetic Westerner in Johannesburg said of Gandhi in 1908: "The skin was dark, the eyes dark, but the smile which lighted up the face, and that direct and fearless glance, simply took one's heart by storm." (Doke 1909, 6)

to weave such a mat, and he asked us please to make one for him. I thought he wanted to test our skill and, more important, our ability to follow through. We got the leaves promptly and within a couple of days made the mat. We did it quite well, except that in our eagerness to give it to him we quite forgot to trim away the sharp ends of the leaves. (Mythri was now 13; I was 15.) When we took it to him, he beamed and said it was a wonderful mat, and then put his hand on it and said, still smiling, "Ah! — you want to remind me that since I am a leader, I must sit on a throne of thorns." (He meant, of course, that a political leader has to make difficult choices.) "You have made a very beautiful mat, but let me show you how to make it even better...." We apologized, and a few minutes later came back with it properly trimmed, and he used it for some time thereafter.

On this visit, Mythri's "bread-labor" included road-sweeping and gardening. Mine was to pick tomatoes in the garden and guava in the orchard, wash them with water, dry them with a towel, and put them in rows on trays so that they could readily be cut up and served. The place where I did the washing and drying was just opposite to Gandhi's wash-room and it happened that I was there every day at the time that he went to take his bath. He would always smile at me as he passed by; then one day he came over and asked what I was doing. I explained, and he asked, in a teasing and yet probing way, "Are you just washing them or are you eating them also?" — "I'm just washing them!" — "Why don't you eat them?" —

"I'm not expected to eat them." — "Then why are you doing the work?" — "So that they can be served at lunch and dinner. *Then* I'll eat some of them." Now came the sharpest probe: "Suppose they aren't served to you. What then?" I reflected, and answered, "Well, perhaps in that case I might eat some while washing them." Gandhiji beamed and said, "Yes, there you are! You are honest because you know you will be justly rewarded for your work," and slowly walked away. I have never forgotten that moment. Like every great politician, Gandhi had a knack for tuning himself to the other person's wave-length.

We spoke in a pâtois of English, Telugu and Hindi. Gandhi understood a little Telugu, and I a little English and Hindi. Later, when I was 15, he urged me to learn Hindi, and I did, studying full-time with a teacher for two years. (It was only in the 1960s that I learned English, teaching myself.) Gora and Gandhi always conversed in English. The only member of our family who at that time spoke Hindi fluently was my aunt.

Since our family and associates were the only residents who did not attend the daily prayers, there was some grumbling, soon after we arrived, from various members of the ashram. Gandhi heard about this in the daily briefings from his secretaries, and asked for detailed reports about us so he would know if the grumbling was justified. He liked what he heard, however: we were free of snobbery, we worked well, and we had taken to the diet (prescribed for everyone by Gandhi himself, as he had his own ideas about that) with no complaints and, unlike most newcomers, no illnesses. So he encouraged us to ignore the grumbling: one evening not long after we had arrived, when he and his entourage happened to meet a group of us during our respective evening walks, he smiled and said to my aunt in Hindi, "I hear you folks are made of granite," and thereafter made it a point to smile and greet each of us when our paths crossed.

The fact that our group included peasants as well as intellectuals helped us work efficiently. Some of us were very quick, for instance, at separating wheat from chaff and pebbles. One task the manager set for us was to remove a big pile of manure to a compost heap. He thought it would take a month, but our men and women did it in ten days because they were experienced farmworkers. On the other hand, when a Communist leader visited soon after two Congress members had written a book in Telugu condemning their politics in our province of India, and Gandhi wanted to know what the book said about them, my father and my uncle translated it into English. (Alas, it was too superficial to be of any use.) And, recently my attention was called to an extant note from Gandhi to Gora at this time in Sevagram, saying: "The enclosed is a rough draft of the scheme along with details as to its estimated budget. Give it shape and return it to me. It will be placed before the Committee."

With children and youngsters, Gandhi was never a remote figure. With teenagers he would manage to criticise and support at once, as when he taught Mythri and me to trim the palm-leaf mat. Another example of this was the way he encouraged Mythri and our elder sister Manorama, one afternoon when they were doing their daily spinning, to salvage the scraps that fell to the floor and integrate them into the main strand: he told them not to follow blindly what they were taught, but to try to improve on it.[18]

With younger children Gandhi would be gentler. In 1945 my youngest brother, Niyanta, four years old, was already a veteran of jail since mother had carried him in her arms when she was sentenced for participating in the resistance movement. The British rules were that bread and milk, which happened to be the only kinds of food that Niyanta would eat when he was first weaned, were not to be served on Sundays. In his hunger Niyanta had cried, so the Indian warden had brought some bread and milk from his own home to get around the rules. Perhaps because of this successful experience with crying at mealtime as a baby, Niyanta formed at home, when the jail-term was over, a habit of demanding that the food for the whole family's meal be put in front of him alone until he had eaten his fill. But now on the first evening at Sevagram, we all

18. Spinning had a special significance. Gandhi considered it indispensable to Indian self-reliance, and told Gora that it would be improper to order a spinning-wheel from outside. We all learned the basic techniques, and my mother and Manorama and Mythri learned a good deal more. All our clothing was made from homespun yarn. My mother would not go to bed without having spun for at least half an hour on a very full day or perhaps for as much as three hours on an otherwise not very active day. The cloth is beautiful and a spinning-wheel costs less than an exercise machine.

sat down to eat together, so he made quite a fuss, and this was, as it happened, a few moments after Gandhi had joined us to ask how we were settling in. My father explained the difficulty — he could hardly avoid doing so, as Niyanta was making a royal ruckus — and Gandhi said, "We have to adjust to the children's way because they don't know any better." My mother agreed, "We all have to be patient in our work!", and then at Gandhi's suggestion a small amount of food — enough for Niyanta and one or two other, hypothetical people — was put in the big serving-dishes, and everyone else had their food in little, separate bowls. Niyanta stopped crying, and this regime was carried on for several days until finally he accepted a normal arrangement.

On another occasion, outside the kitchen a group of children were sifting and grinding grain and cleaning and cutting vegetables and fruits from the garden. Niyanta and our in-between brother Samaram (who was six years old) helped by handing them fruits. Gandhi happend to pass by and, after watching for a moment, asked Samaram and Niyanta, "Why don't you eat some of the fruit now?" Mythri translated the question and their answer: "We'll eat at mealtime."[19] Perhaps because they were so young, he did not follow up with the more probing question that he put to me, but was content to say to another adult who was nearby, "You see, they have security; that is

19. In recalling all this, we have been unable to work out which of the interrogations took place first. Only Gandhi was present at both of them.

why they don't steal. When people have this kind of security, they become honest."

Perhaps Gandhi with that question was conducting a mini-survey to ascertain the moral quality of boys brought up with no fear of a god. It may seem curious, especially to a modern Westerner, that he did not ask Mythri whether *she* was munching the fruit. In fact he never put a probing question even to my mother, but was content to ask her how we were all getting on, and to tell her, "You are doing a good job, you are sincere and honest."

My youngest sister, Maru, was only a few months old at this time, having been born two weeks after mother came out of jail. There was no such thing as a cradle at Sevagram (even married couples had to take a vow of chastity while living there[20]), so my mother improvised a hammock from a sari — still today a common device in India among women who have no cradle — in order to rock Maru to sleep. The next day when Gandhi visited he noticed Maru in the hammock, declared "That can't be very comfortable," and asked Prabhakar to fetch a cradle from the village.

Gandhi could, on the other hand, be quite tough with grown-up men. My father used to tell of the doctor who sought Gandhi's endorsement of an elaborate therapy he had invented.

20. My parents were the only exceptions. Gora had said to Gandhi, "I have denied everything else to my wife, I don't want to deny my self." Gandhi in turn had explained, "I don't want to make the ashram a maternity home."

After waiting for three days he was given a five-minute interview, which Gandhi cut short, without hearing out the account of how the therapy was supposed to work, by asking the doctor to cure a certain patient at the ashram. (He couldn't do it.) Then there was the man who was granted ten minutes and took seven to explain his problem. Gandhi advice was: "The fact that you taken so long to describe the problem shows that you have not understood it.... Go and work. Work will solve your difficulties."[21]

Gandhi's wife, Kasturba, had died in 1944, and soon afterwards a memorial trust was established with donations from all over India. Gandhi wanted the money to be used for the benefit of rural women and children. Gora applied for a center to be established at Mudunúr. After the usual protests ("An atheist!") the matter was referred to Gandhi, who spoke with Gora, decided that Mudunúr would be the site of the first center to be operated by the trust, and put my aunt in the first class of trainees for the national organization. All the trainees were women older than 40 and with no more formal education than the women they would serve. The lessons were conveyed without a textbook: "Always wear homespun cotton and no jewelry." "Consider everything from the other person's point of view." "Favor no caste or religion." "Join in all the village decision-making and in every kind of physical work." "Before

21. *G*, 39.

cutting vegetables, wash them and also the knife; afterwards wash the knife, but not again the vegetables."[22]

Gora and Gandhi corresponded several times in 1945. Most of the letters have disappeared over the years, but one of which a copy has survived, from Gandhi to Gora in October 1945, suggests that Gora was full of enthusiasm for various projects which Gandhi, preoccupied as he was with the independence movement and national unity and trying to quell religious strife, couldn't help with, or at least not yet. The letter discusses five proposals which Gora had evidently made: for a revised edition of a booklet on health that Gandhi had written; for a new design, promoting "service of labor," of a flag for the Congress; for a national "sweepers' conference"; for a maternity home; and for an edition in India, with a preface by Gandhi, of Booker T. Washington's *Up from Slavery*. In regard to this last project Gandhi asked Gora to "wait a little longer and remind me when I have settled down after the tours I have in mind"; for each of the other four there was some reason why Gandhi felt that he could not really be of service.

An idea which engaged his immediate and active response, however, was my parents' choice of a husband for Manorama. Arjun Rao was an "untouchable" from a nearby village who had been a volunteer at the Atheist Center, had gone to jail along with my father, and in 1944 had attended a camp at

22. For many Indian villagers, vegetables on the table would be luxurious novelty.

Sevagram for a hundred or so young men and women from all over India. My parents considered him a good man to be their son-in-law, and Manorama liked him. There was no Hollywood-type romance, but there was the romance of idealism in marrying a fellow *satyagrahi* (non-violent protester) and atheist who had been in the lowest of the castes.

In January 1946, Gandhi visited Madras on the occasion of the silver-jubilee celebrations of the founding of the movement to make Hindi (with appropriate modifications from Urdu) the national language. At his request, Gora brought Manorama to Madras, together with some women who were working in our Kasturba-Foundation project. In regard to the betrothal Gandhi's first step was to ascertain Manorama's true feelings. He asked a Telugu-speaking Brahmin colleague to interview her and see if she was under duress.[23] To test her gumption, this good man told Manorama that the marriage was really a poor idea: there would be so many difficulties, Arjun was penniless, and so on. (For a rough analogy, one might imagine a kindly white Protestant clergyman speaking with concern to Dean Rusk's daughter when she was about to announce her engagement to a Negro.) But Manorama was unequivocal — "We are working for social equality and the eradication of untouchabil-

23. Since Gandhi had read the Koran more than once (see Reading 310 on page 217), maybe he recalled the story (referred to in Chapter XXXIII, Verses 37-38) of the marriage which Mohammed arranged between his high-born cousin Zeinab and his low-born adopted son Zaid, and which then turned out to be unhappy.

ity" — and when this was reported to Gandhi, he told Gora, "Now they are *my* children. Let them wait for two years, and in the meantime let us announce their engagement."

Arjun was sent for and came promptly to Madras to be introduced to Gandhi, who addressed him as *Hari* ("God") and, having found him a presentable and self-confident young man who could get by in Hindi, arranged for him to spend the next two years at Sevagram, while Manorama, who spoke no Hindi, would study at a Kasturba-Foundation nurses' and midwives' training center in a Telugu-speaking part of India.

Before going to Sevagram, Arjun wanted to put his affairs in order at the Atheist Center and say goodbye to his colleagues. Gandhi agreed and suggested that when his own train for Wardha came north from Madras, Arjun join it at Vijayawada.

Meanwhile Gora, who was mindful of the ripples which our absence from the daily prayers at Sevagram had caused, and who would always handle embarrassing questions candidly, asked Gandhi, "What shall be his position in relation to attendance at the prayers, Bapu?" Gandhi replied immediately, "Let him attend the prayers as a matter of discipline of the ashram, but let him not recite the verses if he does not believe in them." After a moment he asked Gora, in his characteristically probing way, "Suppose in the two years that Arjun Rao sits regularly at the prayers, he turns towards theism?" — "I will be very happy, Bapu. I do not want anyone to be an atheist with a closed mind. He should be an atheist out of conviction. If he takes to theism out of conviction, I will welcome such a change in him." — "Oh, yes, I know you are not a fanatic! Instead of Arjun Rao taking to theism, it looks as if both of you will carry this old man into your camp."

Arjun duly joined the train at Vijayawada. When it arrived at Wardha, Gandhi sought him out, patted him on the back, and told him, as they walked out of the station, "This marriage is based on an important principle, so you should be careful. I will introduce you to many visitors who come to the ashram. Please improve your Hindi, and study Hindustani, and make yourself at home by taking part in all the activities of the ashram. I will be quite busy [Sevagram was in some ways the capital of the national independence movement], but I will meet you from time to time." A day or so later he issued a statement to the press. Many visitors came to the ashram to meet Arjun, to offer their congratulations and ask about his background. They would smile when he mentioned that he was an atheist. (Many of them knew about Gora.) After four days Gandhi called for him and asked how he was getting on and with whom he was studying Hindi and Hindustani. (He was studying Hindi with his roommate, a Brahmin from North India who looked after the cows and is today — in 1996 — the only resident of the ashram who goes back so far.) Gandhi encouraged Arjun to educate himself as much as possible, and told him: "You should become like Ambedkar. You should work for the removal of untouchability and of caste. Untouchability must go at any cost."

Soon afterwards, Gandhi left for Bengal to try to cope with the religiously inspired mass killing there. While he was away, Arjun wrote to him now and then, in Hindustani, and Gandhi replied, encouraging him to keep up his studies but on one occasion advising him also not to forget his mother-tongue (Telugu). When Gandhi returned to Sevagram, later in 1946, he found to his delight that Arjun was now very fluent in Hindi. Soon the manager put him in charge of the kitchen — there may have been a special point in this as it meant that everyone would systematically be eating food handled in one way or another by an "untouchable," which was taboo to orthodox Hindus — and before long everyone took to calling Arjun "Mother" because he was providing for their needs. This was not derisive, but an honor: a grand-niece of Gandhi's (Manu) wrote a book about Gandhi entitled *Bapu, My Mother*.

Gandhi and Arjun did not meet again. Gandhi was assassinated in Delhi two days before he was to come home to Sevagram on February 1st, 1948. Gora had proposed that the wedding be celebrated on the day of India's independence in 1947, but Gandhi had said that that day was of no special significance to him[24] and next April would be a nice time for the wedding (which he was to perform).[25]

---

24. He was so saddened by the carving up of India to make Pakistan a separate state that he declined to attend the ceremonies establishing India's independence.

25. See Readings 196 and 415. Arjun and Manorama then returned to the Atheist Center to assist Gora for two years (except that at the request of

In the meantime Gora and Gandhi had met several times here and there, for instance in Delhi when Gora was working there, though without pay, for the All-India Congress Committee. They also collaborated by mail in an effort to bring about the opening to "untouchables" of a Hindu temple, and Gandhi published (with "hearty congratulations") in the 15 September 1946 issue of his journal, *Harijan*, an account of our "assiduous work" in establishing the right of "untouchables" to obtain water from public wells in various villages.

It remains for me to tell of Mythri's last meeting with Gandhi. It was during that visit to Madras. Since her last visit to Sevagram she had been inspired, by Gandhi's example, to study Hindustani and Tamil (the language spoken in Madras) as well as Hindi and English. Perhaps this diligence, as well as the fact that she was growing up, enabled her to overcome her shyness with Gandhi. She wanted to make him laugh again in that loving way of his, so when she met him — he was seated on the floor, working a spinning-wheel — she greeted him by folding her hands and exclaiming the first words of a rousing patriotic poem: "*Vande Mataram,* Bapu!" ("Love our motherland, Bapu!"). He laughed with pleasure: "Oh, very nice!" So when she left a while later, she said, "*Jai Hind,* Bapu!" ("Victory to India, Bapu!") to make him laugh again, and he did.

---

the Sevagram Ashram members, she went to their clinic in July 1949 to give birth to her first child).

Mythri's recollections of that trip are vivid. Every evening there were vast public meetings — tens of thousands of people, and all the incoming trains packed with them throughout the morning and night. She was thrilled at the way Gandhi stirred up in everyone a sense of freedom and self-confidence. This was one of the happiest episodes of the last few years of his life, before the horrendous wave of religious violence in northern India was set in motion.

One thing that impressed Mythri was the apparent honesty of the hundreds of volunteers who would pass through the throngs, collecting donations in their caps and sari-aprons for Gandhi's campaigns for national freedom and for the Harijans. Later when she went with Gora to meet Gandhi, they had to wait in the hallway for half an hour until he was free to see them, and during that time they helped count some of the vast heaps of coins that had been collected and were lying about here and there on the floor. Anyone who happened to pass by was asked to help count the money so that it could be tallied and taken to the bank. There were no inspectors to prevent stealing. Mythri thought, "Gandhi has taught everyone this honesty!" Forty years later, when she saw the glamorous English film about him, she was most touched by the scene of his walking, in his loincloth, up the steps of Buckingham Palace. "He knew he was not one whit inferior to the elaborately dressed people around him, and he made us all feel the same way." Gandhi did indeed have this effect — and among many women as well as men.

As far as I have been able to determine, Gandhiji when speaking with my mother or with her children never once mentioned or evoked the idea of any kind of god or supernatural force. I have often wondered which was the main reason for this: to avoid implying disrespect for my father, or merely to concentrate anyway on the down-to-earth concerns of human service that bound us together? Toward the end of that visit in the first part of 1945 when the whole family was at Sevagram he told my parents, "You are working with a big family, and at the same time following atheism. So, you may have more difficulties than other people. But you must go ahead with confidence." It seemed clear to my mother that whereas Gandhi was very alert to the fact that he had to work in a tradition-bound society, his own mind was free.

CHAPTER 3

ABIDING AND EVOLVING CONCERNS

Students of Gandhi are bound to wonder what were his deepest concerns, the ones that shaped his intuitive as well as his conscious decisions. We think that to some extent these guiding concerns changed throughout his maturity as well as during his childhood and adolescence. In 1932 he described his "spiritual growth" as constant:

[10] *1932*: "My spiritual growth has been unnoticed like the growth of hair on our heads." (Desai, 1968, I, 275)

One of us (Lavanam) saw first-hand in the mid-1940s that Gandhi was, though very old, still evolving.

Our hypotheses as to his main concerns will be sketched under the following headings:

— truth; non-violence; self-discipline and vegetarianism;
— self-respect; public-mindedness; Indian strength and dignity;
— humanitarianism and alleviation of abject poverty;
— love of religion and of Hinduism; yearning for *moksha*.

Readers unfamiliar with the course of his life may find it helpful to consider these issues against the background of an analytical breakdown of it into a few main phases:[26]

---

26. Any such division is to some extent arbitrary. Backianadan 1991, xiii-xv, puts the main divisions at 1915, 1926/27 and 1942. One of the periods thus delineated includes the salt-tax protest and its gestation but excludes Gandhi's internment during World War II.

—1869-87: his childhood and adolesence (including his arranged marriage).

—1888-92: his legal studies in London and failed legal career in India.

—1893-1914: his successful legal and political career in South Africa (with visits to England and India), where he invented *satyagraha*: the political use of civil disobedience by highly disciplined, non-violent volunteers.

—1915-30: the first phase of his maturity in India. He expected Britain to grant India a significant degree of self-rule in return for her loyal support in World War I; but Britain's postwar policy of repression led him to inaugurate in 1920 a campaign of non-coöperation with the colonial authorities. Finding himself unable to maintain the discipline of non-violence amongst his hundreds of millions of ostensible followers, he called this off in 1922, and was thereupon sentenced to jail for six years. During that time he refrained from explicitly anti-British activities (even after being released in 1924 because of poor health) and concentrated on rudimentary social concerns such as famine and destitution (he had begun in 1921 to dress only in a loincloth), economic self-sufficiency (symbolized by making homespun cotton), and the doctrine and practice of untouchability. Then he made his next big anti-imperial move, the salt-tax protest of 1930, which secured his place at the head of the independence movement.

—1930-45, during which his non-violent movement for self-rule was successful. Some milestones in this development were: his visit to London for a "round-table conference" in 1931; in 1935, a Government-of-India Act providing for a degree of Indian home-rule at the provincial level after elections to be held in 1937; the victory of the Indian National Congress in those elections; in 1940, Churchill's reversion (upon replacing Chamberlain as prime minister) to a policy of sowing factional dissension in India; Gandhi's response, the "Quit India" movement, and hence his internment until 1944, when he was again released because of ill health; and then Churchill's electoral defeat in 1945, after which it was inevitable that India would soon achieve her independence (which she did in 1947).

—1945-48: a new phase of development in Gandhi's thinking, as he began to reconsider some of his most basic social and religious beliefs. He began to hedge his opposition to large-scale industry.[27] Having meanwhile failed to prevent the use of religious hatred to divide Pakistan from India, and having admitted that the caste system could (as Ambedkar had argued in the 1930s) never really purge itself of the practice of untouchability, he changed his religious views to the extent of *(1)* advocating the removal of religion from politics; *(2)* fasting in the name of Truth and explicitly not in the name of God; and yet perhaps — the evidence that we will

27. See the last letters published in Nehru 1958.

adduce is suggestive but inconclusive[28] — *(3)* dying with a Moslem evocation of God on his lips.

Truth

Anyone familiar with Gandhi's life would say that virtually from childhood he cultivated a deep and abiding concern for moral truth. We use the term, "moral truth" — which he did not use — to distinguish his value-laden concept (involving that which one ought to do) from the familiar Western idea of objective truth about matters of fact (that which *is*) regardless of normal human interests: the objective truth about, say, nuclear physics as dispensed by an expert to an insane terrorist. Like Gandhi himself we will often write "Truth" with a capital "T" for his concept (which we will not try to describe at length, however, because we are not philosophers).[29]

In his mid-50s Gandhi said that Truth had, already in his teens, become his "sole objective":

[11] *Childhood* (recalled later): "This play — *Harishchandra* — captured my heart.... I must have acted [it] to myself times without number. 'Why should not all be truthful like Harishchandra?' was the question I asked myself day and night. To follow Truth and to go through all the ordeals Harischchandra went through was the one ideal it inspired in me. I literally believed in the story.... The thought of it all often made me weep....

---

28. See Chapter 5.

29. For a more extensive recent analysis, see Backianadan 1991, 7-9, 40-43, 110-119 and 215-218.

"One thing took deep root in me — the conviction that morality is the basis of things, and that Truth is the substance of all morality. Truth became my sole objective. It began to grow in magnitude every day, and my definition of it also has been ever widening." (*A*, I, ch. 2, ch. 10)

Various episodes from his childhood and teenage years suggest to us that this was not an unduly exaggerated claim.

As a boy, Gandhi "cried in deep anguish" when a the headmaster of his high school held, mistakenly, that he had told a lie:

[12] *Childhood* (recalled later): "I had formed a habit of taking long walks [which] gave me a fairly hardy constitution.

"The reason for my dislike for gymnastics [at school] was my keen desire to serve as a nurse to my [ailing] father. As soon as the school closed I would hurry home and begin serving him.... I asked Mr. Gimi to exempt me from gymnastics so that I might be free to serve my father. But he would not listen to me. Now it so happened that one Saturday, when we had no school in the morning, I had to go from home to the school for gymnastics at 4 o'clock in the afternoon. I had no watch, and the clouds deceived me. Before I reached the school the boys had all left. The next day Mr. Gimi, examining the roll, found me marked absent. Being asked the reason for absence, I told him what had happened. He refused to believe me and ordered me to pay a fine....

"I was convicted of lying! That deeply pained me. How was I to prove my innocence? There was no way. I cried in deep anguish. I saw that a man of truth must also be a man of care." (*A*, I, ch. 5)

Gandhi could never be false to his wife (to whom he was married when he was twelve years old), because of his "innate passion" for Truth:

[13] *Early 1880s and since*: "About the time of my marriage, little pamphlets ...used to be issued in which conjugal love, thrift... and other such subjects were discussed.... Lifelong faithfulness to the wife, inculcated in these booklets as the duty of the husband, remained permanently imprinted on my heart. Furthermore, the passion for truth was innate in me, and to be false to her was therefore out of the question." (*A*, I, ch. 4)

[14] *Early 1880s* (recalled later): "My friend once took me to a brothel.... It was all pre-arranged; the bill had already been paid.... I sat near the woman on her bed, but I was tongue-tied. She naturally lost patience with me and showed me the door, with abuses and insults." (*A*, I, ch. 7)

To deceive his parents was so distasteful that he gave up smoking, confessed abjectly to a petty theft (such as many teenagers lapse into before they have become quite aware of the moral implications), and gave up eating meat even though he approved of it morally and thought it was good for him:

[15] *1885*: "Though it is essential to eat meat, and also essential to take up food reform, yet deceiving and lying to one's father and mother is worse than not eating meat. [Henceforth] in their lifetime, therefore, meat-eating must be out of the question. When they are no more and I have found my freedom, I will eat meat openly." (*A*, I, ch. 7)

[16] *mid-1880s* (recalled later): "A relative and I became fond of smoking [surreptitiously]. ...But we had no money. So we began pilfering.... I was 12 or 13, possibly less. The other theft was committed when I was 15.... I made up my mind to confess it to my father.... I asked adequate punishment for it, and closed with a request to him not to punish himself for my offence. I also pledged myself never to steal in future." (*A*, I, ch. 9)[30]

In England he maintained this devotion to Truth. At the age of 20 he was thrilled to hear Annie Besant say that her dearest wish was to live and die for truth:

[17] *1889*, recalled after nearly 30 years: "I went to Queen's Hall [in London]... to listen to [Mrs. Besant]. And the words she uttered then as she rose to answer the charge of inconsistency [she had given up her atheism for Theosophy] have never faded from my memory. She said as she wound up her great speech, which held her audience spellbound, that she would be quite satisfied to have the epitaph written on her tomb that she lived for truth and she died for truth.... Ever since I have followed her career with unabated interest... [but] I have also been hurt to feel at times that she has lost her robust independence of 1888 and her uncompromising search after and adherence to truth at all cost." (*C*, XV, 201f)[31]

When a British viceroy (Curzon) declared publicly in 1904 that "the highest ideal of truth is to a large extent a Western

30. For a detailed account see *E*, 211f.

31. Shortly after writing this, he told her, "It saddens me to see in your writings a new Mrs. Besant, and not the old Mrs. Besant who... stood for truth." (*C*, XXVI, 300f)

conception," Gandhi published a collection of dozens of passages from Hindu scripture extolling Truth and truthfulness.[32] Four years later he denounced the entire law profession for teaching immorality — by which, as anyone who has dealt with lawyers will know, he must have meant deceit:[33]

[18] *1909*: [Critical comment posed for Gandhi's consideration:] "To denounce such an estimable class of men is to spell injustice, and you are abusing the liberty of the press by decrying lawyers." [His response:] "At one time I used to think exactly like you. I have no desire to convince you that they have never done a single good thing.... Lawyers are also men, and there is something good in every man.... All I am concerned with is to show you that the profession teaches immorality." (*S*, 143)

In the 1920s he declared, in his autobiography, that from experience he knew there is "no other God than Truth":

[19] *Middle and late 1920s*: "The experiments I am about to relate... are spiritual, or rather moral; for the essence of religion is morality....

"My uniform experience has convinced me that there is no other God than Truth." (*A*, introduction and last chapter)

---

32. *I*, 1/iv/1905, 204f. *C*, IV, 392ff.

33. Gandhi was one of those rare lawyers who avoid deception. In America today a common attitude in the profession is that of Harvard professor Alan Dershowitz, who justifies his high-paid work for criminals by saying, "I'm just their representative, not their conscience. I would never do many of the things in my personal life that I have to do as a lawyer" (*ABA Journal*, May 1995, p. 40). For Gandhi's views in detail, see S. B. Kher, ed., 1962 and C. Shulka, ed., 1949, 231-2.

He advocated truth "in thought" and "in action" as well as in speech:[34]

[20] *1930*: "Generally speaking, [observance of] truth is understood merely to mean that we must speak the truth. But we in the ashram should understand the word 'satya' or 'Truth' in a much wider sense. There should be truth in thought, truth in speech and truth in action." (*C*, XLIV, 40f)

[21] *1945*, as recalled later by Gora: "Then he [Gandhi] inquired into my conception of morality. I replied, 'I do what I say and I say what I do — that is my definition of moral behavior....'

"'Exactly,' said Bapuji... [and] described to me some of his hard experiences in trying to live openly." (*G*, 45)

At Sevagram he posted in his own room (where it remains today) a warning, attributed to John Ruskin, not to indulge in the practice of misleading people while steering clear of an explicit lie:

[22] **Attributed to John Ruskin**: "The essence of lying is in deception and not in words; a lie may be told by silence, by equivocation, by the accent on a syllable, by the glance of the eye attaching a particular significance to a sentence; and all these kinds of lies are worse and baser by many degrees than a lie plainly worded."

---

34. See also *S*, VI, 127f, and *H*, 9/vi/1946, 171 (criticizing Bertrand Russell).

Non-violence (ahimsa)

Gandhi's concern for non-violence — *ahimsa*[35]— was secondary in that he saw it as a great method to be developed in the even greater quest for Truth:

[23] *1936*: "By instinct I have been truthful, but not non-violent. As a Jain *muni* [sage] once rightly said, I was not so much a votary of ahimsa as I was of Truth, and I put the latter in the first place and the former in the second.... It was in the course of my pursuit of Truth that I discovered non-violence." (*H*, 28/iii, 49)

He considered it susceptible to development like a scientific method:

[24] *1939*: "Ahimsa is a science. The word 'failure' has no place in the vocabulary of science. Failure to obtain the expected result is often the precursor to further discoveries." (*C*, LXIX, 166)

[25] *1946*: "[The existence of violence] can never mean that the creed of non-violence has failed. At best it may be said that I have not yet found the technique required for the conversion of the mass mind." (*C*, LXXXVI, 134)

His devotion to it emerged gradually. In later years he saw it

35. "Himsa" means "violence"; the prefix "a-" is cognate with its English counterpart in such Greek-derived words as "anonymous" and "atheist." We can offer here only a brief sketch of Gandhi's concept, to which many books have been devoted. For a good discussion — of moderate length yet with citations and with a sense of Gandhi's growth over the years — see Backianadan 1991, 23-30, 73-88, 169-197 and 235-244.

in the way his father had received his teen-age confession of a petty theft:

[26] *1885* (recalled later): "I was trembling as I handed the confession to my father.... He read it through, and pearl-drops trickled down his cheeks, wetting the paper.... If I were a painter I could draw a picture of the whole scene today.... Those pearl-drops of love cleansed my heart and washed my sin away....

"I could read in it nothing more than a father's love, but today I know that it was pure ahimsa.... This sort of sublime forgiveness was not natural to my father. I had thought that he would be angry." (*A*, I, ch. 8)

He saw a further step forward in his intuitive use of diplomacy when he had dealt with some corrupt South African policemen in the early 1900s:

[27] *1903* (recalled later): "I had nothing against them personally [when gathering evidence with a view to having them prosecuted]. They were aware of this themselves, and when in their straits [after their dismissal] they approached me, I helped them too. They had a chance of getting employed by the Johannesburg municipality in case I did not oppose the proposal, and I agreed not to thwart them, and they succeeded.

"This attitude of mine put the officials with whom I came in contact perfectly at ease, and though I had often to fight in earnest with their department and use strong language, they remained quite friendly with me. I was not then quite conscious that such behavior was part of my nature. I learned later that it was... an attribute of ahimsa." (*A*, IV, ch. 9)

And he had learned from his wife:

[28] *1938*: "I used to let loose my anger upon her. But she bore it all meekly and uncomplainingly. I had a notion that it was her duty to obey me, her lord and master.... But her unresisting meekness opened my eyes and slowly it began to dawn upon me that I had no such prescriptive right over her. If I wanted her obedience, I had first to persuade her by patient argument. She thus became my teacher in non-violence." (*C*, LXVIII, 46)

He distinguished, however, between the weak ahimsa of the weak and the strong ahimsa of the strong:

[29] *1926*: "Non-violence presupposes the ability to strike. It is a conscious, deliberate restraint put upon one's desire for vengeance.... The desire for vengeance comes out of fear of harm, imaginary or real. A man who fears no one on earth would consider it troublesome even to summon up anger against one who is vainly trying to injure him. (*C*, XXXI, 292)

[30] *1940*: "I have not concentrated upon [the ahimsa of the physically or militarily strong] or given it the weight I might have. This... had the result of retarding the growth of pure ahimsa, so that today we are not even within the ken of the ahimsa of the strong." (*C*, LXXII, 280)

[31] *1948*: "What I and the people with me termed non-violence was not the genuine article but a weak copy known as passive resistance. Naturally, passive resistance can avail nothing to a ruler." (Bose 1953: 3)

Moreover, his concept of ahimsa was far from indiscriminate, particularly in comparison with the traditional Jain precept of non-violence to all forms of life, which was, as we will see in Chapter 5, familiar to him from his childhood years. He considered it non-violent for a woman to slap and scratch while resisting rape:

[32] *1932*: "The woman will not even till death surrender herself to the man. Her anger, her alarm, proclaims for herself as well as for the man her preparedness to die.... Her slap or scratching indicates this resolve. It... is not violence, but it has the power to move a lecherous mind and to awaken the woman who administers the slap." (*C*, LI, 18ff)

He said that anyone who felt humiliated by a bully's insults should hit the bully to vindicate his self-respect:

[33] *1940*: "The use of force, in the circumstance, would be the natural consequence if you are not a coward. But if you have assimilated the non-violent spirit, there should be no feeling of humiliation within you. Your non-violent behavior should then either make the bully feel ashamed of himself and prevent the insult, or make you proof against it so that the insult would remain, so to say, in the bully's mouth and not touch you at all." (*H*, 9/iii, 31)

And he said it would be sheer self-deception to imagine oneself wholly non-violent while benefitting from, say, a farmer's killing of pests during a famine:

[34] *1925*: "I have not the capacity for preaching universal non-violence. I preach... non-violence restricted strictly to the purpose of winning our freedom and, therefore,

perhaps for preaching the regulation of international relations by non-violent means." (*C*, XXVII, 51f)

[35] *1946*: "In life it is impossible to eschew violence completely. The question arises, where is one to draw the line? ...To allow crops to be eaten up by animals in the name of ahimsa while there is a famine in the land is certainly a sin. Evil and good are relative terms. What is good under certain conditions can become an evil or a sin under a different set of conditions." (*C*, LXXXIV, 231)

Notwithstanding this, everyone knows that non-violence was a basic concern of Gandhi's. He said it distinguishes humanity from brutes and is indispensable for the realization of Truth:

[36] *1920*: "Non-violence is the law of our species as violence is the law of the brute. The spirit lies dormant in the brute and he knows no law but that of physical might. The dignity of man requires obedience to a higher law — to the strength of the spirit." (*C*, XVIII, 133)

[37] *Late 1920s*: "If every page of these chapters does not proclaim to the reader that the only means for the realization of Truth is ahimsa, I shall deem all my labor in writing these chapters to have been in vain." (*A*, last chapter)

According to Gandhi, the key to peace among religions is a non-violent regard for truth; indeed, it would be better for the masses of India's people to be non-violent atheists than violent upholders of religion as they became on the eve of India's independence.

[38] *1940*: "I have come to the conclusion that, if it is proper and necessary to discover an underlying unity among all religions, a master-key is needed. That master-key is that

of truth and non-violence.... Unless and until we realize this fundamental unity, wars in the name of religion will not cease." (*C*, LXXII, 254)

[39] *1947* (as reported later): "Pandit Sundarlal ...revealed... a particular remark that Bapuji made to him when they both had met at Delhi at the time of a communal riot. Bapuji wished the communities turned atheists, if that served to stop communal hatred and riots." (*G*, 50)

Self-discipline

When Gandhi first sailed for England in 1888 — which was many years before he became interested in ahimsa — his main concerns appear to have been quite simple: in the long run, to succeed his father, and in the short run, to keep some vows that he had taken to his mother:

[40] *1888* (recalled later): "An old friend and adviser of the family... said, 'The times are changed and none of you can expect to succeed to your father's *gadi* [office] without having had a proper education.... Think of that barrister who has just come back from England. How stylishly he lives! He could get the diwanship [the position Gandhi's father had held] for the asking. I would strongly advise you to send Mohandas to England this very year.'" (*A*, I, ch. 11)

[41] *1888* (recalled later): "Someone had told [my mother] that young men got lost in England. Someone else had said that they took to meat; and yet another that they could not live there without liquor.... I said, 'I swear that I shall not touch any of those things.'... — 'But how can I trust you in a distant land? I am dazed and know not

what to do....' A Jain monk... came to my help, and said: 'I shall get the boy solemnly to take the three vows, and then he can be allowed to go.' He administered the oath and I vowed not to touch wine, women and meat." (*A*, I, ch. 11)

During his first few weeks abroad Gandhi maintained under such pressure his vow to remain vegetarian that we may consider self-discipline to have been already a deep concern of his. Anyone acquainted with English-style boiled vegetables — a tasteless semi-mush — will smile at his troubles:

[42] *1888* (recalled later): "An English passenger [during the voyage from India], taking kindly to me, drew me into conversation.... He laughed at my insistence on abjuring meat, and said in a friendly way when we were in the Red Sea: 'It's all very well so far, but... it is so cold in England that one cannot possibly live there without meat'... — 'I thank you for your kind advice, but I have solemnly promised my mother.'...

"[In London] my food... became a serious question. I could not relish boiled vegetables cooked without salt or condiments. The landlady was at a loss to know what to prepare for me. We had oatmeal porridge for breakfast, which was fairly filling, but I always starved at lunch and dinner:... spinach and bread and jam.... [My] friend ...said, 'What is the value of a vow made before an illiterate mother and in ignorance of conditions here? It is no vow at all.'... One day the friend began to read to me Bentham's *Theory of Utility*. I was at my wits' end. ...'These abstruse things are beyond me. I admit it is necessary to eat meat. But I cannot break my vow.'...

"I told [my next landlady] about my vow.... Here too I practically had to starve.... Everything was insipid. I launched out in search of a vegetarian restaurant.... I would trot 10 or 12 miles each day, go into a cheap restaurant and eat my fill of bread, but would never be satisfied." (*A*, I, chh. 13-14)

This episode culminated in his apparently sudden conversion to a belief in vegetarianism, which he never abandoned and which may thus be considered, in a way, the first ideology that he adopted:

[43] *1888* in London (recalled later): "During these wanderings I once hit on a vegetarian restaurant in Farringdon Street. The sight of it filled me with the same joy that a child feels on getting a thing after its own heart. Before I entered I noticed books for sale exhibited under a glass window near the door. I saw among them [Henry] Salt's *Plea for Vegetarianism.* This I purchased for a shilling and went straight to the dining room. This was my first hearty meal since my arrival in England. God had come to my aid.

"I read Salt's book from cover to cover... [and] blessed the day on which I had taken the vow before my mother. I had all along abstained from meat in the interests of Truth [toward her] and of the vow I had taken, but had wished at the same time that every Indian should be a meat-eater and had looked forward to being one myself freely and openly some day, and so enlisting others in the cause. The choice was now made in favor of vegetarianism, the spread of which henceforward became my mission." (*A*, I, ch. 14)

The themes of self-discipline and diet were often intertwined in Gandhi's later years:

[44] *1909*: "I had read ...that... saltless diet was better for the health. I had deduced that a *bramachari* [a self-disciplined, celibate person] benefitted by a saltless diet. I had read and realized that the weak-bodied should avoid pulses [beans and peas]. I was very fond of them.

"Now it happened that [my wife] Kasturbai, who had a brief respite after her operation, had again begun getting haemorrhage.... When all my remedies had failed, I entreated her to give up salt and pulses. She would not agree..., saying that even I could not give up these articles if I was advised to do so. I was pained, and [yet] delighted ...in that I got an opportunity to shower my love on her. ...'If I was ailing and the doctor advised me to give up those or any other article, I should unhesitatingly do so. But there! Without any medical advice, I give up salt and pulses for one year, whether you do so or not.'... — 'Forgive me. Knowing you, I should not have provoked you. I promise to abstain from these things, but for heaven's sake take back your vow. This is too hard on me.' — 'It is very good of you to forego these articles.... As for me, I cannot retract a vow seriously taken. And it is sure to benefit me, for all restraint, whatever prompts it, is wholesome.'...

"After this Kasturbai began to pick up... and I added somewhat to my reputation as a quack.... I was all the better for the new denials. I never craved for the things I had left.... I found the senses to be more subdued than ever.... I continued the abstention... until long after [the year of the vow]." (*A*, IV, ch. 29)

[45] *1920*: "A genuine fast cleanses the body, mind and soul. ...Purity thus gained, when it is utilized for a noble purpose, becomes a prayer." (*C*, XVII, 110)

Gandhi regarded self-control as the main cause of the spiritual strength of Rajchandra, the poet and merchant who was as near to a religious guru as he ever had:[36]

[46] *1926*: "We shall have to wander from existence to existence, whereas [he] may have only one life more to live....

"During the two years [1891-93] I remained in close contact with [him], I felt in him every moment the spirit of *vairagya* [renunciation].... One rare feature of his writings is that he always set down what he had felt in his own experience. There is in them no trace of unreality. I have never read any line by him which was written to produce an effect on others....

"His eyes... were extremely bright and free from any sign of impatience or anxiety.... These qualities can exist only in a man of self-control. A man cannot become free from attachments by making a show of being so.... The Poet made me feel that this state of freedom from attachment was spontaneous to him." (*C*, XXXII, 2-7)

At various times Gandhi linked a variety of virtues with self-discipline, including spiritual strength, civilization, democracy, and freedom of conscience:

[47] *1924*: "It is my own firm belief that the strength of the soul grows in proportion as you subdue the flesh." (*Y*, 23/x, 354)

36. See Reading 240.

[48] *1930*: "Civilization, in the real sense of the term, consists not in the multiplication, but in the deliberate and voluntary restriction of wants. This alone promotes real happiness and contentment, and increases the capacity for service." (*S*, IV, 230)

[49] *1939*: "A born democrat is a born disciplinarian. Democracy comes naturally to him who is habituated normally to yield willing obedience to all laws, human and divine. Let those who are ambitious to serve democracy qualify themselves by satisfying first this acid test of democracy." (*H*, 27/V, 136)

[50] *1931*: [Q.] "What is Truth?"

[A.] "A difficult question, but I have solved it for myself by saying that it is what the voice within tells me. How then, you ask, [do] different people think of different and contrary truths?

"Seeing that the human mind works through innumerable media and that the evolution of the human mind is not the same for all, it follows that what may be truth for one may be untruth for another and hence those who have made these experiments have come to the conclusion that there are certain conditions to making experiments. Just as for science there is an indispensable course common for all, even so it is true for persons who would make experiments in the spiritual realm — they must submit to certain conditions. And since everybody says it is his inner voice which speaks,... we have the belief based upon uninterrupted experience that those who would make diligent search after Truth — God — must go through these vows: the vow of truth — speaking and thinking of truth; the vow of bramacharya [celibacy], of non-violence, poverty, and non-possession. If you do not take these five vows you may not embark on the experiment.... Those who have made these experiments know that it is not for everyone to claim to hear the voice of conscience." (*C*, XLVIII, 405f)

[51] *1924*: "Willfulness is not conscience.... Conscience is the ripe fruit of strictest discipline.... A conscientious man hesitates to assert himself." (*C*, XXV, 23f)

In 1920 Gandhi said that anger if controlled can be transmuted into a power that can "move the world," and in 1942 his secretary remarked that Gandhi was entirely self-controlled with regard to anger, ambition and sex, and hence generated a "tremendous energy" which was the source of his hold on people:

[52] *1920*: "I have learnt through bitter experience the one supreme lesson to conserve my anger, and as heat conserved is transmuted into [other forms of] energy, even so our anger controlled can be transmuted into a power which can move the world." (*C*, XVIII, 246)

[53] *1942* as recalled by an American visitor: "I had been listening carefully to Gandhi and studying my notes and wondering all the time what was the source of his hold on people; I had come to the tentative conclusion that it was his passion.

"'That is right,' [Mahadev] Desai [Gandhi's secretary] said.

"'What is the root of his passion?' I asked.

"'This passion,' Desai explained, 'is the sublimation of all the passions that flesh is heir to.'

"'Sex?'

"'Sex and anger and personal ambition.... Gandhi is under his own complete control. That generates tremendous energy and passion.'" (Fischer 1950, 378f)

Gandhi recounted in 1934 a charming incident that illustrates how this radiant energy, derived from his self-discipline, could move other people to remarkable feats of discipline. During his campaign of 1933-34 against untouchability, a teen-age girl came forward to donate some jewelry to be sold for the cause, and then, in spite of his protests ("Have you the permission of your parents?"), proceeded to strip herself, one by one, of every piece she had — whereupon he told her, and she agreed, that she was not to have them replaced:[37]

[54] *1934*: "I had just finished my speech [and] had made a reasoned appeal to the women present for [donations of] jewelry,... when gently walked up to the platform... a girl, 16 years old. She took out one bangle and asked me if I would give my autograph. I was preparing to give it, when off came the other bangle.... 'You need not give me both. I shall give you the autograph for one bangle only.' She replied by taking off her golden necklace.... 'But have you the permission of your parents?'... Her hands automatically went to her ears and out came her jewelled ear-rings, amid the ringing cheers of the public.... Someone told me that her father was present... [and] was as generous as his daughter in giving to worthy causes. I reminded [her] that she was not to have ornaments replaced. She resolutely assented.... As I handed her the autograph, I could not help prefacing it with the remark, 'Your renunciation is a truer ornament than the jewelry you have discarded.'" (*T*, III, 241f)

37. He subsequently interviewed her to see whether she was certain she wished to keep the vow.

Gandhi put such a high value on self-discipline that he opposed the spread of knowledge about contraception and declared that sexual union in marriage is of no benefit to the partners:

[55] *1936*: "Eradication of disease is an utter impossibility unless the people learn to observe the elementary rule of self-discipline.... The Birth Control League... should understand that spread of contraceptive knowledge and practice can only aid the growth of self-indulgence and abuse and its inevitable concomitants, misery and diseases." (*H*, 12/xii, 354)

[56] *1936*: "It is not proved to my satisfaction that sexual union in marriage is in itself good and beneficial to the unionists. To the contrary effect I can bear ample testimony from my own experience and that of many friends. I am not aware of any of us having derived any benefit, mental, spiritual or physical. Momentary excitement and satisfaction... was invariably followed by exhaustion.... Indulgence interfered with my work.... Self-restraint is responsible for the comparative freedom from1 illnesses that I have enjoyed for long periods and for my output of energy and work both physical and mental which eye-witnesses have described as phenomenal.... Is it or is it not correct to say that the only right use of the generative organ is to confine it solely to generation and that any other use is its abuse? If it is, no difficulty in achieving the right use and avoiding the wrong should baffle the scientific seeker [of Truth]." (*C*, LXII, 310)

This became a basic concern of Gandhi's. He and his wife became friendlier to each other and more able to "render real service to humanity" after they took a vow of mutual chastity when they were 36 years old. Gandhi later said this had been in the "heyday of his youth," and thereby justified a ban on intercourse between young married folk at his ashram.[38]

Self-respect; Public-mindedness

In spite of his shyness Gandhi must have had, when he arrived in South Africa in 1893, more self-respect than most people; otherwise he would not have reacted with quite such indignation to his first insulting encounters there with the color-bar. The following episode illustrates the kind of insults that stirred him so deeply:

[57] *1893* (recalled in the 1920s): "A first-class seat [on the train] was booked for me.... The train reached... the capital of Natal at about 9 p.m.... A passenger came [in] and looked me up and down. He saw that I was a 'colored' man. This disturbed him. Out he went and came in again with one or two officials. They all kept quiet when another official came to me and said, 'Come along, you must go to the van compartment.'

"'But I have a first class ticket.'...

"The constable came. He took me by the hand and pushed me out. My luggage was also taken out. I re-

---

38. *H*, 7/vii/1946, 214. Gandhi said that although his wife was "never the temptress" (*A*, III, ch. 7), in the early years of the marriage he had cultivated a "devouring passion" for her; "the thought of nightfall and our subsequent meeting was ever haunting me" (*A*, I, ch. 4); yet in the daytime they often quarreled in those early years. One may readily imagine a link between this and Gandhi's later esteem for chastity.

fused to go to the other compartment and the train steamed away. I went and sat in the waiting room.... It was winter, and... extremely bitter. My overcoat was in my luggage, but I did not dare to ask for it lest I should be insulted again, so I sat and shivered....

"I began to think of my duty. Should I fight for my rights or go back to India?" (*A*, II, ch. 8)

[58] *1893* (recalled in 1938): "One experience... that changed the course of my life... occurred seven days after I had arrived in South Africa. I had gone there on a purely selfish mission. I was just a boy returned from England wanting to make some money. Suddenly the client who had taken me there asked me to go to Praetoria from Durban. It was not an easy journey. There was the railway journey as far as Charlestown and [then] the coach to Johannesburg. At Maritzburg where the beddings were issued [on the train] the guard came and turned me out and asked me to go the van compartment. I would not go and the train steamed away leaving me shivering in the cold. Now the creative experience comes here. I was afraid for my very life. I entered the dark waiting-room. There was a white man in the room. I was afraid of him. What was my duty, I asked myself. Should I go back to India, or should I go forward, with God as my helper, and face whatever was in store for me?" (*C*, LXVIII, 171)

Gandhi's positive decision must have been due only in part to the fact that he was a London-trained barrister and had come to South Africa as a first-class passenger; a deeper reason for it, and also for his emerging public-mindedness, must have been that he was the son of an esteemed public official who had devoted a great deal of love to him and had made it implicitly clear that he too should one day become occupied with governmental affairs:

[59] *Early 1880s* (recalled later): "My father would never ask any of the servants to do anything for him, but would insist on my doing it. If it was water that he wanted, or a shampoo of his legs, or any other personal service small or big, there was sure to be a call for me. He simply doted on me; it is hard to find a father as loving as he was.

"That day when I tried to see the drama is indelibly carved in my memory. Oh, the tears he shed, and the punishment he inflicted upon himself then! This was how it all happened. That day I was pressing his legs, as usual, but my heart was far away. The single thought: 'Oh, if only Bapu spared me today to let me see the play!' revolved in my mind. 'Bapu...,' I broached the subject timidly. But he had chosen to be deaf; he had sensed, of course, that the boy's heart was not in the massage. 'Bapu,' I ventured again, 'an excellent play is to be enacted today.' No answer. But my craze to see the performance blinded me to the plainest signs. The third time I pressed: 'Bapu, there is an excellent program. Shall I go to see it?' — 'Ye...s' came out from his trembling lips, but the meaning was clearly 'No.' Even that did not deter me. I stuck to the letter of his permission and went.

"The curtain was only just lifted and the first scene was on, when a man came from home and told me, 'Bapu is weeping like anything and beating with his palm

> his forehead in anguish.' I came out, sped home, and fell at Bapu's feet. He spoke not a word, not one word of anger or reproach. He showed his dislike merely through a stream of tears and gesticulation. Never after that day did I see a single play as long as he was alive.
>
> "He was a very strict disciplinarian. 'No; you will do this, not that.' — 'This has got to be done.' — 'What's this nonsense?' — 'Who did it this way?' would come out from his lips with irresistible finality. He insisted on having his way always. Even when the most confidential consultations [in his work as chief administrator of Rajkot] were going on, or when the most celebrated state representative was visiting him, he would have me by his side." (Desai 1968, 60f)

This last sentence casts light on a basic difference between Gandhi and the Communist anti-colonial leaders: while fighting for independence, Gandhi always had vividly in mind — from his experience at his father's side — that success would bring with it the task of governing. He was not the kind of leader who is a genius at getting the foreigners out of his country, and then, having helped to destroy the social and legal fabric of his homeland, becomes a monstrous bull in a china-shop when it comes to governing. He would always understand sympathetically the viewpoint of his adversary to the extent that it had to do with the responsiblities of governing. And it was for the same reason that he found it always more important to attend to the quality of his political means than to have a detailed idea of his political goal.

Indian Dignity

This combination of self-respect and public-mindedness generated Gandhi's simple yet, in the event, very strong decision, when the lawsuit which had brought him to South Africa had been settled, to stay for a while and build up an effective opposition to the government's proposed disenfranchisement of the Indian community:

[60] *1894*: "This Bill, if it passes into law, will... [be] the first nail in our coffin. It strikes at the root of our self-respect." (*A*, II, ch. 16)

The struggle lasted longer than he had imagined it would, and when he finally in 1914 negotiated an agreement in writing with General Smuts, many of his supporters felt that he settled for too little in the way of legislative and administrative changes. But he said that their chivalry had left an "invisible yet potent impress" and had "enhanced the prestige of the Indians." He asked them to be patient and by honorable means to educate the public and thereby enable the government to go further in future.[39]

We are struck by the fact that for some time after the conclusion of that first, historical non-violent political struggle, Gandhi's humanitarianism was still so weak that in 1918 he pleaded with his fellow Indians to take up arms in defence of the British Empire because he considered this a good way to

---

39. *S*, III, chh. 47-50.

win political advantage for India. He wanted Indian youngsters to kill German-speaking and Turkish youngsters in a war that did not concern India, because he imagined that Britain would then, out of gentlemanly gratitude, grant India a significant degree of self-rule:

[61] *1918*: "Sisters and brothers...: You have just emerged from a glorious satyagraha campaign.... You have successfully demonstrated how you can resist [the] government with civility and how you can retain your self-respect without hurting theirs. I now place before you an opportunity of proving that you bear no hostility to [the] government despite your having given it a strenuous fight.... It is our duty to enlist ourselves in the army [in World War I].... There can be no friendship between the brave and the effeminate. We are regarded as a cowardly people. If we want to become free from that reproach, we should learn the use of arms.... The easiest and the straightest way to win *swaraj* [self-rule] is to participate in the defence of the Empire." (*C*, XIV, 439f)

After the war Britain did not, alas, act as Gandhi had hoped. Instead, she curtailed such political rights as the Indians had already enjoyed, massacred civilians in 1919 and followed up with other brutalities. Gandhi's concern for national honor now became so keen that he said that to fail to "right the injustice," even if the effort cost India all the wealth she had, would be to sacrifice her soul for a "mess of pottage":

[62] *1920*: "Undoubtedly a cause must be grave to warrant the drastic method of non-coöperation.... I cannot imagine a graver wrong than the massacre... and the barbarity that

followed it, the whitewash of the... Committee... [and] the refusal to remove [British] officials who made the lives of the Punjabis a hell during the martial-law period. These acts constitute a complete series of continuing wrongs against India which, if India has any sense of honor, she must right at the sacrifice of all the material wealth she possesses. If she does not, she will have bartered her soul for a mess of pottage." (*T*, I, 299)

Patriotism dominates Gandhi's first book, *Indian Home Rule* (1909), and in that work his detailed criticism of Western ways — particularly its medical, legal and industrial practices — sank to the level of chauvinism:

[63] *1909*: "Indian civilization is the best.... The European is a nine days' wonder. Such ephemeral civilizations have often come and gone and will continue to do so." (*S*, IV, 198)

Now and then in his last years, his love of India might still cause him, perhaps in some moment of fatigue in the midst of passionate noise all around him, to echo such a drum-thumping kind of patriotism:

[64] *1946*: "Prayer is the first and the last lesson in learning the noble and brave art of sacrificing self in the various walks of life culminating in the defence of one's nation's liberty and honor." (*C*, LXXXIII, 372)

Humanitarianism

More significant than Gandhi's patriotism was the development, in the 1920s, of the deeper humanitarian concerns with-

[70] *1933*: **[Q.]** "Will it not hasten the removal of untouchability if caste Hindus take Harijans as domestic servants?"

[A.] "I fear that receiving Harijans as domestic servants will be, when it becomes at all general, not a spur to the removal of untouchability, but a sign of removal. Nevertheless, it is the duty of every reformer who has got rid of untouchability from his own household to have a Harijan domestic servant. No doubt, for the reformer it would be better still if he would take a Harijan boy or girl, not as a servant, but as a member of his family." (*C*, LVI, 1f)

Gandhi's growing humanitarianism led him in the 1920s to criticize other aspects of contemporary religious practice. He encouraged a 22-year-old Hindu man to resist his parents' inhumane demand that he marry a 9- or 10-year old girl:

[71] *1929*: **[Q.]** My parents want me to be married this very year.... Child-marriage is the rule [and] in my case... girls of nine or ten years of age only are available [from within our sub-caste].... I am... 22 years of age. My parents will not hear of my marrying a [young] widow or outside my caste. What am I to do in the circumstances?'

[A.] "...It seems to me that in all such contingencies it is not only the right but the religious duty of young men and young girls not to be afraid of the parents' wrath. It has been my experience that when a grown-up boy or girl takes up a just and right position and adheres to it with absolute firmness,... the parents, when once they realize that the resolution of their children is absolutely unalterable,... get reconciled to it.... My advice... is to refuse to be a party to the... sin of marrying a child girl.

> ...Consider it a virtue to marry [instead] outside [your] sub-caste or to marry a widow subject to the necessary limitations [e.g. within the same varna]." (*C*, XXXVIII, 431f)

He said women should not have to veil their faces,[43] and told Moslems that regardless of any ancient authority in favor of execution by stoning they should reject it as repugnant to their sense of humanity, which is the basis of "all true religion":

[72] *1925*: "I am very glad to find [from my correspondent] that there is no penalty of stoning to death in the Koran.... But [another Moslem correspondent], whilst saying that the penalty is not prescribed in the Koran, energetically argues that it has nevertheless a place in Islam.... What I would like my Moslem friends to do is unhesitatingly to condemn, irrespective of its source, what the world's reasoned opinion rejects as contrary to humanity. I am glad therefore that [two other Moslem correspondents] condemn the penalty of stoning altogether....

"There are undoubtedly things in the world which transcend reason.... Such is the mystery of the deity. It is not inconsistent with reason, it is beyond it. But stoning to death is no more beyond reason than, say, the practice of honesty.... The stoning incident is a matter... of public morality and general humanity which is the basis of all true religion." (*C*, XXVI, 415f)

He also opposed, as one might expect, the religious advocacy of wars. On that account he criticized the practices of Islam and Christianity, which he said were contrary to the teachings of their respective founders:

43. See Readings 305-307.

[73] *1927*: "I have given my opinion that the followers of Islam are too free with the sword. But that is not due to the teaching of the Koran. That is due, in my opinion, to the environment in which Islam was born. Christianity has a bloody record against it, not because Jesus was found wanting but because the environment in which it spread was not responsive to his lofty teaching." (*C*, XXXII, 588)

[74] *1936*: "I am convinced that it [Christianity] has distorted the message of Jesus. He was an Asiatic whose message was delivered through many media, and when it had the backing of a Roman emperor it became an imperialist faith as it remains to this day." (*H*, 30/v, 122)

An important new aspect of Gandhi's evolving humanitarianism during this period was his concern, in the wake of what he saw in India, about abject poverty.[44] He had not been concerned about this in South Africa; the Indians there, though insulted and politically cheated, were not starving, and he was not an advocate for the Blacks. Later, he recalled how in 1894 he had begun to develop direct contacts with Indian indentured laborers:

[75] *1894* (recalled later): "Although the members of the Natal Indian Congress included ...the clerical class,... the indentured laborers were still outside its pale. They could

44. Had he advocated the use of contraception as a form of discipline, there would be much less such poverty today. It did not seem to him a form of discipline, however, partly because "A friend who advocates birth-control frankly admits that he does not believe in the moral tie and that promiscuous intercourse is an ideal state." (*C*, XXVII, 96).

> not afford to belong to it by paying the subscription and becoming its members. The Congress could win their attachment only by serving them. An opportunity offered itself when neither the Congress nor I was really ready for it. I had put in scarcely three or four months' practice, and the Congress was still in its infancy, when a Tamil man in tattered clothes, head-gear in hand, two front teeth broken and his mouth bleeding, stood before me trembling and weeping.... The master, getting angry with him, had lost self-control and had beaten [him] severely....
>
> "I called upon the [master] and said to him, 'I do not want to proceed against you and get you punished. I think you realize that you have severely beaten the man. I shall be satisfied if you will transfer the indenture to someone else.' To this he readily agreed....
>
> "[The] case reached the ears of every indentured laborer and I came to be regarded as their friend. I hailed this connection with delight. A... stream of indentured laborers began to pour into my office and I got the best opportunity of learning their joys and sorrows." (*A*, II, ch. 20)[45]

Here we see Gandhi, having earned his spurs as an attorney, joining a white-collar work-ethic to a religiously derived ideal of suffering (in the form of tedious and conscientious litigating or negotiating) in order to serve a fellow Indian who needed his help but could not pay for it.

Then in 1904 a book by Ruskin showed Gandhi the value of physical work, which thereupon became one of his deepest beliefs:

---

45. For a detailed account see *E*, 493-95.

[76] *1904* (recalled later): "[A book] that brought about an instantaneous and practical transformation in my life was [Ruskin's] *Unto This Last*. I translated it....

"The teachings of *Unto This Last* I understood to be: *(1)* that the good of the individual is contained in the good of all; *(2)* that a lawyer's work has the same value as the barber's, inasmuch as all have the same right of earning their livelihood from their work; *(3)* that a life of [physical] labor, i.e. the life of a tiller of the soil and the handicraftsman, is the life worth living. The first of these I knew [already]. The second I had dimly realized. The third had never occurred to me. *Unto This Last* made it as clear as daylight for me that the second and third were contained in the first. I arose with the dawn, ready to reduce these principles to practice." (*A*, IV, ch. 17)

Yet for a long time he remained far more alert to the cause-and-effect chain: sacrifice – voluntary poverty – enlightenment than to its ugly counterpart: involuntary poverty – drudgery – degradation:[46]

[77] *1916*: "In South Africa, where I had the privilege of associating with thousands of our countrymen on most intimate terms, I observed almost invariably that the greater the possession of riches, the greater was their moral turpitude. Our rich men, to say the least, did not advance the moral struggle of passive resistance as did the poor....

"Jesus, Mohammed, Buddha, Nanak, Kabir [and several others]... were all men who deliberately embraced poverty as their lot." (*C*, XIII, 312ff)

46. See also *H*, 21/vii/1946, 232.

In his writings it appears that only after his definitive return to India in 1915, and then perhaps gradually, did Gandhi became distressed by the abject poverty around him. In 1917 he was astonished to learn that some women did not own two saris:

[78] *1917* (recalled in the late 1920s): "It may not be out of place here to narrate an experience that I have described before now at many meetings.... I happened to visit a... village ...and found some of the women dressed very dirtily. So I told my wife to ask them why they did not wash their clothes. She spoke to them. One of the women took her into her hut and said, 'Look now, there is no box or cupboard here containing other clothes. The sari I am wearing is the only one I have. How am I to wash it? Tell Mahatmaji ["Mr. Great Soul"] to get me another sari, and I shall then promise to bathe and put on clean clothes every day.' This cottage was not an exception, but a type to be found in many Indian villages. In countless cottages in India people live without any furniture, and without a change of clothes, merely with a rag to cover their shame." (*A*, v, ch. 18)

The list of problems to which Gandhi in 1919 thought that the method of satyagraha might be applied — political problems, the condition of women, some evil customs, some religious problems and the hardships of the "untouchables" — may refer vaguely to poverty, but does not evoke it specifically:

[79] *1919*: "Satyagraha is not limited to the relationship between the rulers and the ruled. For social reform too it is a priceless weapon, one without a parallel. The condition of women, our many evil customs, the difficulties which arise between Hindus and Moslems, the hardships of the

'untouchables' — a great many such problems can be solved in this way." (*C*, XVI, 93)

During the 1920s and after, however, Gandhi's humanitarian distress about involuntary poverty grew deeper. In 1921 he said that to ignore the masses of abjectly poor yet inarticulate people would be, for someone who was aware of their condition, less than human:

[80] *1921*: "I would be less than human if, with all my knowledge of avoidable misery pervading the land..., I did not feel with and for all the suffering but dumb millions of India." (*C*, XXI, 458)

When he was sentenced in 1922 to a six-year prison term, he told the court that in South Africa in the 1890s he had believed that the unfair treatment of Indians there was an excrescence upon a system that was "intrinsically and naturally good," and so he had given the government his "voluntary and hearty coöperation"; but that later in India, the poverty which he saw there had changed his mind:

[81] *1922*: "I came reluctantly to the conclusion that the British connection had made India more helpless than she ever was before, politically and economically.... She has become so poor that she has little power of resisting famines.[47] ...Little do [town-dwellers] realize that the government established by law in British India is carried on for this exploitation of the masses. No sophistry, no jugglery

47. Nanda 1958, 91: "There were seven famines in India in the first half of the nineteenth century; there were twenty-four in the second half."

in figures can explain away the evidence the skeletons in many villages present to the naked eye." (*C*, XXIII, 117)

After his release in 1924 on grounds of poor health (three weeks after an operation for appendicitis), he felt morally constrained not to assume an active political role until the end of the six-year period; but this did not prevent him from conveying in other ways his passionate concern about poverty:

[82] *1924*: "You regard me as a mahatma, not because of my truth, nor for my non-violence, but on account of my deep attachment to the poorest of the poor. Whatever happens, I can never desert the poor in their rags. That is why you feel that Gandhi counts for something.... I am convinced that the sole cause for your love for me is that I have identified myself with the poor." (*C*, XXV, 59f)

Gandhi never cultivated elegant secular poetry, yet even in rejecting aestheticism he spoke inadvertently in poetic terms when he declared in 1925, after seeing famine in the poorest province of India, "Orissa haunts me / in my waking hours / and in my dreams":

[83] *1925*: [Q.] "May not... some artists be able to see truth in and through beauty?" [A.] "Some may, but ...to the millions we cannot give that training to acquire a perception of beauty in such a way as to see Truth in it. Show them Truth first, and they will see beauty afterwards. Orissa haunts me in my waking hours and in my dreams. Whatever can be useful to those starving millions is beautiful to my mind. Let us give today first the vital things of life, and all the graces and ornaments of life will follow." (*C*, XXV, 255f)

In 1931 he said that God could appear only in the form of food to those who had but one daily meal, and an American visitor found that he cared far more about their hunger than about any other issue:

[84] *1931*: "How am I to talk of God to the millions who have to go without two meals a day? To them God can only appear as bread and butter." (*Y*, 15/x, 310)

[85] *1931*, according to a friend's later recollection: "He had the economic needs of the half-starved Indian villagers constantly in mind; he cared far more about them than about any political issue.... I have heard him say that, if he believed that the British would really be single-minded in treating the problem of poverty as the first problem to be tacked in India, he would be happy to see them continue to rule India indefinitely, even though he might be the only Indian to ask them to stay — though he hastened to add that he was convinced that this could never be, as every alien government was bound to make its own security its first concern." (H. Alexander 1969, 55)

In the 1940s he predicted a violent and bloody revolution unless there were a voluntary sharing of wealth to alleviate hunger; he warned rich people not to presume that their privileged wants are real needs; and he told his followers always to ask themselves if their activities were of any use to the poorest and weakest people they had come across:

[86] *1945*: "A non-violent system of government is clearly an impossibility so long as the wide gulf between the rich and the hungry millions persists.... A violent and bloody revolution is a certainty one day unless there is a volun-

tary abdication of riches and the power that riches give and sharing them for the common good." (*S*, IV, 350)

[87] *1946*: "Let no one try to justify the glaring difference between the classes and the masses, the prince and the pauper, by saying that the former need more." (*H*, 31/iii, 63)

[88] *1947*: "Whenever you are in doubt, or when the self becomes too much with you, apply the following test. Recall the face of the poorest and weakest man whom you may have seen, and ask yourself if the step you contemplate is going to be of any use to *him*.... Will he gain anything by it? Will it restore [to] him... control over his own life and destiny? In other words, will it lead to swaraj [self-rule] for the hungry and spiritually starving millions? Then you will find your doubts and ...self melting away." (*L*, II, 65)

This long crescendo of humanistic concern for the poor made Gandhi a far greater person at the time of his death than he had been when he was first addressed, in 1914, as a *mahatma*.[48]

Love of Religion

Gandhi's love of religion — he spent more than an hour each day in prayer — changed accordingly in those years. His father had given him an abiding respect for religion in general, and his mother a latent disposition to Hindu religiosity:

[89] *1870s and '80s* (recalled later): "My father... had that kind of religious culture which frequent visits to temples and

48. Goswami 1971, 68.

listening to religious discourses make available to many Hindus....

"The outstanding impression my mother has left on my memory is that of saintliness. She was deeply religious. She would not think of taking her meals without her daily prayers. Going to... temple... was one of her daily duties.... She would take the hardest vows and keep them without flinching.... To keep two or three consecutive fasts was nothing to her." (*A*, I, ch. 1)

His love of Hinduism, nourished by his having seriously considered Christianity in England and in South Africa, found its strongest mature expression at moments of anguish over what he regarded as its greatest curse, the doctrine and practice of untouchability:

[90] *1924*: "If untouchability is not eradicated during my lifetime and if I am to take another birth, I wish to be born a Bhangi [a bottom-rung 'untouchable']. If untouchability persists and I have the strength to abandon the Hindu religion, I shall read Kalma or become a Christian. I have, however, such great faith in my religion that I must live and die in it. For this reason also, I would wish to be born a Bhangi were I to be reborn." (*C*, XXV, 60)

[91] *1933* (in a letter to Nehru): "There is nothing so bad in all the world [as untouchablility], and yet I cannot leave religion and thereby Hinduism. My life would be a burden to me if Hinduism failed me. I love Christianity, Islam and many other faiths through Hinduism. Take it away and nothing remains for me." (*C*, LV, 96)

By the time of his death, however, he seemed on the verge of a broader religious identification. His prayers were a mixture of scriptures from every major religion.[49] His last words are sometimes translated into English as "Oh God," and in Chapter 5 we will show that this is the safest translation inasmuch as various witnesses have recorded versions of them that contradict each other and differ significantly from yet another, similar-sounding expression, exemplifying Hindu-Moslem harmony, which Gandhi himself said, a few months before, would be his last utterance if he were killed. Just a few hours before his assassination, he said:

[92] *1948*: "If someone were to end my life by putting a bullet through me — as someone tried to do with a bomb the other day — and I met his bullet without a groan and breathed my last taking God's name, then alone would I have made good my claim [to be a man of God]." (*L*, II, 766)[50]

Moksha

We come now to a concern which Gandhi described in the introduction to his autobiography as having been central to him ever since the 1890s:[51] the traditional Hindu yearning to

49. Gandhi's most revered spiritual disciple in India, Vinoba, followed him in this regard until 1955, and then decided that public prayer is less worthy of a religious person than to ask his or her companions to join in silent contemplation of truth, non-violence and compassion (see note 194, page 277).

50. An earlier related statement is recorded in *L*, II, 195 and *C*, LXXXVI, 522.

achieve *moksha* (salvation). This allegedly consists of escaping from a chain of successive worldly rebirths, and from the suffering that they entail, so that the bit of soul (*atman*) that has been attached to one's various worldly existences can be united, eternally and serenely, with a universal soul (*paramatman*) free of any corporeal existence.

[93] *Late 1920s*: "What I have been striving and pining to achieve these thirty years is self-realization, to see God face to face, to attain moksha." (*A*, Introduction)

It seems clear that Gandhi for at least most of his life took for granted the traditional Hindu belief in transmigration of the soul through a succession of worldly lives:[52]

[94] *Late 1920s*, discussing his wedding night: "We were certainly too shy.... But no coaching is really necessary in such matters. The impressions of the former birth are potent enough to make all coaching superfluous." (*A*, I, ch. 3)

[95] *1931*: "It is Nature's kindness that we do not remember past births.... Life would be a burden if we carried such a tremendous load of memories. A wise man deliberately forgets many things, even as a lawyer forgets the cases and their details as soon as they are disposed of. Yes, 'death is but a sleep and a forgetting'." (*C*, XLV, 115)

In 1908 he expressed the hope of achieving moksha at the end of his soul's next wordly life:

---

51. Patel 1981, 42, observes in regard to the years 1910-12 that "Gandhiji's Gujarati letters of this period are full of discussions of *moksha* and the means of attaining it."

52. See also Readings 115 (the first long paragraph), 116, 120, and 217.

[96] *1908*: "I have not yet reached the stage when I can attain liberation but I do believe that if I leave this body while treading the path along which my thoughts are nowadays running, I shall be reborn and speedily attain to moksha at the end of that life."[53] (*C*, VIII, 254)

His famous remark of 1924 that "there are no politics devoid of religion" was not a statement of intent to manipulate other people's religious sentiments for a political cause, but a confession of hope that his patriotic activities would help earn him the release of moksha:

[97] *1924*: "I am striving for the kingdom of heaven which is moksha.... For me the road to salvation lies through incessant toil in the service of my country and therethrough of humanity.... So my patriotism is for me a stage in my journey to the land of eternal freedom and peace. Thus it will be seen that for me there are no politics devoid of religion." (*C*, XXIII, 349)

Later that same year, he expressed a similar idea in apparently Christian terms when he told a Roman Catholic priest that since he yearned to see God face to face, he was struggling to reach the status of the lowliest of God's (human) creatures by serving them, which he could not do without entering politics. The priest had complained to him about "letters appearing under flaring captions in the nationalist press, drawing a comparison between your life and activities and that of Christ."

53. See also Reading 46.

[98] *1924*: "I lay claim to nothing exclusively divine in me. I do not claim prophetship. I am but a humble seeker after Truth and bent upon following It. I count no sacrifice too great for the sake of seeing God face to face. The whole of my activity, whether it may be called social, political, humanitarian or ethical, is directed to that end. And as I know that God is found more often in the lowliest of His creatures than in the high and mighty, I am struggling to reach the status of these. I cannot do so without their service. Hence my passion for the service of the suppressed classes; and... I cannot render this service without entering politics." (*C*, xxv, 117)

We have been struck by the paucity of references to moksha in the writings available from Gandhi's last years. According to the index to his *Collected Works*, the last reference is in the following remarks of about *mukti* (release):

[99] *1944*: "We all desire mukti but, perhaps, we do not know precisely what it means. Deliverance from the cycle of birth and death is one of its several meanings.

"The poet-saint Narsinh says: 'A man of God seeks not deliverance from birth and death; he asks to be born again and again.' Viewed from this angle, mukti takes on a somewhat different form.

"Extreme non-attachment is salvation, according the the *Gita*.... How to develop non-attachment? This can be done by regarding joy and sorrow, friend and foe, mine and thine, as all alike. Thus another name for non-attachment is equanimity.

"As drops add up to make the ocean, we can be friendly and become an ocean of friendliness. The world would be transformed if everyone in the world lived in a spirit of mutual amity." (*C*, LXXVII, 394)

Gandhi in these passages adopted a here-and-now outlook and avoided suggesting that he himself believed in transmigration. And when in 1947 a British journalist asked him why, since he had earlier made so much of moksha, it had not recently been "emphasized sufficiently," he replied with a tepid and in some ways equivocal endorsement of the idea, in contrast to the way he had written about it in his autobiography twenty years before:

[100] *1947* (as reported): [Q.] "From a reading of Gandhi's writings [someone] had gathered that the root of all Gandhi's activities was the desire for moksha, emancipation. But why was not this aspect emphasized sufficiently?" [A.] "Gandhiji... said the desire for moksha was indeed there, but it was not meant for anyone other than the individual himself. The world was interested in the fruits, not the root.... Was not a tree judged by its fruits?

"He was still a soul yearning to be free, but ever failing to reach the ideal which he knew to be true. Hence, it would be enough if he could take care of the immediate task before him, whether great or small, with all the care and freedom from bias or mental worries which he could bring to bear upon it." (*H*, 28/ix, 340)

In August 1947 Gandhi cited again, in a letter of consolation to a friend, the proverb, "Death is but a sleep and a forgetting,"[54] and thereupon explained, without suggesting that the explanation was applicable to certain people only:

---

54. This is an echo of "Our birth is but a sleep and a forgetting" in William Wordsworth's "Ode on Intimations of Immortality in Early Childhood."

[101] *1947*: "When the isolated drops melt, they share the majesty of the ocean to which they belong. In isolation they die but to meet the ocean again." (*C*, LXXXIX, 24)

Subtle evidence of this kind makes it reasonable to doubt that Gandhi in his last years believed in any form of afterlife for anyone.

Summary

To sum up the hypotheses outlined in this chapter — which we invite other students of Gandhi to improve upon — it seems to us that an active love of moral truth was central to his personality from early adolescence throughout his life. His sense of self-discipline, his love of Hinduism, and his humanitarianism were somehow latent from childhood, but came to the fore only at successively later stages of his life: the self-discipline in London, the love of Hinduism in South Africa (as a result of his study of Christianity), the humanitarianism in India.

He was converted to vegetarianism soon after arriving in London and it remained constantly important to him for the rest of his life.

In South Africa his sense of self-dignity, combined with a public-mindedness and a concern for non-violence that were latent from his childhood, led to his famous invention of political satyagraha in the service of Indian dignity. A cherishing of physical work dawned upon him in 1904 and remained strong for the rest of his life.

His return to India brought in its wake a blossoming of his love of Hinduism, and, more gradually, a broadening of his humanitarianism, a deep concern with starvation and involuntary poverty, and finally, an ever more desperate, indeed fatal, dedication to inter-religious harmony. His concern for moksha, which had been strong since sometime around the turn of the century and had helped sustain his dedication to politics in the discouraging mid-1920s, seems rather to have faded in his last years.

In India today Gandhi is most often celebrated for having led her to political independence from the British empire. We think this was never a very deep concern of his. He spent years in jail for it, but in his heart he felt that formal political independence was but an honorable (and eventually indispensable) means to other, more important ends.

CHAPTER 4

GANDHI'S HINDUISM

Much of this chapter will focus on the issue of caste, which is a unique and pivotal feature of traditional Hinduism.[55] In his last years Gandhi progressed in his attitude toward caste (as we saw first-hand at the time) by adapting his views to new circumstances and influences. We will consider also, though more briefly, his ideas about how humans should treat animals (who according to Hindu belief have souls in exactly the same way as humans), as this topic too will serve to show his undiminished capacity, in his last years, to become more humanistic.

Gandhi was not the kind of Hindu who accepts the authority of a priest or even attends temple. His religious activities consisted mainly of praying each day,[56] making (and keeping) vows, and working for religious reforms. All the essential ideas of traditional Hinduism were of course instilled in him during his youth. Among the most significant of these were beliefs in:

—the recurring transmigrations and reincarnations of the individual soul (*atman*) as a part of the universal soul (*paramatman*): a drop of the spiritual ocean.

—the possibility of eventual salvation (*moksha*) or self-realization in the sense of the atman's release (*mukti*) from the cycle of rebirths so that it can return to the universal ocean

55. Caste is more rigid than class. Your inherited caste identity is immutable.

56. For a representative selection of his prayers (in 1930) see C, XLIV, 386-97.

(as it were) and thus no longer be subject to the sufferings which have to be endured in any incarnation.

—each human being's inheritance, due to the degree of spiritual merit (*karma*) achieved in his or her most recent previous incarnation, of membership in one of four main types of caste (four *varnas*): *(1)* priestly (*Brahmin*); *(2)* military and administrative; *(3)* farmer and merchant (such was Gandhi's caste); *(4)* servant (*Shudra*) — or else in an even lower, "untouchable" caste.[57]

—Non-violence (*ahimsa*); courage; self-discipline; vegetarianism; the sacredness of the cow.

Also significant is that Hinduism is not a religious cult with a founder, but a broad tradition embracing many ancient native cults of India. There is no central body of Hindu leaders; the word "Hinduism" was coined by foreigners to distinguish between the religions native to India and those introduced from elsewhere; and Hindus have traditionally been cosmopolitan and tolerant of other religions, rather than proselytizing.[58]

Some formative influences

Gandhi's caste was not Brahmin, so he did not as a youth study the most ancient Hindu scriptures, the vedas,[59] from which a few of the precepts that we have mentioned can be

57. It is reckoned that about 20% of Hindus are in a formerly "untouchable" caste. About half of the other 80% are in a Shudra caste.

58. See Reading 227. (In this light the "Hare-Krishna" proselytizers in the USA may be seen as a recent aberration.) For an account by Gandhi in 1905, of the "tenets of Hinduism" at large, see *C*, IV, 408f.

derived.[60] Nor was he ever especially well read in the philosophical upanishads,[61] though he may have read some of the eleven earliest ones (there are more than a hundred later ones), each of which interprets or expands upon part of one of the classical vedas. He was fond of reciting the most famous mantra from one of the most highly venerated of the upanishads, which may be translated as follows:

[102] **Ancient Hindu philosopher:** "Enveloped by Consciousness is everything whatever that fluctuates [every phenomenon] in the universe. Therefore, enjoy with renunciation [and] do not covet that which is due to others." (Isa Upanishad, beginning)

In terms of scripture his Hinduism was based mainly on three sources:

—the *Ramayana*, the story of an ancient prince, Rama, who in order to honor a promise made by his father, went away to the forest for 14 years so that his younger half-brother could inherit the throne. He overcame many hardships, killed

59. The term "veda" comes from the Sanskrit word *vid*, meaning "to know," and thus a veda was originally regarded as nothing other than a compendium of knowledge. There are four basic classical vedas, the oldest of which, the Rig Veda, is regarded by many scholars as the earliest known book.

60. Untouchability and the sacredness of the cow are traditional concepts with no basis in ancient scriptures. In the vedas and the Gita there are passages referring to four types of people or four types of work, but without implying inherited vocations or castes. Hence the logic of a reformed Hinduism rejecting these latter concepts.

61. This term comes from two Sanskrit words meaning "to sit beneath" and thus evokes discipleship.

many demons and rescued his bride, Sita, from the demon-king of "Lanka" (probably Ceylon) before returning home to India to become a benevolent king. One of Rama's notable virtues was faithfulness to his word; he showed himself willing to sacrifice his life for its sake. He is considered by traditional Hindus to have been one of several epoch-making earthly incarnations (avatars) of the god Vishnu.

—a chapter from the *Mahabharata* (which is one of the two most famous ancient Indian epics, along with the Ramayana) known as the *Gita* (or *Bhagavad Gita*). This is a dialogue between the compassionate ancient Prince Arjuna and his royal charioteer, Krishna. Looking out at a prospective battlefield, the men discuss justice and Krishna explains to Arjuna the duty of defending it courageously, even at the expense of compassion.

—the *Bhagavata*: a long poem about this same Krishna, who ranks, like Rama, as a divine avatar. Krishna is the most prominent single figure in classical Hindu art. While he is depicted as a delightfully impish child and as a handsome young cowherd dallying with nubile milkmaids, the tone of the Bhagavata is of blissful religious devotion.

The following excerpts from Gandhi's autobiography show how he was introduced to some of this lore, and to his favorite magic spell:

[103] *Childhood* (recalled later): "Being born in the Vaishnava faith [a major Hindu cult, worshipping Vishnu], I had often to go to the [temple of Vishnu], but it never appealed to me. I did not like its glitter and pomp. Also I heard rumors of immorality being practiced there....

"My nurse, an old servant of the family,... suggested as a remedy for... [my] fear of ghosts and spirits... the repetition of Ramanama [i.e. the name, "Rama"] ...and so at a tender age I began repeating Ramanama to cure my fear of ghosts and spirits.... I think it is due to the seed sown by that good woman... that today 'Ramanama' is an infallible remedy for me [in any illness]....

"A cousin of mine who was a devotee of the Ramayana arranged for my second brother and me to learn Ram Raksha [a famous prayer]. We got it by heart, and made it a rule to recite it every morning after the bath. The practice was kept up as long as we were in Porbandar. As soon as we reached Rajkot [when Gandhi was seven years old] it was forgotten. For I had not much belief in it. I recited it partly because of my pride in being able to recite Ram Raksha with correct pronunciation.

"What, however, left a deep impression on me was the reading of the Ramayana before my father... [by a man who] had a melodious voice. He would sing the *doha*s [couplets] and *chopai*s [quatrains] and explain them, losing himself in the discourse and carrying his listeners along with him. I must have been 13 at that time, but I quite remember being enraptured by his reading. That laid the foundation of my deep devotion to the Ramayana [which] I regard as the greatest book in all devotional literature.

"The Bhagavata... used to be read [at Rajkot once every two weeks].... I attended the reading, but the reciter was uninspiring. Today I see that the Bhagavata is a book which can evoke religious fervor....

"In Rajkot... I got an early grounding in toleration for all branches of Hinduism and sister religions.... My father and mother would visit the [temple of Vishnu] and also Shiva's and Rama's temples, and would take or send us youngsters there." (*A*, I, ch. 10)

Amongst these temples, that of Rama had been the nearest and dearest:

[104] *Childhood* (recalled in 1933): "I used daily to visit the Ramji Mandir [Temple of Rama] adjacent to my ancestral home. My Rama then resided there. He saved me from many fears and sins." (*C*, LIV, 112)

Now and then throughout his life, Gandhi would express an intensely sentimental love of Rama:

[105] *1924*: "My mother, my father, my brother — He [Rama] is everything to me. My life is His. In Him I live. I see Him in all women, and so regard every one of them as mother or sister.[62] I see Him in all men and therefore look on everyone as father, brother or son according to his age." (*C*, XXIV, 197)

[106] *1931*: "To me that name ['God'] makes no appeal, but when I think of Him as Rama, He thrills me." (*C*, XLVIII, 127)

[107] *1934*: "Learn to repeat the blessed name of Rama with such sweetness and such devotion that the birds will pause in their singing to listen to you." (*C*, LVII, 446)

We have seen (Reading 89) how Gandhi's mother was saintly, with her daily prayers and attendance at temple and her vows and fasting, and also how moral Truth became Gandhi's "sole objective" already in his childhood (Reading 11). The following passage is about a precept which served him well

62. Gandhi had no daughters.

in his political work and which Christians are taught in the Sermon on the Mount:

[108] *Mid-1880s* (recalled later): "A Gujarati didactic stanza... gripped my mind and heart. Its precept — return good for evil — became my guiding principle:...

> For a bowl of water, give a goodly meal;
> For a kindly greeting, bow thou down with zeal....
> But the truly noble [behavior] all men know as one
> And return — with gladness — good for evil done."
> (*A*, I, ch. 10)

In England, his Hindu heritage was awakened by some Theosophist friends:

[109] *1889* (recalled later): "Towards the end of my second year in England I came across two Theosophists... [who] talked to me about the Gita. They were reading Sir Edwin Arnold's translation — *The Song Celestial* — and they invited me to read the original with them.... I was constrained to tell them that I had not read the Gita..., still I hoped to be able to understand the original to the extent of telling where the translation failed to bring out the meaning.... The verses in the second chapter:

> ...If one
> Ponders on objects of the senses, there springs
> Attraction; from attraction grows desire;
> Desire flames to fierce passion; passion breeds
> Recklessness; then the memory — all betrayed —
> Lets the noble purpose go, and saps the mind,
> Till purpose, mind and man are all undone

made a deep impression on my mind and they still ring in my ears. The book struck me as one of priceless worth... [and] the impression has ever since been growing on me.....

"The brothers also recommended *The Light of Asia* by Sir Edwin Arnold... [and] once I had begun it I could not leave off. They... introduced me to Madame Blavatsky [the inventor of Theosophy] and Mrs. Besant... [and] advised me to join the [Theosophical] Society, but I politely declined.... Madame Blavatsky's *Key to Theosophy*... stimulated in me the desire to read books on Hinduism and disabused me of the notion fostered by the [Christian] missionaries that Hinduism was rife with superstition." (*A*, I, ch. 20)

His sense of Hindu identity grew stronger and more substantial during his years in South Africa:

[110] *1894* (recalled later): "Raychandbhai [Rajchandra] was guiding me [by letters from India].[63] Some friends sent me Narmadashanker's book, *Dharma Vichar*.... I read with interest Max Muller's book, *India – What Can it Teach Us?*, and the translation of the upanishads by the Theosophical Society. All this enhanced my regard for Hinduism." (*A*, II, ch. 23)

[111] *1903* (recalled later): "Theosophist friends [in South Africa]... expected that I should be helpful to them.... I felt like a triton among the minnows. I started reading Swami Vivekananda's *Rajayoga* with some of these friends and M. N. Dvivedi's *Rajayoga* with others. I had to read Patanjali's *Yoga Sutras* with one friend and the Bhagavadgita with quite a number. We formed a sort of Seekers' Club where we had regular meetings....

"I decided to get by heart one or two verses [of the Gita] every day.... I turned to this dictionary of conduct for a

63. See Reading 241.

ready solution of all my troubles and trials. Words like *aparigraha* [meaning 'non-possession'] and *samabhava* [meaning a feeling of oneness and equality with others] gripped me." (*A*, IV, ch. 5)

Selectiveness

Gandhi's capacity for idiosyncratic interpretation is illustrated by the way he downplayed the most likely historical meaning of the Gita[64] in order to interpret it as a tract against violence, and so had to defend his view with remarks like:

[112] *1925*: "Although ...[Chapter 2] lends itself to a violent interpretation, the concluding verses seem to me to preclude any such interpretation. The fact is that a literal interpretation of the Gita lands one in a sea of contradictions. The letter truly killeth, the spirit giveth life." (*C*, XXVI, 289)

In the early 1920s his sense of Hindu identity was perhaps more vivid than during any other part of his life, but even then he could hardly be described as a religious conformist:

[113] *1920*: "My unconventionality [as a Hindu] I carry to the point of rejecting the divinity of the oldest *shastras* [scriptures] if they cannot convince my reason. But I have found by experience that if I wish to live in society, ...I must limit the points of utter independence to matters of first-rate importance." (*C*, XVIII, 44)

64. Nanda 1958: 69f.

Later he would describe Hindu society as rife with gender bias:[65]

[114] *1932*, recalling the early days of his marriage: "I did not give ...[Kasturba] the same freedom of action which I enjoyed, and she did not have the capacity to exercise it either. Hindu women never have such capacity. That is a defect of Hindu society." (*C*, L, 354)

When he encountered, in the meantime, strong religious opposition to his movement to abolish untouchability, he claimed the status of an orthodox and conservative Hindu. In reading the following remarks, however, one should allow for the fact that probably most of the readers to whom he addressed them remained unconvinced:

[115] *1921*: "It has been asked why I call myself an orthodox *sanatani* [conservative] Hindu and why I regard myself as a Vaishnava.... The answer will cover the definition of a sanatani Hindu and include a complete description of a Vaishnava.

"According to my belief, a Hindu is anyone who, born in a Hindu family in India, accepts the vedas, the upanishads and the puranas [epic myths] as holy books; who has faith in the five yamas of truth, non-violence, etc. [celibacy, non-possession and voluntary poverty], and practices them to the best of his ability; who believes in the existence of the atman and the paramatman and believes, further, that the atman is never born and never dies but, through incarnation in the body, passes from existence to existence and is capable of attaining moksha; who believes that

65. P. Joshi 1988 is an anthology of Gandhi's remarks about women.

moksha is the supreme end of human striving and believes in varnashrama [the laws of the four basic castes and four stages of spiritual growth in a person's life] and cow-protection. Whoever, besides believing in all these, has been born in a family belonging to the Vaishnava sect [the sect of Vishnu] and has not forsaken the Vaishnava way; who possesses in some measure the qualities described in Narasinh Mehta's devotional song entitled "Vaishnava-jana" and strives to cultivate these qualities in perfection is a Vaishnava. It is my firm belief that I possess in a large measure the characteristics described by me and I have been striving to strengthen them. I do not, therefore, hesitate to call myself with all firmness, though humbly, a strict sanatani Hindu and a Vaishnava.

"I believe that the most important outward form of Hinduism is cow-protection. I regard the Hindu world as impotent because at present not a single Hindu is capable of giving that protection. Among these impotent people, I believe myself to be the least impotent....

"I believe that the essence of Hinduism is truth and non-violence. I have not seen anyone among those whom I know respect truth so scrupulously as I have been doing right from my childhood. The active manifestation of non-violence is love — absence of ill will. I firmly believe that I am overflowing with love. I have not felt ill will against anyone even in a dream. I entertain no such feeling against Dyer, his wicked deeds notwithstanding.[66] Wherever I have seen misery or injustice, I have felt troubled in my soul.

---

66. General Dyer at Amritsar in 1919 ordered his troops to fire without warning at a nearby crowd of peaceful Indian civilians in an enclosed space, and later justified his having marched his soldiers away without doing anything about the more than 1000 wounded survivors (many

"The central principle of Hinduism is that of moksha. I am ever striving for it. All my activites are for moksha. I have as much faith in the existence of atman and in its immortality as I am certain of the existence of my body and its transience.

"For these reasons I am happy to declare myself a staunch sanatani Hindu.

"If anybody asks me whether I have made any deep study of the shastras [scriptures], I would say that I have and I have not. I have not studied them from a scholar's point of view. My knowledge of Sanskrit is almost nil; even of the translations available in modern Indian languages, I have read only a few. I cannot claim to have fully read even a single veda. Nevertheless, I have understood the shastras from the point of view of *dharma* [duty]. I have grasped their real meaning. I know that one can attain moksha without reading the vedas.

I have found the right method for reading — for understanding — the shastras. If any injunction in a shastra is opposed to truth, non-violence and bramacharya, it is unauthentic, whichever the shastra in which it is found. The shastras are not above reason.... That shastra which teaches me drinking liquor, eating meat and wicked ways cannot be called a shastra.

"...I have always believed that there are no more than four varnas [general castes]. I believe that one acquires one's caste by birth....

"...[Specific] castes are subject to increase and decrease [in number]. Only the man himself can leave Hinduism, though he may be expelled from the [specific] caste. Ex-

---

others were killed), on the grounds that the victims did not at the time apply to him for help.

communication by the caste is a mode of punishment and ought to be available to every community.

"It is certainly necessary that the numerous castes should become fewer, and this can be brought about by the councils of the various castes without injury to Hinduism....

"Now remains the issue of untouchability. Nobody can trace the origin of this practice.... That an untouchable cannot live in our neighborhood and cannot own land, that an untouchable must, on seeing us, shout: 'Please keep at a distance! Do not touch me!'... — this is not Hinduism. This is Dyerism....

"I have found the homes of Bhangis ['untouchable' scavengers] far cleaner than many Vaishnava houses. I have been astonished at the truthfulness, simplicity, kindness, and other such qualities in some of them. It is my conviction that we [Hindus] have fallen [into impotence] because of the entry into Hinduism of the demon of untouchability, and have, in consequence, also become powerless to ensure the protection of mother cow. So long as we have not rid ourselves of this Dyerism, we have no right to ask that we should be freed from the Dyerism of the British." (*C*, XIX, 327-332)

The first part of the following, more succinct statement is notable for its hedging phrases; the second part shows a link between Gandhi's selective use of Hindu scriptures and his tendency, which became stronger as he grew older, toward a similarly selective eclecticism.

[116] *1921*: "I call myself a sanatani Hindu because: *(1)* I believe in... all that goes by the name of Hindu scriptures, and therefore in avatars and rebirth, *(2)* I believe in

varnashrama dharma [duties entailed by varna] in a sense in my opinion strictly vedic but not in its present popular and crude sense, *(3)* I believe in the protection of the cow in its much larger sense than the popular; *(4)* I do not disbelieve in idol-worship....

"[Yet] I believe the Bible, the Koran, and the Zend-Avesta to be as much divinely inspired as the vedas. My belief in the Hindu scriptures does not require me to accept every word and every verse as divinely inspired." (*C*, XXI, 245f)

In either context — Hindu or "all-religions"— the criteria for his selectiveness would be reason and humanitarian morality:

[117] *1927*: "In trying to explore the hidden treasures of ancient culture, I have come upon this inestimable boon that all that is permanent in ancient Hindu culture is also to be found in the teachings of Jesus, Buddha, Mohammed and Zoroaster.... Then you can see how safe the road becomes in front of you and me when we summarily and mercilessly reject untouchability, the devadasi institution [religiously sanctioned prostitution], drunkenness, [and] sacrifice of animals... because they do not appeal to our moral sense." (*C*, XXXV, 327f)

[118] *1935*: "[Not] every word of the printed works passing muster as shastras is, in my opinion, a revelation.... Nothing in the shastras which is manifestly contrary to universal truths and morals can stand. Nothing in the shastras which is capable of being reasoned can stand if it is in conflict with reason." (*C*, LXII, 121)

The issue was not just academic. The opposition to Gandhi's proposed reforms was so strong that he predicted they might provoke his assassination:[67]

[119] *1932*: "I find no warrant for untouchability in this Book of Life [the Gita]. On the contrary, it compels me, by an appeal to my reason and a more penetrating appeal to my heart, in language that has a magnetic touch about it, to believe that all life is one and that it is through God and must return to Him.

"According to sanatana dharma [the orthodox Hindu concept of religious duty], life does not consist in outward rites and ceremonies but the uttermost inward purification and merging oneself, body and soul, in the divine essence. I have gone to the masses in their millions with this message from the Gita burnt into my life, and they have listened to me, not for any political wisdom or for eloquence, but because they have instinctively recognized me as one of them, as one belonging to their faith. As days have gone by, my belief has grown stronger that I could not be wrong in claiming to belong to sanatana dharma, and if God wills it, He will let me seal that claim with my death." (*C*, LI, 345)

Caste and vocation

In Gandhi's day, the traditional Hindu caste distinctions involved four basic rules:

— to follow your parent's vocation;

— to marry within your caste;

— not to eat together with anyone lower-caste than yourself;

— to avoid touching or, in Malabar, even looking at an "un-

67. This prediction did not come true. He was assassinated in 1948 for advocating amity with Pakistan.

touchable" if you were not one yourself — which in turn meant that the "untouchables" had to reside outside the proper confines of the village.

Gandhi's first main proposal for reforming Hinduism was that untouchability should be abolished. The "untouchable" castes should become Shudra (servant) castes and the former untouchables should thus be allowed to enter temples, walk on public roads, and draw water from the same wells as other people. In Chapter 3 we have seen how Gandhi had already as a child disbelieved in untouchability (Reading 67). We will cite below a few of his later remarks about it.

His other main proposal was to fuse the castes within each of the four varnas. This idea can be found in the first paragraph of the following passage. The first sentence of the second paragraph suggests that one of his reasons for clinging to the idea of inherited vocations was a certain revulsion for the contemporary Western alternative:

[120] *1920*: "I believe that caste has saved Hinduism from disintegration. But like every other institution it has suffered from excrescences. I consider the four divisions alone to be fundamental, natural and essential. The innumerable sub-castes are sometimes a convenience, often a hindrance. The sooner there is fusion [within each of the four varnas], the better....

"One of my correspondents suggests that we should abolish the caste [system] but adopt the class system of Europe — meaning thereby, I suppose, that the idea of heredity in caste should be rejected. I am inclined to think that the law of heredity is an eternal law and any attempt to alter that law must lead us, as it has before led [others], to utter confusion.... If Hindus believe, as they must believe, in reincarnation [and] transmigration, they must know that Nature will, without any possibility of mistake, adjust the balance by degrading a Brahmin, if he misbehaves himself, by reincarnating him in a lower division, and translating one [of a lower caste] who lives the life of a Brahmin in his present incarnation to Brahminhood in his next. (*C*, XIX, 83f)

Around 1920, Gandhi's belief in the four varnas and in inherited vocations was just as passionate as other people's belief at that time in untouchability:

[121] *1920*: "The beauty of the caste system is that it does not base itself upon distinctions of wealth-possessions. Money, as history has proved, is the greatest disruptive force in the world.... Caste is but an extension of the principle of the family. Both are governed by blood and heredity. Western scientists are busy trying to prove that heredity is an illusion and that milieu is everything. The ...experience of many lands goes against the conclusions of these scientists; but even accepting their doctrine of milieu, it is easy to prove that milieu can be conserved and developed more through caste than through class.... As we all know, change comes very slowly in social life, and thus, as a matter of fact, caste has allowed new groupings to suit the changes in lives. But these changes are [as] quiet and easy as a change in the shape of the clouds. It is difficult to imagine a better harmonious human adjustment.

"Caste does not connote superiority or inferiority. It simply recognizes different outlooks and corresponding modes of life. But it is no use denying the fact that a sort of hierarchy has been evolved in the caste system, but it cannot be called the creation of the Brahmins. When all castes accept a common [religious] goal of life, a hierarchy is inevitable, because all castes cannot realize the ideal in equal degree." (*C*, XIX, 174ff)

[122] *1921-22*: "I believe that if Hindu society has been able to stand, it is because it is founded on the caste system.... A community which can create the caste system must be said to possess unique power of organization....

"To destroy the caste system and adopt the Western European social system means that Hindus must give up the principle of hereditary occupation which is the soul of the caste system. [The] hereditary principle is an eternal principle. To change it is to create disorder.... It will be a chaos if every day a Brahmin is to be changed into a Shudra and a Shudra is to be changed into a Brahmin. The caste system is a natural order of society.... I am opposed to all those who are out to destroy the caste system." (*B*, IX, 275f)

He felt that even if you have managed somehow to learn a profession other than your "hereditary" one, you must not earn a living by it:[68]

[123] *1925*: "There is no harm if a person belonging to one varna acquires the knowledge or science and art specialized in by persons belonging to other varnas. But as far as the way of earning his living his concerned, he must follow the occupation of the varna to which he belongs,

68. In 1915 he had become acquainted with, and admired, a tailor "who earns Rs. 15 a month — which is just what he needs — working [as a tailor] an hour a day, and gives the rest of his time to public work" (*A*, V, ch. 3).

which means he must follow the hereditary profession of his forefathers.

"The object of the varna system is to prevent competition and class struggle and class war. I believe in the varna system because it fixes the duties and occupations of persons.... Varna means the determination of a man's occupation before he is born.... In the varna system no man has any liberty to choose his occupation. His occupation is determined for him by heredity." (*B*, IX, 277)

[124] *1926*: "In accepting the fourfold division I am simply accepting the laws of Nature, taking for granted what is inherent in human nature and the law of heredity. We are born with some of the traits of our parents. The fact that a human being is born only in the human species shows that some characteristics [comprising] caste are determined by birth. There is scope enough for freedom of the will inasmuch as we can to a certain extent reform some of our inherited characteristics. [But] it is not possible in one birth entirely to undo the results of our past doings." (*C*, XXIX, 410f)

Yet now and then he would soften the tone of his argument. In 1920 he had said that while "caste does not connote superiority or inferiority," nonetheless "a hierarchy is inevitable" (Reading 121), but by the mid-1920s he would downplay the latter idea:

[125] *1925*: "The caste system has in my opinion a scientific basis. Reason does not revolt against it. If it has disadvantages, it has also its advantages. It does not prevent a Brahmin from serving his Shudra brother. Caste creates a social and moral restraint [and is therefore good]. [However,] the doctrine of caste cannot be extended [beyond that

of varna]; [so] I would restrict it to four divisions. Any multiplication would be an evil. I would reform the castes and rid them of undoubted abuses, but I can find no reason for their abolition. For me there is no question of superiority or inferiority. A Brahmin who regards himself as a superior being born to look down upon the other castes is not a Brahmin. If he is first [in status] he is so by right of [spiritual] service." (*C*, XXVI, 289)

[126] *1927*: "In [my] conception of the law of varna no one is superior to any other.... A scavenger has the same status as a Brahmin." (*C*, XXXV, 260)

In 1931, he met Ambedkar (1891-1956), who was soon to become the most articulate critic of his views on caste. Ambedkar was born into an "untouchable" caste traditionally responsible for such tasks as sweeping the streets and carrying away dead cattle. However, his grandfather and father had served in the colonial British army, and his unusual intelligence as a child had prompted some reform-minded Hindus to pay for most of his higher education. In 1916 he took a Ph.D. degree in economics at Columbia University (in New York), where he delivered a paper entitled, "The Castes in India — their Mechanism, Genesis and Development." After serving as a professor of economics in Bombay from 1918 to 1920, he went abroad again; in 1923 he was awarded a D.Sc. degree by the London School of Economics and became a barrister (a lawyer qualified to plead in British courts). Returning to India in 1923, he practiced law and undertook a variety of social, educational and political projects for the advancement of the untouchables.[69]

Ambedkar was less diplomatic than Gandhi. Their first meeting, in Bombay in 1931, did not end very cordially. (Gandhi later explained, "I did not know he was a Harijan; I thought he was some Brahmin who took deep interest in Harijans and therefore talked intemperately.")[70] But Gandhi respected Ambedkar and was influenced by his criticisms. This seems evident already in the novel (for Gandhi) nuances of the following statements:

[127] *1931*: "I do not believe in caste in the modern sense. It is an excrescence and a handicap on progress. Nor do I believe in inequalities between human beings. We are all absolutely equal. But equality is of souls and not bodies. ...We have to realize equality in the midst of this apparent inequality. Assumption of superiority by any person over any other is a sin against God and man. Thus caste, in so far as it connotes distinctions in status, is an evil.

"I do however believe in varna which is based on hereditary occupations. Varnas are four to mark four universal occupations — imparting knowledge, defending the defenceless, carrying on agriculture and commerce, and performing service [to other humans] through physical labor. These occupations are common to all mankind, but Hinduism, having recognized them as the law of our being, has made use of it in regulating social relations and conduct.[71] Gravitation affects us all whether one

69. Khairmoday 1972. Alas, Busi 1997 came to our attention too late to be of use in preparing this book.

70. Desai 1953, I, 52.

(71: see next page)

knows its existence or not. But scientists who knew the law have made it yield results that have startled the world. Even so has Hinduism startled the world by its discovery and application of the law of varna....

"[Yet] according to my definition of varna there is no varna in operation at present in Hinduism. The so-called Brahmins have ceased to impart knowledge. They take to various other occupations. This is more or less true of the other varnas." (*C*, XLVI, 302)

[128] *1932*: "No matter what was the position in ancient times, no one can nowadays go through life claiming to belong to a high class. Society will not willingly admit any such claim to superiority, but only under duress. The world is now wide awake....

"There are four varnas, all equal in status, and they are determined by birth. They can be changed by a person choosing another profession, but if varnas are not as a rule determined by birth, they tend to lose all meaning....

"The varna system implies the obliteration of all distinctions of high and low. If the carpenter is held to be superior to the shoemaker, and the pleader or doctor is superior to both of them, no one would willingly become a shoemaker or carpenter and all would try to become pleaders or doctors. They would be entitled to do so and to be praised for doing so....

---

71. Other societies had traditional occupations and social regulations without limiting a young man's vocational choice to his father's occupation. A young man in neo-Confucian China would enter government service by doing well in written national examinations (with the candidates' identities concealed from the evaluators). In Medieval and Renaissance Europe, he could be apprenticed to someone in a different occupation from that of his father if it suited him better.

"But when it is suggested that everyone should practice his father's profession, the suggestion is coupled with the condition that the practitioner of every profession will earn only a living wage and no more.... This principle then is an integral part of the varna system: that learning is not a trade and may not be used in order to amass riches. Therefore in so far as ministrations may be necessary, the lawyer or doctor ought by practicing his profession to earn only living wage. And such was actually the case formerly.... Such is the varna system which the ashram is trying to resuscitate....

"Boys [between 9 and 16 years of age] should be taught their parents' avocation in such a way that they will by their own choice obtain their livelihood by practicing the hereditary craft. This does not apply to the girls.... [From] 16 to 25 [years of age]... every young person should have an education according to his or her wishes and circumstances." (*C*, L, 233)

[129] *1932*: "My own opinion is that the varna system has just now broken down. There is no true Brahmin [caste priest] or true Kshatriya [caste warrior] or Vaishya [caste merchant]. We are all Shudras [caste servants], i.e. one varna. If this position is accepted, then the thing becomes easy. If this does not satisfy our vanity, then we are all Brahmins. Removal of untouchability does mean root-and-branch destruction of the idea of superiority and inferiority." (*C*, LI, 199f)

Gandhi would evoke this all-Shudra idea from time to time thereafter:

[130] *1933*: "Today... there is utter confusion of varna, and I wish that all the Hindus will voluntarily call themselves Shudras." (*T*, III, 196)

It had initially come to him from considering a related idea which he had encountered soon after returning to India from South Africa.

[131] *1915*, recalled later: "[Someone suggested] that formerly all were Brahmins, and that now too all should be recognized as such and that the other varnas should be abolished. It appeared to me then, as it appears to me now, as a wierd suggestion. It is the so-called superior that has to descend from his heights, if the reform is to be peaceful." (*C*, xxxv, 262f)

And yet Ambedkar's view of the matter would sometimes provoke Gandhi into arguing that it was not really important even to reduce the number of castes to four:

[132] **Ambedkar**, *1933*: "There will be outcastes as long as there are castes, and nothing can emancipate the outcaste except the destruction of the caste system."
Gandhi: "Dr. Ambedkar is bitter. He has every reason to feel so.... [Yet] I do not believe the caste system, even as distinguished from varnashrama [the four varnas and four ideal stages of spiritual growth in an individual life], to be an 'odious and vicious dogma.' It has its limitations and defects, but there is nothing sinful about it, as there is about untouchability, and if [untouchability] is a by-product of the system, it is only in the same sense that an ugly growth is of a body, or weeds of a crop." (*T*, III, 192f)

He did now admit, however, that his ideal of a varna system with everyone enjoying equal economic and social status probably had no historical warrant:

[133] **Interviewer,** *1934*: "Do you not think that in ancient India there was much difference in economic status and social privileges between the four varnas?"
Gandhi: "That may be historically true. But misapplication or an imperfect understanding of the law must not lead to the ignoring of the law itself. By constant striving we have to enrich the inheritance left to us. This law determines the duties of man. Rights follow from a due performance of duties. It is the fashion nowadays to ignore duties and assert or rather usurp rights." (*C*, LIX, 319f).

The contrast between Gandhi's and Ambedkar's views of varna and inherited vocations was heightened by their respective relations to the most radical contemporary reform-Hindu movement. An energetic organization founded in 1875, the *Arya Samaj* ("Society of Aryans"), had in the late 19th and early 20th centuries overtaken the somewhat older *Brahmo Samaj* as the most successful such movement, with its membership growing from some 40,000 in 1891 to half a million by 1921.[72] While proclaiming that Hinduism was far better than any other religion, the Arya Samaj criticized sharply a number of conservative Hindu practices and precepts, among them the multiplicity of castes based on birth alone. Then, around 1930, a small offshoot of the Arya Samaj, the *Jat-Pat Todak Mandal* ("Caste-Breaking Society") dedicated itself to promoting a casteless Hinduism by advocating marriages between people of different varnas. Gandhi felt:

---

72. Sarkar 1983: 74.

[134] *1932*: "If eradication of castes means the abolition of varna I do not approve of it. But I am with you if your aim is to end the innumerable [sub]caste distinctions." (*C*, LI, 264)

Yet Ambedkar and the Jat-Pat Todak Mandal between them caused the tone of Gandhi's statements about caste to change considerably. In 1935 Gandhi said:

[135] *1935*: "Caste has to go. Varnashrama of the shastras is today nonexistent in practice. The present caste system is the very antithesis of varnashrama. The sooner public opinion abolishes it the better.

"...Prohibition there is [in varnashrama] of change of one's hereditary occupation for purposes of gain. The existing practice is therefore doubly wrong in that it has set up cruel restrictions about interdining and intermarriage and tolerates anarchy about choice of occupation....

"The most effective, quickest and most unobtrusive way to destroy caste is for reformers to begin the practice with themselves and, where necessary, take the consequences of social boycott. The change will be gradual and imperceptible." (*C*, LII, 121f)

In 1936 the Jat-Pat Todak Mandal invited Ambedkar to preside at their annual convention. However, upon seeing the typescript of his proposed presidential address, in which he not only outlined a comprehensive program of Hindu reform including the selection of priests by state examinations rather than by heredity, but also implied that he would probably leave Hinduism altogether,[73] they asked him to modify the text. He refused; they cancelled the convention; and his speech was published independently. Here is a brief excerpt pertinent to our immediate topic:

[136] **Ambedkar,** *1936*: "The mass of people [in India have] tolerated the social evils to which they have been subjected... [because they] have been completely disabled for direct action on account of this wretched system of chaturvarnya [the four varnas]. They could not bear arms and without arms they could not rebel.[74] ...On account of the chaturvarnya, they could receive no education, [so] they could not think out or know the way to their salvation.... Not knowing the way of escape and not having the means of escape, they became reconciled to eternal servitude, which they accepted as their inescapable fate." (*B*, I, 63)

Gandhi invited Ambedkar to express his views in *Harijan*. Ambedkar declined, but Gandhi called attention to them anyway, and commented:

[137] *1936*: "Dr. Ambedkar... has quoted chapter and verse in proof of his... indictment.... No Hindu who prizes his faith above life itself can afford to underrate the importance of this indictment.... [Yet there are] flaws in [it].... Caste has nothing to do with religion. It is a custom whose origin I do not know.... Varna [has] nothing to do with castes. The law of varna teaches us that we have each one of us to earn our bread by following the ances-

73. Ambedkar converted to Buddhism in the last year of his life.

74. A traditionalist could reply that India might thus indeed lose wars but at least would not stop tending her crops for the sake of military mobilization.

tral calling.... The essence of Hinduism is contained [however] in its enunciation of the one and only God as Truth and its bold acceptance of ahimsa as the law of the human family.

"I am aware that my interpretation of Hinduism will be disputed by many besides Dr. Ambedkar. That does not affect my position. In my opinion the profound mistake that Dr. Ambedkar has made in his address is to pick out *[1]* texts of doubtful authenticity and value and *[2]* the state of degraded Hindus who are no fit specimens of the faith.... Judged by the standard applied by Dr. Ambedkar, every known living faith will probably fail [to be found worthy of acceptance]." (*C*, LXIII, 135 and 153f)

Ambedkar responded with a virtuoso display of academic and barrister-like disputation. It is almost a pity merely to print the following long extracts; they ought rather to be delivered by a powerful actor in a dramatic setting:

[138] **Ambedkar**, *1936*: "The first point made by the Mahatma is that the texts cited by me are not authentic. I confess I am no authority on the matter. But... the texts cited by me are all taken from the writings of... a recognized authority on the Sanskrit language and on the Hindu shastras.... The masses... are too illiterate to know the contents of the shastras. They have believed what they have been told and what they have been told is that the shastras do enjoin as a religious duty the observance of caste and untouchability.

"...The saints... did not preach that all men were equal. They preached that all men were equal in the eyes of God[75] — a very different and a very innocuous propo-

75. See Reading 127.

sition which nobody can find difficult to preach or dangerous to believe in.... [Moreover,] the masses have been taught that a saint might break caste but the common man must not....

"That religion should be judged not by its worst specimens but by its best is true enough, but does it dispose of the matter? I say it does not. The question still remains — why the worst number so many and the best so few. To my mind there are two conceivable answers to this question: *[1]* That the worst by reason of some original perversity of theirs are morally uneducable and are therefore incapable of making the remotest approach to the religious ideal. Or *[2]* That the religious ideal is a wholly wrong ideal which has given a wrong moral twist to the lives of the many, and that the best have become best in spite of the wrong ideal — in fact by giving to the wrong a twist, a turn in the right direction. Of these two explanations I am not prepared to accept the first.... To my mind the second is the only logical and reasonable explanation unless the Mahatma has a third alternative to explain why the worst are so many and the best so few. If the second is the only explanation then obviously the argument of the Mahatma that a religion should be judged by its best followers carries us nowhere except to pity the lot of the many who have gone wrong because they have been made to worship wrong ideals.

"...The Mahatma seems to me to suggest... that Hindu society can be made tolerable and even happy without any fundamental change in its structure if all the high-caste Hindus can be persuaded to follow a high standard of morality in their dealing with the low-caste Hindus. I am totally opposed to this kind of ideology. I can respect those of the caste Hindus who try to realize a high social ideal in their life. Without such men India would be an uglier and a less happy place to live in than it is. But nonetheless anyone who relies on an attempt to turn... caste Hindus into better men by improving their personal character is in my judgement wasting his energy and hugging an illusion. Can personal character make the maker of armaments a good man, i.e. a man who will sell shells that will not burst[76] and gas that will not poison? If it cannot, how can you expect personal character to make a man loaded with a consciousness of caste a good man, i.e. a man who would treat his fellows as his... kinsmen and equals? As a matter of fact, a Hindu does treat all those who are not of his caste as though they were aliens, who could be discriminated against with impunity and against whom any fraud or trick may be practiced without shame. This is to say that there can be a better or a worse Hindu, but a good Hindu there cannot be. This is not because there is anything wrong with his personal character. In fact what is wrong is the entire basis of his relationship to his fellows....

"...Does the Mahatma practice what he preaches? One does not like to make personal reference in an argument which is general in its application. But when one preaches a doctrine and holds it as a dogma, there is a curiosity to know how far he practices what he preaches.... The Mahatma is a Bania [a member of a certain merchant caste] by birth. His ancestors had abandoned trading in favor of ministership which is a calling of the Brahmins. In his own life, before he became a mahatma, when occasion came for him to choose his career he preferred law to scales. On abandoning law he became half saint and half politician. He has never touched trading

76. A rare instance (during World War II) is depicted in the celebrated film (1993), "Schindler's List."

which is his ancestral calling. His youngest son... has married a Brahmin's daughter and has chosen to serve a newspaper magnate. The Mahatma is not known to have condemned him for not following his ancestral calling. It may be wrong and uncharitable to judge an ideal by its worst specimens. But surely the Mahatma as a specimen has no better and if even he fails to realize the ideal then the ideal must be an impossible ideal quite opposed to the practical instincts of man....

"Why does the Mahatma cling to the theory of everyone following his or her ancestral calling? He gives his reasons nowhere [nowadays; but]... years ago, writing on caste versus class in his *Young India*, he argued [Reading 121] that the caste system was better than the class system on the ground that caste was the best possible adjustment of social stability. If that be the reason why the Mahatma clings to the theory of everyone following his or her ancestral calling, he is clinging to a false view of social life.... Stability is wanted, but not at the cost of change when change is imperative.... Adjustment is wanted, but not at the sacrifice of social justice. Can it be said that the adjustment of social relationship on the basis of caste, i.e. on the basis of each to his hereditary calling, avoids those two evils? I am convinced that it does not. Far from being the best possible adjustment, I have no doubt that it is of the worst possible kind inasmuch as it offends against both the canons of social adjustment — namely fluidity and equity.

"...I must admit that the vedic theory of varna as interpreted by Swami Dayanand [the founder of Arya Samaj] and some others is a sensible and an inoffensive thing. It did not admit birth as a determining factor in fixing the place of an individual in society. It only recognized worth. The Mahatma's view of varna... makes nonsense of the vedic varna [and] makes it into an abominable thing [instead]. [Vedic] varna and caste are two very different concepts. Varna is based on the principle of each according to his worth, while caste is based on the principle of each according to his birth. The two are as distinct as chalk from cheese.... If the Mahatma believes as he does in everyone following his or her ancestral calling, then most certainly he is advocating the caste system and in calling it the varna system he is... causing confusion....

"Does he regard [his concept of hereditary] varna as the essence of Hinduism? One cannot as yet give any categorical answer. Readers of his article on 'Dr. Ambedkar's Indictment' will answer 'No.' In that article he does not say that the dogma of varna is an essential part of the creed of Hinduism. Far from making varna the essence of Hinduism, he says [Reading 137], 'The essence of Hinduism is contained in its enunciation of one and only God as truth and its bold acceptance of ahimsa as the law of the human family.' But readers of his [other] article... will say 'Yes.' In that article he says [Reading 191], '...I do not know how a person who rejects caste, i.e. varna, can call himself a Hindu.' Why this prevarication? Why does the Mahatma hedge? Whom does he want to please? Has the saint failed to sense the truth? Or does the politician stand in the way of the saint? The real reason why the Mahatma is suffering from this confusion is probably to be traced to two sources. The first is the temperament of the Mahatma. He has almost in everything the simplicity of the child with the child's capacity for self-deception. Like a child he can believe in anything he wants to believe. We must therefore wait till such time as it pleases the Mahatma to abandon his faith in [hereditary] varna as it has pleased him to abandon his faith in caste. The second course of confusion is the double role which

> the Mahatma wants to play — of a mahatma and a politician. As a mahatma he may be trying to spiritualize politics. Whether he has succeeded in it or not, politics have certainly commercialized him. A politician must know that society cannot bear the whole truth; if he is speaking the whole truth, it is bad for his politics. The reason why the Mahatma is always supporting caste and varna is because he is afraid that if he opposes them he will lose his place in politics. Whatever may be the source of this confusion, the Mahatma must be told that he is deceiving himself and also deceiving the people by preaching caste under the name of varna.
>
> "The Mahatma says that the standards I have applied to test Hindus and Hinduism are too severe.... [But] my quarrel with Hindus and Hinduism is not over the imperfections of their social conduct. It is much more fundamental. It is over their ideals." (*B*, I, 87-92)

It was undoubtedly beyond Gandhi to answer in detail an argument as elaborate, sincere and aggressive as this. Its immediate effect on him does not seem to have been decisive: late in 1936 he argued at length in *Harijan* that his "ideal Bhangi" would do sanitation work and thereby "possibly even excel" a Brahmin in rendering service.[77] But in the long run, Gandhi would have to admit that Ambedkar's view of inherited varna was correct.

Meanwhile, a younger opponent of caste and varna, Gora (1902-1975), who had been disowned by his own (Brahmin) caste in 1928 and then a few years later was dismissed from his job as a college biology teacher for saying that the idea

77. *C*, LXIV, 86ff.

of divine beings was untrue, began to walk to villages on weekends and during school vacations, speaking out against superstition, caste and economic inequality. Years later he would publish the views he had been expounding throughout the 1930s, among them:

[139] **Gora,** *1949*: "This thorn-bush [caste] is in our path. It is useless to argue about who put it there, why, and when; the whole thing is against the interest of the people and we must simply remove it." (*Sangham*, 17/iv)

Gandhi heard about Gora's social work in the early 1940s and invited him to Sevagram when they were released from detention in 1944. He found him courteous, free of fanaticism, and hard-working.[78] Gandhi's views of caste now moved closer to those which Gora shared with Ambedkar. A day after writing a letter to a disciple of Gora's who had initially brought them together, Gandhi completed a lengthy preface to a new edition of a little book of his own from the 1920s extolling the varna system. In the new preface, entitled "Key to My Writings," he argued that everyone must nowadays perform service to his fellow humans — property-owners, for instance, must manage their holdings exclusively for the benefit of others — and therefore everyone was now in the same, service-performing varna:

[140] *1945*: "I do not have the time to read this book again. I do not even wish to. I have many other things to do.

78. See Chapter 2 and Readings 411-416.

79. See Readings 129-130.

80. See page 36.

"In my opinion a man daily moves either forward or backward. He never stands still. The whole world is moving and there is no exception....

"Where are the four varnas of the Gita today?... There prevails only one varna today, that is, of 'Shudras,'[79] or, you may call it, 'Ati-Shudras'.... If I can bring round the Hindu society to my view, all our internal quarrels will come to an end....

"A man should consider himself not the owner of his property but its trustee... [using] it for the service of society. He will accept only that much for himself as he has earned with his [physical] labor. If that happens, no one will be poor and no one rich. In such a system, all religions will naturally be held equal. Therefore all quarrels arising out of religion, caste and economic differences will be ended.

"This is the swaraj [self-rule] of my dreams. I yearn for that. I want to live for the attainment of it. I am devoting every breath of my life to that effort.

"The reader is therefore requested to discard anything in this book which may appear to him incompatible with my views given above." (*C*, LXXX, 222ff)

A very clear and brief statement of Gandhi's latter-day view of caste — namely, that his long-cherished ideal of varna must be given up in order to eradicate untouchability — is in the following remark to Gora's prospective son-in-law (who had been born an untouchable):

[141] *1946.* "You should become like Ambedkar. You should work for the removal of untouchability and caste. Untouchability must go at any cost."[80]

An American visitor described as follows Gandhi's view of caste at this time:

[142] *1946* (as reported): "He said he was trying to create a classless and casteless India. He yearned for the day when there would be only one caste, and Brahmins would marry Harijans. 'I am a social revolutionist,' he asserted. 'Violence is bred by inequality, non-violence by equality.'" (Fischer 1946, 425)

As to when that day — a classless *and entirely casteless* India — might come, his own goal would be to see the dawn within 50 years:

[143] *1946*: **[Q.]** "In your recent correspondence... you have said that caste ought to go root and branch if untouchability is to be completely eradicated.[81] Then, why do you not make anti-untouchability work part of a wider crusade against the caste system itself? If you dig out the root, the branches will wither by themselves."
[A.] "It is one thing for me to hold certain views and quite another to make my views acceptable in their entirety to society at large. My mind, I hope, is ever growing, ever moving forward. All may not keep pace with it. I have therefore to exercise the utmost patience and be satisfied with hastening slowly.... I am wholly in agreement with you in principle. If I live up to 125 years, I do expect to convert the entire Hindu society to my view." (*C*, LXXXV, 24)

To have abolished "all distinctions of class and caste" (in the

81. The sentence in question was, "Caste must go if we want to root out untouchability." (*C*, LXXXI, 24f)

Indian National Army) was, he said, Subhas Chandra Bose's "greatest and lasting act."[82]

Hindu sophists argued that Gandhi contradicted himself by saying that caste must go and yet he would now be a Harijan (and thus in a caste). His response was:

[144] *1946*: "A Harijan by birth may repudiate his varna but how can I, who have become a Harijan by choice? I have not hesitated to suggest to caste Hindus that today they have all to become atishudras if the canker of caste feeling is to be eradicated from Hinduism and Hinduism is not to perish from the face of the earth." (*C*, LXXXIV, 247)

Yet with all this, and notwithstanding his realization that "when all became casteless, ...monopoly of occupations would go,"[83] he would still sometimes — with hedging expressions like "more or less" and "generally" — say that the unusual person who masters an occupation other than "the one he is born in" must nevertheless earn his living by "his hereditary occupation" and not by the new one:

[145] *1947*, as reported: "[The] vocational organization of society, held Gandhi, may be vertical and competitive, or horizontal and coöperative. Under the former, remuneration is... on the basis of the law of supply and demand; in the latter all occupations... are paid equal wages ...[and] a person will choose an occupation, not because of the personal prospects it offers, but because he has a special skill or aptitude for it. And since skills and aptitudes

82. *C*, LXXXVI, 383f.

83. *C*, LXXXVI, 484.

generally follow the line of heredity more or less, the average person in the normal course would, if there were no inequalities of remuneration to lure him away from it, tend to follow the occupation he is born in.... Would that mean that one would be debarred from changing his hereditary occupation, if he felt a special urge? 'No,' said Gandhiji, 'not so long as one does not depend on it [the new occupation] for one's living.' Such cases will naturally be few. Thus Buddha was [by heredity] a ruling prince, Socrates a sculptor, St. Paul a tent-maker. Yet Buddha became the Enlightened One, Socrates the prince of philosophers and St. Paul an apostle; but none of them regarded their [new] calling as a means of livelihood." (*L*, I, 541f)

Had Ambedkar commented on this, he would surely have mentioned the lack of evidence that any society pays equal wages to all professions,[84] or that Buddha earned his keep exclusively by being a king, St. Paul by making tents and Socrates by sculpting. It seems to us that Gandhi's thinking in this regard was so unrealistic that one may dismiss as sentimental one of his last recorded statements on the subject:

[146] *1947*: "I would wish with all my heart to have a brave, selfless and pure-hearted scavenger girl to be our first President [of India]. It is no vain dream. We can certainly come across such Harijan girls if we make an effort to find them." (*C*, LXXXVIII, 63)

---

84. Gandhi nearly admitted this: "Indian society may never reach the goal [of equal wages for all] but it is the duty of every Indian to set his sail towards that goal and no other if India is to be a happy land." (*H*, 16/iii/1947; see *C*, LXXXVII, 10)

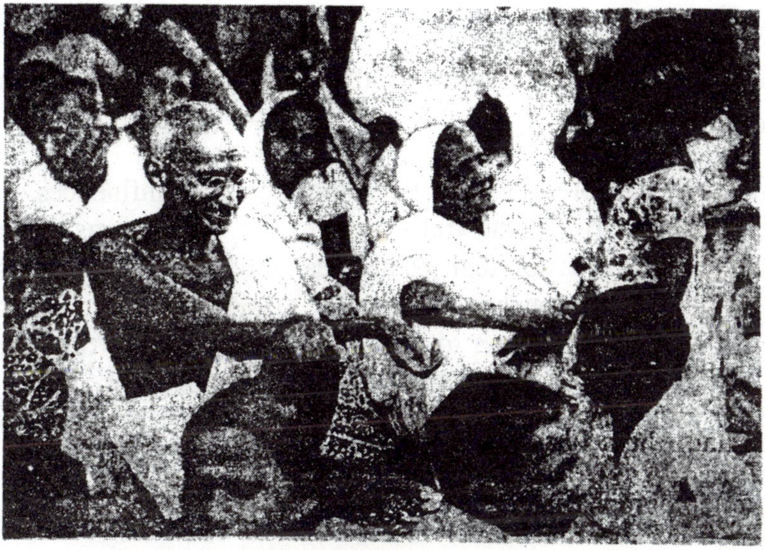

Breaking the taboo: Gandhi and his wife greeting "Untouchable" children

Untouchability

Despite his conservativism about Indian social structure in general, Gandhi was deeply concerned to eliminate the doctrine and practice of untouchability, which he had even as a youngster never accepted (Reading 67). In a letter of 1921 to a Christian friend, he outlined briefly the history of his feelings about it:

[147] *1921* "Before I came under the Christian influences in South Africa... the truth came to me when I was yet a child. I used to laugh at my dear mother for making us bathe if we touched any pariah. [Then] in 1897... I was prepared in Durban to turn Mrs. Gandhi away from the house because she would not treat on a footing of equality Lawrence who she knew belonged to the pariah class and whom I had invited to stay with me." (*C*, XIX, 289)

His autobiography includes a more ample account of the incident in South Africa (and assigns it to 1898):

[148] *1897 or '98*, recalled later: "When I was practicing [law] in Durban, my office clerks often stayed with me.... One of the clerks was a Christian, born of Panchama [untouchable] parents.

"...The clerks who made themselves completely at home would naturally clean their own [chamber-] pots, but the Christian clerk was a newcomer, and it was our duty to attend to his bedroom. My wife managed the pots of the others, but to clean those used by one who had been a Panchama seemed to her to be the limit, and we fell out. She could not bear the pots being cleaned by me, neither did she like doing it herself. Even today I can

> recall the picture of her chiding me, her eyes red with anger, and pearl drops streaming down her cheeks as she descended the ladder, pot in hand....
>
> "I was far from satisfied by her merely carrying the pot. I would have her do it cheerfully. So I said, raising my voice: 'I will not stand this nonsense in my house.'
>
> "The words pierced her like an arrow.
>
> "She shouted back, 'Keep your house to yourself and let me go.' I forgot myself, and the spring of compassion dried up in me. I caught her by the hand, dragged the helpless woman to the gate, which was just opposite the ladder, and proceeded to open it with the intention of pushing her out. The tears were running down her cheeks in torrents, and she cried: 'Have you no sense of shame? Must you so far forget yourself? Where am I to go? I have no parents or relatives here to harbor me. Being your wife, you think I must put up with your cuffs and kicks? For Heaven's sake behave yourself, and shut the gate. Let us not be found making scenes like this!'
>
> "I put on a brave face, but was really ashamed and shut the gate. If my wife could not leave me, neither could I leave her." (*A*, IV, ch. 10)

It has been said that Gandhi wrote and spoke more about untouchability than any other subject.[85] Many of his statements about it are available in a series of topical volumes issued by his publishing house in Ahmedabad. The ones that appeared within his lifetime are entitled *The Bleeding Wound!* (1932), *My Soul's Agony* (1932), and *Untouchability* (1944). Those

---

85. B. Kumarappa, ed. 1954, *The Removal of Untouchability*, by M. K. Gandhi (Ahmedabad), p. iii.

published next after his death — *The Removal of Untouchability* (1954) and *For Workers Against Untouchability* (1954) — reflect the fact that even though the Constitution of the Republic of India had been adopted in 1950, its injunctions against untouchability were not yet very effective. This was especially true in the villages where some 80% of the people lived (today 70%). In the cities, the desegregation of buses, cinemas, tea shops etc. meant that even the most devout and fastidious members of a varna could never tell if they were being "polluted."

Untouchability is now a thing of the past except in some very remote places; but it prevailed throughout India when Gandhi arrived home from South Africa in 1915. The following excerpts from his autobiography are from a chapter entitled "On the Anvil":

[149] *1915* (recalled in the 1920s): "I received a letter from [an enlightened Hindu social worker] to this effect: 'A humble and honest untouchable family is desirous of joining your ashram. Will you accept them?' I was perturbed.... I shared the letter with my companions. They welcomed it....

"The family consisted of Dudabhai, his wife Danibehn and their daughter Lakshmi, then a mere toddling babe. ...Their admission created a flutter amongst the friends who had been helping the ashram.... The man in charge of the water-lift objected that drops of water from our bucket would pollute him.... All monetary help... was stopped...." (*C*, XXXIX, 315ff)

Some years later he recalled:

[150] *1915* (recalled in 1932): "The ashram was founded in order to serve and if necessary to die in the service of Truth. If therefore while holding that untouchability is a sinful thing, it did not do something positive in order to end it, it could hardly deserve the name of Satyagraha Ashram.... Within a month of the foundation of the ashram, Dudabhai applied for admission along with his family.... The arrival of Dudabai was the signal for a storm breaking upon the placid atmosphere of the ashram.... Things came to such a pass that Kasturba [Gandhi's wife] should either observe the rules or else leave.... But the argument that a woman in following in her husband's footsteps incurs no sin appealed to her and she quieted down. ...No one could uphold untouchability and still live in the ashram. It would have been extremely painful to me if my wife had had to leave....

"[My nephew] Maganlal Gandhi's case was harder than mine. He packed up his things.[86] ...I could endure to be separated from all the world besides, but not from Maganlal. I therefore suggested that he should go to Madras with his family. He and his wife would learn more of weaving there [presumably from an untouchable, as weavers were normally of such a caste] and would have more time to

---

86. At Phoenix Settlement in South Africa, Maganlal's wife had routinely, before using brass utensils used also by the Moslem members for non-vegetarian cooking, "purified" them with fire. Eating in the company of the Moslems had also been problematic for Maganlal and his wife; but they had overcome their religious scruples for the sake of Gandhi's more cosmopolitan ideals. (Pyarelal 1986, 441)

Maganlal's service as executive director of Satyagraha Ashram was invaluable to Gandhi and to his cause.

ponder over the situation that had developed. So they went and lived in Madras for six months. They mastered the art of weaving and after mature consideration also washed their hearts clean of untouchability.

"The internal storm thus blew over. But there was a storm outside the ashram too. The chief person who financed the ashram discontinued his assistance.... But... a sum of 13,000 rupees was received from an unexpected source. Thus the ashram ordeal in keeping Dudabai at any cost was not so severe as it might well have been.... [Today] 'untouchable' families come to the ashram freely and live in it. Dudabhai's daughter Lakshmi has become a full member of the family." (*C*, L, 221ff)

When Gandhi in 1933 recommended that reform-minded Hindus adopt Harijan children (Reading 70), he doubtless had in mind his own adoption of Lakshmi. Normal religious belief, however, was very different:

[151] **Gandhi**, *1925*: "Is it fair to exclude a whole section of Hindus, because of their supposed lower birth, from public roads which can be used by non-Hindus, by criminals and bad characters, and even by dogs and cattle?"

Temple trustee: "But how can it be helped? They are reaping the reward of their karma."

Gandhi: "No doubt they are suffering for their karma by being born as untouchables. But why must you add to the punishment? Are they worse than even criminals and beasts?"

Temple trustee: "They must be so, for otherwise God would not condemn them to be born untouchables." (Zelliot 1972, 79f)

Still in 1938 Gandhi's wife and that of his secretary, Mahadev Desai, would worship in such a temple. When Gandhi learned of it he was so angry that he fell ill. He told Desai:

[152] *1938*: "What is the use of your writing articles... on untouchability... when you do not carry the message to your own home?" (*T*, IV, 238)

Desai lost a night's sleep and in despair asked to be sent away; Gandhi upbraided him for reacting hysterically instead of "repairing his folly by going to the temple with a band of Harijan satyagrahi pilgrims."

Almost throughout his political career in India, Gandhi used strong and characteristically eloquent language on this subject. Here are a few examples:[87]

[153] *1920*: "I consider untouchability to be a heinous crime against humanity. It is not a sign of self-restraint but an arrogant assumption of superiority. It has served no useful purpose and it has suppressed, as nothing else in Hinduism has, vast numbers of the human race who are not only every bit as good as ourselves but are rendering in many walks of life an essential service to the country.... I know of no argument in favor of its retention and I have no hesitation in rejecting scriptural authority of a doubtful character in order to support a sinful institution. Indeed I would reject all authority if it is in conflict with sober reason or the dictates of the heart. Authority sustains and ennobles the weak when it is the handiwork of reason but it degrades them when it supplants reason sanctified by the still small voice within." (*C*, XIX, 85)

87. See also Reading 68 and *C*, XLVIII, 298.

[154] *1932*: "The caste Hindus are responsible for whatever bad habits are to be observed among the Harijans. The so-called higher castes have deprived them of the facilities for keeping themselves clean and also the incentive for doing so. As for the occupations of scavenging and tanning, they are no more dirty than many other occupations I can name. What may be admitted is that these occupations, like several others, are carried on in a dirty manner. That is due to the high-handed indifference and criminal neglect of the 'high caste.' I can say from my experience that both scavenging and tanning can be done in a perfectly healthy and clean manner.

"Every mother is a scavenger in regard to her own children.... It is only ceaseless effort that can raise these downtrodden fellow beings ['untouchables'] from degradation [and] purify Hinduism." (*T*, III, 181f)

[155] *1934*: "Nearly 20,000 people [have] died in an earthquake. ...Why should this calamity come upon us?... The wrong we have done is staring us in the face. We believe, in the name of religion, that thousands of our own countrymen are born 'untouchables'." (*C*, LVII, 49)[88]

[156] *1938*: "It is my daily prayer, as it should be the prayer of you all [at the ashram], that if untouchability does not perish, it were far better that Hinduism perished." (*T*, IV, 239)

---

88. Nehru and Tagore were appalled by Gandhi's several remarks in this vein (see also *C*, LVII, 44, 50ff, 76, 86f, 101 and 164ff). Nehru recalled in his autobiography (p. 490): "I read with a great shock Gandhi's statement to the effect that the earthquake had been a punishment for the sin of untouchability.... The ideas of... divine wrath and man's relative importance in the affairs of the universe... take us back a few hundred years, when the Inquisition flourished in Europe ...[or to the time when] Boston divines attributed earthquakes in Massachusetts to the impiety of lightning rods."

But he would use very moderate language and actions when dealing with his religious antagonists:[89]

[157] **Correspondent,** *1933*: "For many centuries, rightly or wrongly, untouchables have not been allowed access to public temples.... I do not see what right has the majority to override the intention of the founder [of the temple]...."
Gandhi: "I thank you for your valuable letter.... I appreciate your argument.... [Yet] Hinduism has never been a rigid faith. It has kept abreast of the times.... I would like you therefore to reconsider your position, and if there is a flaw in my deductions from your argument, I would like you to strive with me. For I have no desire to see any injustice done to any party or person." (*C*, LIII, 432)

[158] *1933*: **[Q.]** "Do you know that some temples which had been opened to Harijans were subsequently closed to them? What is your solution?" **[A.]** "For the time being we have to assume that such temples were opened under some sort of coercion or that the trustees have been since coerced into closing them against Harijans.... For the time being we should suffer this deprivation." (*C*, LVI, 3)

89. The next four citations are from Gandhi's famous tour of 1933-34. Its Its primary objective was to secure for Harijans the right to enter temples. While telling Ambedkar that he regarded this as "a spiritual matter through which everything else will bear fruit" (*C*, LIII, 500), Gandhi begged the religious leaders to "show... by our acts that varnashrama [the religious law of varna] is not a vertical line but... a horizontal plane on which all the children of God occupy absolutely the same status, though they may be engaged in different pursuits of life and... have different qualities" (*C*, LIII, 337). For a detailed account of the tour, based on British intelligence reports, see Baren Ray 1996.

[159] *1933*, **in regard to three social workers who sought his advice about legal redress against fellow villagers who ostracized them for having let some 'untouchables' drink water from their glasses which they — the owners — had then washed:** "What the villagers have condemned as a sin I consider a meritorious deed.... It [now] becomes the duty of the three young men by their firmness, purity, *tapasya* [penance], sacrifice, patience and generosity to change the hearts of these villagers lost in darkness and at the same time to teach the Harijans the habits of cleanliness. They can under no circumstance take the matter to a court of law." (*C*, LV, 174)

[160] **Correspondent**, *1934*: "As a sanatanist I have a difficulty about temple-entry by Harijans. Supposing among temple-goers of a particular temple there is a majority of 99 to 1 in favor of Harijans entering the temple and the temple is opened, What about the minority of one who has objection to worshipping in a temple visited by Harijans? If reformers have their way, will it not be an undue interference with the right of worship which belongs to the sanatanists from time immemorial?..."

Gandhi: "...If the one solitary sanatanist has the right, as he undoubtedly has, what about the majority? Have they no rights?... It should be remembered that the minority is free to build a temple for itself. And so far as I am concerned, I have given my opinion that even a minority of one should have its prejudices so far respected that a special hour may be set apart so as to enable it to offer worship free from the intrusion, whether of reformers or of Harijans." (*C*, LIX, 309f)

[161] *1942*: **[Q.]** "Should we [campaigners against untouchabiity] seek the coöperation of the Harijans, and if so, to what extent?"

[A.] "[Such] coöperation is necessary, but we must not take the Harijans in a body and invade the [varna-members'] quarters. We should [for instance] visit the wells, ascertain the classes of people using them, and reason with these to let the Harijans use them.... The Harijans should invariably be asked to use clean vessels and observe all the ordinary rules of cleanliness.... The Harijans have to be taught to assert themselves firmly and non-violently, and the [varna members] may be gently reminded that injustice cannot last for ever...."

[Q.] "Can't we insist on the admission of Harijan boys to [student] hostels where all non-Harijan Hindu boys are admitted?"

[A.] "Of course, but care must be taken to see that the hostel is not exclusively for a particular community or section of Hindus." (*C*, LXXV, 206f)

And he could sometimes lapse into a remarkably patronizing stance, as when he asked a Christian missionary not to preach to untouchables who lacked "the mind and intelligence to understand":

[162] *1936*: "Would you... preach the Gospel to a cow? Well, some of the 'untouchables' are worse than cows in understanding. I mean, they can no more distinguish between the relative merits of Islam and Hinduism and Christianity than a cow." (*C*, LXIV, 37)

[163] *1937*, referring to this last passage: "I have no remorse about the propriety of the analogy. There could be no offence meant to Harijans, because the cow is a sacred animal. I worship her as I worship my mother. Both are givers of milk. And so far as understanding is concerned, I do maintain that there are, be it said to the discredit of superior-class Hindus, thousands of Harijans who can no

more understand the merits and demerits of different religions than a cow. That after a long course of training Harijans can have their intelligence developed, in a manner [which] a cow's cannot, is irrelevant to the present discussion." (*C*, LXIV, 218)

(One can just imagine Ambedkar's feelings.) Gandhi in 1931 had told the British:

[164] *1931*: "I claim myself in my own person to represent the vast mass of the untouchables... and I say that it is not a proper claim which is registered by Dr. Ambedkar when he seeks to speak for the whole of the untouchables of India." (*C*, XLVIII, 297f)

And in 1937 the Indian National Congress under Gandhi's unofficial guidance eclipsed Ambedkar's political party in the first elections for provincial assemblies in India.

In the meantime Gandhi and Ambedkar had differed as to whether, in those elections, separate constituencies should be established for the untouchables, as had already been done (in some less important types of elections) for the Moslems in 1909 and the Sikhs in 1919. In 1932 Gandhi conducted — in prison — a "fast unto death" to protest against *(a)* this proposal, which the colonial government was about to adopt, and *(b)* the precept and practice of untouchability. After five days he obtained a modicum of satisfaction on both counts. In the "Poona Pact," he and Ambedkar worked out a compromise about the rules for the elections (and the British went along),[90] and a

90. There would be no separate constituencies of "untouchable" voters, but

group of conservative Hindu leaders signed a document saying that henceforth:

[165] *1932*: "Among Hindus no one shall be regarded as untouchable by reason of his birth, and those who have been so regarded hitherto, will have the same right as other Hindus to the use of public wells, public schools, public roads and other public institutions." (*T*, III, 174)

During his current prison term Gandhi's political journal, *Young India*, had ceased publication. Soon afterwards he founded a new journal, entitled *Harijan* — a term of his devising which means literally "child(ren) of God" and which he used thereafter instead of "untouchable." Then after his next jail term he embarked, in 1933, on a nationwide campaign for "Harijan uplift." This was a matter partly of consciousness-raising in the hope of giving some substance to the Poona Pact's ostensible abolition of untouchability, partly of fund-raising to pay for schools and student hostels, and partly of keeping the Harijans within the national anti-imperialist movement.

Yet as we have seen, Gandhi did not want better-educated Harijans to work in any jobs different from those of their parents. His view of Harijan uplift was still subsumed in his view of inherited varna. In 1925 he had been explicit that for the Harijans the proper varna would be Shudra:

---

a certain procedure (described in the agreement) for selecting the candidates would ensure that at least a specified number of the people elected to each provincial legislature would be from those castes. See *C*, LI, 463f.

[166] *1925*: "A Panchama [a member of a supposed fifth varna, lower than Shudra] should be regarded as a Shudra because there is no warrant for belief in a fifth caste." (*Y*, 23/iv)

In 1931 he was vague about the label but still fairly explicit about the intention:

[167] *1931*: "'Untouchables' should... be regarded as honored members of Hindu society, and should belong to the varna for which their occupation fits them." (*C*, XLVI, 302)

And again in 1937:

[168] *1937*: "[Every]one born a scavenger must earn his livelihood by being a scavenger, and then do whatever else he likes. For, a scavenger is as worthy of his hire [to carry feces] as a lawyer [is of being hired to plead or negotiate a case] or your President [to lead a nation]. That, according to me, is Hinduism." (*H*, 6/iii, 27)

So even though Gandhi would declare:

[169] *1933*: "My goal is quite clear. It is not to have Harijans regarded as a separate body in Hinduism or outside it. I shall be satisfied with nothing less than complete removal of untouchability as it is known today." (*C*, LV, 319)

—Ambedkar would respond:[91]

[170] **Ambedkar**, *1945*: "The Untouchables... have grounds to say: 'Good God! Is this man Gandhi our saviour?'" (Zelliot 1972, 69)

---

91. Ambedkar's rhetoric was even tougher in his Maruti than in his English writings. See Talwakar 1997.

With Gandhi's encouragement,[92] Ambedkar was in 1946 elected chairman of the Drafting Committee of the Constitution of the Republic of India. Article 17 reads:

[171] **Ambedkar, Munshi** *et al.*, *1948*: "'Untouchability' is abolished and its practice in any form is forbidden. The enforcement of any disability arising out of 'Untouchability' shall be an offence punishable in accordance with law." **(Constitution of the Republic of India)**

The Constituent Assembly adopted this article amidst shouts of *Mahatma Gandhi ki jai!* ("Victory to Mahatma Gandhi!").[93]

Meanwhile Gora wrote to Gandhi in 1946 to congratulate him for arranging to live in the huts of Harijans during a visit to Bombay, as he had recently done in New Delhi:

[172] **Gora**, *1946*: "I and my co-workers have been trying this method of residing and eating with the Harijans for the last five or six years. Our experience proves that it is an efficient method to remove the social isolation of the untouchables. But our work is spreading slowly. If a man like Bapuji took it up, as he did at Bombay, it is bound to gain wide publicity and attract more workers to the method." (*G*, 50f)

When Gora was working in New Delhi without pay for the All-India Congress Committee, Gandhi asked him to describe his program for the eradication of untouchability. Gora's suggestion of "regular cosmopolitan dinners on a mass scale" prompted the following exchange:

---

92. Nauriya 1996, p. 45.

93. B. S. Rao *et al.*, 1969, p. 205.

[173] **Gandhi**, *1946*: "Would cosmopolitan dinners be sufficient to catch the imagination of the people?"
Gora: "Then, intermarriages.... " (*G*, 51)

Intercaste dining and marriage

Hinduism taught its devotees not only to follow their parents' occupation and to avoid contact between "untouchables" and members of a varna, but also to marry someone from the same subcaste and never to take nourishment in the company of anyone in a lower caste or subcaste (nor let such a person touch one's utensils, etc.). For each of these latter taboos — against "intermarrying" and "interdining" — there were nuances, for instance depending on whether the violation was across mere subcaste distinctions within the same varna, or between members of two different várnas, or between an "untouchable" and a member of a varna.

Gandhi often referred to interdining and intermarrying in the same statement. But of course intermarriage is more enduringly subversive of old-fashioned beliefs.

When Gandhi in the 1880s went abroad to England — thereby violating yet another taboo, for which he was declared outcaste[94] — he dined now and then with all sorts of "unclean" people (such as his friends in the Vegetarian Society). He thus became too cosmopolitan to heed privately the injunction against interdining:

[174] *1892*, recalled later: "In Bombay I started a household with a cook as incompetent as myself. He was a Brahmin. I did not treat him as a servant but as a member of the household.... I had no scruples about intercaste dining; [he] too came to have none; and so we went on merrily together.... [But alas, he] had sworn to remain dirty and to keep the food unclean!" (*A*, II, ch. 2)

A good summary of his political attitude (until his last years) toward interdining and intermarriage is in the following remarks of 1919:

[175] *1919*: "Interdrinking, interdining, intermarrying, I hold, are not essential for the promotion of the spirit of democracy.... But as time goes forward and new necessities and occasions arise, the custom regarding interdrinking, interdining and intermarrying will require cautious modifications or rearrangements." (*C*, XIX, 83f)

In his ashram, interdining even with "untouchables" was implicit in their acceptance in 1915 as members. But for a long time he took a different stance in regard to Hindu practice at large. Did he hope that Indian religious pride would nourish her political will for independence? (The most fiery Indian patriot of that era, Tilak (1856-1920), had with such hopes revived in 1893 the cult of the elephant-god, Ganapati.) Was his sense of his own Hinduism, deepened by his having in South Africa considered converting to Christianity, now also heightened (as it were) by the veneration accorded to him? Whatever the causes, he was never more outspoken against interdining — and intermarrying — than in the early 1920s:

[176] *1920*: "The restraints about interdining have to a great extent helped the cultivation of will-power and the conservation of certain social virtues." (*C*, XIX, 174f)

[177] *1921*: "Hinduism [has] reached the highest limit of self-restraint. It is undoubtedly a religion of renunciation of the flesh so that the spirit may be set free.... Prohibition against interdining and intermarriage is essential to a rapid evolution of the soul. But this self-denial is no test of varna." (*C*, XXI, 247)

Some of his arguments were lacking in cogency, as when he used a Hindi term evoking "seclusion" in such a way as to obfuscate the difference between doing something alone and doing it in the company of members of your caste:

[178] *1921-22*: "Interdining or intermarriage are not necessary for promoting national unity. That dining together creates friendship is contrary to experience.... Taking food is as dirty an act as answering the call of nature.... Just as we perform the act of answering the call of nature in seclusion, so also the act of taking food must be done in seclusion.

"In India, children of brothers do not intermarry.[95] Do they cease to love because they do not intermarry?... [Hence] the caste system cannot be said to be bad because it does not allow... intermarriage....

"Caste does not allow a person to transgress caste limits in pursuit of his enjoyment. That is the meaning of such caste restrictions as interdining and intermarriage." (*B*, IX, 276)

95. In some parts of India it is common for a man to marry a daughter of his sister, of his paternal aunt or of his maternal uncle.

We may sense a softening of tone in 1925 in regard to interdining:

[179] *1925*: "I would neither object to nor advocate participation in an international or cosmopolitan dinner.... Whilst I... take food that I do not regard as [inherently] forbidden at the hands of anyone so long as it is cleanly dressed, I respect the scruples of those who observe the [traditional] restrictions.... These self-imposed restrictions have a sanitary as also a spiritual value." (*C*, XXVI, 569)

But not yet in regard to intermarriage:

[180] **Correspondent,** *1925*: "I was surprised to read in a recent article [your] repudiation of intermarriage between touchables and untouchables...."
Gandhi: I have repeatedly expressed my view of caste and intermarriage.... I cannot picture to myself a time when all mankind will have one religion. As a rule there will, therefore, be the religious bar; people will marry in their own religion.... The caste restriction is an extension of the same principle. It is a social convenience.... I am opposed to untouchability because it limits the field of service. [But] marriage is not an act of service." (*C*, XXVI, 285)

The more positive tone of Reading 179 may have been due to partly to the fact that a Shudra satyagrahi, famous for his heroic role in a campaign of 1924 to persuade a temple in the village of Vaikom to admit low-caste folk, had in 1925 resigned in disgust from the Indian National Congress because its Brahmin members refused to eat together with the non-

Brahmins (and because the campaign had ended in a compromise whereby low-caste people were allowed to walk on a nearby road, but were still barred from the temple[96]). The disaffection of the "Vaikom hero" may have caused Gandhi to reconsider the value of the interdining taboo outside his ashram.[97]

Moreover, by 1928 he was clear in his mind that he would like people to marry across subcaste lines within the same varna. He attended reluctantly the wedding in 1928 of his son Ramdas and a girl, Nirmala, whom he found personally acceptible but who was of the same subcaste; and this was the last such wedding he attended.[98] Three weddings which he later attended between people in different subcastes of his own varna were those of Rukshmani and Banarasilal (1929), Madalasa and Sriman (1937), and Sharada and Gordhandas (1939). None of these were "love matches," but all of them matches suggested by family friends.[99]

That in itself was, for Gandhi, an important, positive feature. In the late 1920s his youngest son, Devadas, and a Brahmin girl fell in love; they had to wait for five years before

---

96. Sarkar 1983: 229.
97. Reading 399 is from a conversation between them.
98. In 1945 he told a social-worker: "If the marriage is in the same community do not ask for my blessings, however deserving the girl may be. I send my blessings if she is from another community." (*C*, LXXX, 99)
99. The information in this paragraph is from *D*, 77; *C*, LXVIII, 391; and interviews with Nirmala Gandhi in January 1996 and Madalasa Narayan in January 1997.

marrying.[100] And when in 1947 Gandhi's grand-nephew Kanu wanted to marry a Brahmin girl (Abha) with whom Gandhi was well acquainted and of whom he personally approved,[101] he asked them to live apart for a year beforehand, which they did; but he wanted no such delay for his arranged match in 1933 between a reform-Hindu Brahmin lad (Maruti) and his adopted Harijan daughter, Lakshmi (notwithstanding her biological father's reluctance).[102]

This Brahmin-Harijan match, while unique in that Gandhi had assumed personal responsibity for Lakshmi's future, was a harbinger of later developments in his general attitude. His recent statements had been along the following lines:

[181] *1931*: "When Hindus were seized with inertia, abuse of varna resulted in innumerable castes with unnecessary and harmful restrictions as to intermarriage and interdining. The law of varna has nothing to do with these restrictions. People of different varnas may intermarry and interdine. These restrictions may be necessary in the interest of chastity and hygiene. But a Brahmin who marries a Shudra girl or *vice versa* commits no offence against the law of varna." (*C*, XLVI, 302)

[182] *1932*: "The ashram will not help to arrange a marriage between members of the same subcaste, and everyone is encouraged to seek his mate outside his own subcaste." (Translated in *H*, 26/ix/1948, 259)

---

100. See *C*, XXXV, 339f and *D*, 102. (Her father was a politician who might benefit unduly from the link — or even if not, people might criticize it on such grounds.)

101. Bose 1953, 49.

102. See *C*, LIII, 288f, 325, 358 and 438f.

[183] *1932*: "[In the ashram] there are no restrictions on interdining and all ashramites sit to dinner in the same line. But no propaganda in favor of interdining is carried on outside the ashram." (*C*, L, 223)

We have seen (Reading 71) how in 1929 he had advised a 22-year-old lad not in the ashram to insist to his parents that he would marry outside the subcaste, or else marry a widow, rather than accept against his conscience a match with a nine- or ten-year-old girl within the subcaste. In those days, even more extreme examples of taking a child-bride for the sake of marrying in one's subcaste were at issue:

[184] Correspondent, *1930*: "I draw your attention with great shame to the article 'Surfeit of child-marriages...'. These weddings took place in our... Chaturvedi [sub]caste. It is the misfortune of our caste that girls of 2, 2½ and 3 years of age are given in marriage.... It must be pointed out that we, the Chaturvedi community, consider ourselves the highest Brahmins. We consider it a sin to eat food cooked even by other Brahmins."

Gandhi: "What else can the marriages... be called than monstrous?... When scriptures are quoted in their favor, the difficulties multiply. However, satyagraha can become a sure means of overcoming all kinds of tyranny." (*C*, XLII, 439)

And indeed the general religious climate was such that in the last three months of 1932, when the ink was hardly dry on the Poona Pact and Gandhi was beginning to plan his Harijan Uplift campaign, he repeatedly gave assurances that he would not campaign for intermarriage or interdining:

[185] *1932*: "Mixing up the two problems [of untouchability and of too many subcastes] would jeopardize the success of both. For this reason intermarriage and interdining with untouchables are not an integral feature of removal of untouchability; but their practice is not against religion either." (*C*, LI, 264)

[186] *1932*: "I should never dream of making this reform [interdining and intermarriage], however desirable in itself it may be, part of an all-India reform which has been long overdue. Untouchability, in the form we all know it, is a canker eating into the very vitals of Hinduism. Dining and marriage restrictions [merely] stunt Hindu society. I think the distinction is fundamental." (*T*, III, 180f)

[187] *1932*: "I am glad to find that temples in your part of the country are being opened to Harijans. The removal of untouchability does not necessarily include interdining and intermarriage, but it is open to anyone to dine or marry among Harijans. In other words, Harijans should have the same status as the rest of the Hindus in all matters. Interdining does not mean eating out of the same plate. Hence, there can be no question of anybody's saliva being mixed with food." (*C*, LI, 237)[103]

Ten years later he would say:

[188] *1942*: "When I said that removal of untouchability did not include the removal of restrictions on interdining and intermarriage, I had the general Hindu public in mind, not the Congress workers or Congressmen. These have to abolish untouchability from every part of their life." (*C*, LXXV, 207)

103. See also *C*, LI, 176, 188, 199, 206, 231, 241, 248, 264 and 269.

Meanwhile someone in 1933 had noticed that the tone of his publicly stated views on interdining and intermarriage had changed quite perceptibly since the early 1920s:

[189] *1933*: "A correspondent who is a diligent student of my writings finds it difficult to reconcile my recent writings about intercaste dining and intercaste marriage and [my] corresponding writings of some years ago.... [Yet] the mode of life in the ashram in 1921 was absolutely the same as it is now. Therefore my practice has undergone no change. I still believe that restriction imposed by oneself upon interdining and intermarriage is an act of renunciation of the flesh [and therefore good]. There is one word that perhaps I would change if I was writing the article of 1921 [see Reading 177] today. Instead of 'prohibition,' I should... say, 'self-imposed restriction against intermarriage and interdining is essential for a rapid evolution of the soul.'" (*C*, LV, 61)

Amidst all this tugging one way and another, the Jat-Pat Todak Mandal and Ambedkar gradually influenced Gandhi to evolve further:

[190] *1935*: "In [the varna system] there was and should be no prohibition of intermarriage or interdining... [so] there can be no compulsion. It must be left to the unfettered choice of the individual as to where he or she will marry or dine. If the law of varnashrama was observed [in regard to hereditary occupation], there would naturally be a tendency, so far as marriage is concerned, for people to restrict the marital relations to their own varna." (*C*, LXII, 121)

In the following exchange with a representative of the Jat-Pat Todak Mandal, he went so far as to apply to the taboos against interdining and intermarriage an idea which he had for years been applying to untouchability: namely that Hinduism had better shed the evil or else be abandoned:

[191] **Correspondent**, *1936*: "For all practical purposes, in Hindu society caste and varna are... the same thing, for the function of both of them is... the same, i.e. to restrict intercaste marriages and interdining.... When you advocate your ideal of [varna] they find justification for clinging to caste.... To seek the help of the shastras for the removal of untouchability and caste is simply to wash mud with mud."

Gandhi: "If caste and varna are convertible terms and if varna is an integral part of the shastras which define Hinduism, I do not know how a person who rejects caste i.e. varna can call himself a Hindu.

"[Yet] if the shastras support caste as we know it today in all its hideousness, I may not call myself or remain a Hindu, since I have no scruples about interdining or intermarriage." (*C*, LXIII, 225f)

Ambedkar argued — correctly, we believe — that intermarriage was the more basic issue (and that religion was a major impediment to progress):

[192] **Ambedkar**, *1936*: "The real remedy [to caste] is intermarriage. Fusion of blood can alone create the feeling of being kith and kin, and unless this feeling... becomes paramount, the separatist feeling — the feeling of being aliens — created by caste will not vanish....

"...The Hindus observe caste not because they are inhuman... [but] because they are deeply religious [and] their religion... has inculcated this notion of caste." (*B*, I, 67f)

In 1937 Gandhi displayed a cautious quasi-advocacy of inter-varna marriage while discussing with some members of his main social-work organization a proposal that they "give a place to Harijans in their homes, receive Harijans in the same way as they would receive others, seek opportunities to eat with them... [and] bring up some Harijan children":

[193] **Hindu colleague,** *1937*: "This proposal justifies the fear of the sanatanists.... From removal of untouchability you want to proceed step by step to intermarriage."

Gandhi: "For ordinary people, removal of untouchability is enough. But, for you, mere touch is not enough. You must continue to proceed further....

"The Hindu masses still follow quite a few restrictive practices in the matter of interdining and intermarriage. Even I have followed certain restrictions in this [latter] regard. That is why I have not spoken to the masses about these.

"But if I suggest to you that you should go to the extent of interdining and intermarrying with Harijans I would not be violating truth.... You have really not much control in the matter of intermarriage. You should certainly not bring compulsion on your children in this matter. Interdining is a different matter. If your mother says that it is irreligion, you must tell her that you would take the food cooked by her as well as by an untouchable, and it would not matter that you were forsaken by her on that account." (*C*, LXV, 134f)

In 1940 he publicly approved of a high-caste Hindu lad who married a Harijan girl after overcoming the reluctance of their parents:

[194] **Correspondent,** *1940*: "Shri [Mr.] Radhamadhab Mitra married a Harijan girl on 4th March last, strictly according to Hindu rites with Brahmin priests, and the ceremony was attended by about one thousand people of all castes and communities. Radhamadhab is aged about 25. When he was a student he organized a Harijan boys' football team. During your epic fast [in 1932] for Harijans, Radhamadhab with some of his friends lived in a Harijan village, and during that period he and his friends promised to marry Harijan girls. His friends forgot their promise but Radhamadhab carried it out. When the proposal for marriage with a Harijan girl was first made all the relatives and friends used all sorts of pressure to dissuade Radhamadhab from his resolve. When he first consulted me, I depicted a very dark future before him.... There was opposition from the bride's relatives who were afraid of oppression from higher castes and also of divine punishment. But ultimately they agreed.... We tried our utmost to secure the attendance of as many high-class people as possible, and thank God we could get what we wanted.... Just imagine several hundred of high-caste people sitting together with an equal number of Harijans ...and receiving betel from the father of the bride."[104]

Gandhi: "I congratulate Shri Radhamadhab on his courage in breaking through the rock of caste superstition. I hope his example will be copied by other young men. May the union prove happy. I would advise Shri Radhamadhab to arrange for proper education of his wife who, I understand, has not received any scholastic training." (*H*, 22/vi, 173)

---

104. From the letter Gandhi published excerpts, which we have further abbreviated.

In that same year there took place in his immediate circle, and with his approval, an inter-varna wedding between a Brahmin woman (Dr. Saundaram) and a Shudra man (G. Ramachandran), and another between a Harijan woman (Indumati) and a high-caste Hindu man (Dr. A. G. Tendulkar, President of the Goa Congress).[105] These were love-matches, as was also perhaps that of Radhamabhab and his bride (since they braved opposition from her family as well as his); so we can readily imagine that Gandhi's approval of them may have been tinged with a wistful longing — hinted at in Reading 193 — for his cherished ideal of marriage due less to personal attraction than to dedication and discipline. How could those values be combined with the new values of intercaste marriage?

Notwithstanding this concern, he felt by 1945 that at some future time it would become very important for caste-Hindus to marry Harijans:

> [195] *1945*: "If... castes and subcastes as we know them disappear — as they should — we should [then] unhesitatingly accord the highest importance to marriages between Ati-Shudras and caste-Hindus." (*C*, LXXX, 77)

Meanwhile, Gora and his wife in their social work with Harijans were often asked, in the early 1940s, "Although you are helping us and saying 'We are all human,' would you really have your children marry people like us?" Their re-

105. *C*, LXXV, 447 and LXXVII, 396, and correspondence with Prof. C. N. Patel.

sponse was positive (see Reading 21) and when they came out of prison in 1944 they began to consider who, among the young Harijan men who had joined in their work, might be a suitable match for their eldest child, then 16. Within a few months they had a young man in mind and asked their daughter if she was inclined to become engaged and would be willing to marry him. She concurred; they consulted him; he was astonished but accepted the idea. Gora wrote about it to Gandhi, who replied:

[196] *1946*: "I have your letter. I like it.... I am prepared to get the marriage performed in the Sevagram Ashram.... One more thing — Manorama is 17 years old.... I suggest that she should wait for two years...." (*G*, 47; *C*, LXXXII, 432f)

Toward the end of January they all met in Madras (see Chapter 2) and it became clear to Gandhi that this was not a love match but was motivated by dedication to social justice, and with no trace of compulsion or reluctance in either family. In March, Gora wrote to Gandhi:

[197] **Gora**, *1946*: "Side by side with the mixing up [of people born into different castes], an attempt also might be made to discourage the use of labels of caste and creed which raise imaginary barriers between man and man. Not only should the practice of untouchability go, but the Harijan should not be allowed to continue a Harijan.... Similarly the Hindu and Moslem differences might be solved by discarding the labels. Such an attempt will no longer keep the form of communal harmony, but it would lead to the growth of one humanity.... Though a powerful personality like Gandhiji might harmonize [different reli-

gious] communities for a while, when the personal influence weakened, the communities would clash again. So a permanent solution of communal differences is the growth of [the] one-humanity outlook rather than communal harmony." (*G*, 51; *C*, LXXXIII, 440)

Gandhi replied:

[198] *1946*: "Though there is a resemblance between your thought and practice and mine superficially, I must own that yours is far superior to mine." (*G*, 52; *C*, LXXXIII, 390)

(As far as we know, he never praised anyone else quite so strongly and succinctly.) He vowed thereafter to attend only weddings between Harijans and members of a varna,[106] and a hint of this was published at the time, albeit not in *Harijan*:

[199] *1946*: [Q.] "Does the Congress program for the abolition of untouchability include interdining and intermarriage with Harijans?" [A.] "So far as I know the Congress mind today, there is no opposition to dining with Hari-

---

106. Lavanam and several other members of Gora's family (Saraswati, Manorama, Mythri, Arjun Rao), and also the oldest surviving member of Gandhi's family (Nirmala), have recalled the vow of 1946, which Gora's family naturally considered to be of special significance. At Sevagram Ashram it is still honored by allowing only such marriages to be celebrated within its confines. There is a direct reference to it in *L*, I, 63. There is a reference in *H*, 26/ix/1948, p. 259, to Gandhi's having said in 1948 that he would lend his presence to no other type of wedding, and this is echoed by Balvantsinha's vague reference (1962, p. 112) to Gandhi's having "eventually" decided that he would bless only marriages between a Harijan and a caste Hindu. Nanda's account (1985, 26) is as follows: "In 1946, Gandhi made the startling announcement that no marriage would be celebrated in his ashram at Sevagram, unless one of the parties was an 'untouchable' by birth."

jans. But speaking for myself, I have said that we have all to become Harijans today or we will not be able to purge ourselves completely of the taint of untouchability. I, therefore, tell all boys and girls who want to marry that they cannot be married at Sevagram Ashram unless one of the parties is a Harijan.[107] I am convinced that there is no real difficulty in this. All that is needed is a change of outlook." (*The Hindustan Standard*, 5/i)

The following thoughtful exchange now appeared in *Harijan*:

[200] **Correspondent,** *1946*: "Educated [Harijan] girls can be counted on the fingers of one hand. If they marry caste Hindus they will, as a rule, be cut off from their own society and... not be able to work for the uplift of their Harijan sisters from within. If Harijan girls are to marry caste Hindus it should be on condition that the couple will devote their lives to the service of the Harijans.[108] Otherwise, educated Harijan girls should be encouraged to marry educated youths of their own community."

Gandhi: "It is certainly desirable that caste Hindu girls should select Harijan husbands. I hesitate to say that it is better. That would imply that women are inferior to men. I know that such [an] inferiority complex is there today. For this reason I would agree that at present the marriage of a caste girl to a Harijan is better than that of a Harijan girl to a caste Hindu. If I had my way I would persuade all caste Hindu girls coming under my influence to select Harijan husbands." (*H*, 7/vii, 212f)

---

107. This way of putting it suggests that no Harijan had asked to be married at the ashram.

108. The first such marriage we know of was that of Hemalata and Lavanam, at Sevagram in 1960.

At a meeting of the Harijan-uplift society which he had founded in 1932, Gandhi was asked how best to further the cause of intercaste marriage:

[201] *1946*: [Q.] "What is your criterion in this respect?"
[A.] "Are you married?"
[Q.] "I happen to be."
[A.] "Then, have you an unmarried son or daughter? If you have one, get him or her a Harijan for a bride or a bridegroom, as the case may be, in the spirit of a sacrament." (*C*, xxxv, 27)

And his advocacy of interdining was likewise stronger now than ever before:

[202] *1946*: "At one time I did say that interdining was not an essential part of the campaign for the removal of untouchability. Personally, I was for it. Today I encourage it. In fact, today I go even further." (*C*, xxxv, 25)

All this was diametrically contrary to his precept of 1921-1933 that prohibition or at least self-imposed restriction against interdining and intermarriage was essential to a rapid evolution of the soul.

Inter-religious marriage

Gandhi in 1926 prevented his son Manilal from marrying a Moslem girl (and a year later found a Hindu wife for him[109]):

109. *C*, XXXIII, 55f, 73f ,78, 83f, 103f, 130ff, 145f, and 148.

[203] *1926*: "You are of course a free man; so I cannot force you to do anything. But I write to you as a friend.

"What you desire is contrary to dharma [religious duty]. If you stick to Hinduism and Fatima follows Islam, it will be like putting two swords in one sheath.... What should be your children's faith? ...It is adharma [lack of religious duty] if Fatima agrees to conversion just for marrying you....

"Nor is it in the interests of our society to form this relationship. Your marriage will have a powerful impact on the Hindu-Moslem question. Intercommunal marriages are no solution to this problem. You cannot forget, nor will society forget, that you are my son.

"If you enter into this relationship, you may not be able to render any service. I fear you may no longer be the right person to run *Indian Opinion* [which Manilal had been editing since 1917].

"It will be impossible for you, I think, after this to come and settle in India.

"I cannot [even] ask Ba's [Kasturba's] permission.... Her life will be embittered for ever.

In proposing this marriage you have thought only of momentary pleasure.... I want you to get out of your infatuation.... May God show you the right path." (*C*, xxx, 229f)

In the early 1930s his view began to soften:

[204] *1931*: "[As for] marriage outside one's religion... so long as each [partner] is free to observe his or her religion, I can see no moral objection to such unions. But I do not believe that these unions can bring peace. They may follow peace. I can see nothing but disaster following any attempt to advocate Hindu-Moslem [marital] unions so long as the relations between the two [religions] remain

strained. That such unions may be happy in exceptional circumstances can be no reason for their general advocacy." (*C*, XLVI, 303)

[205] *1932*: "If anybody asks my opinion, I would say that marriage between persons following different faiths was a risky experiment.... I do not advocate marriages between persons of different faiths as I advocate inter-caste marriages because I desire the disappearance of sub-castes. I would not agitate against such marriages either. This is an issue on which every man and woman should think and decide for himself or herself. There cannot be a uniform law for all. " (*C*, XLIX, 478)

In 1996 the only surviving member of his family from the next generation did not recall his having ever attended an inter-religious marriage.[110] However, in 1942 Gandhi defended the engagement of Nehru's daughter, Indira, to a Parsi (Feroz Gandhi),[111] and in 1945 he ventured to suggest, though not yet in print, that inter-religious marriages might entail "no difficulty":

[206] *1945*: "Where parents are wise, there should be no difficulty even between persons of different religions. Do we not look upon all religions as equal? ...The offspring may choose either religion. The couple of our conception will give the children liberal education in that regard. In my view this should be quite easy." (*C*, LXXX, 77f)

110. Nirmala Gandhi, interview, 23/1/1996. In South Africa in 1905, Gandhi had sponsored the civil marriage of Millie Graham, a Christian, and H. S. L. Polak, a Jew. According to Gandhi they had a common religion of ethics. (See *A*, IV, ch. 22 and M. G. Polak 1931, 11-14.)

111. *C*, LXXV, 375.

And then his appreciation of the point of view represented in Reading 197 led him to argue that the marriage laws of the Republic of India should provide for non-religious weddings in order to "clear the way for inter-religious marriages":

[207] *1947* (as reported): [Q.] "You advocate intercaste marriages. Do you also favor marriage between Indians professing different religions?... If so, what form should the marriage ceremony take?"
[A.] "Although he [Gandhi] had not always held that view, he had long since come to the conclusion that inter-religious marriage was a welcome event whenever it took place. Marriage in his view was a sacred institution. Hence there must be mutual friendship, either party having equal respcct for the religion of the other. There was no room in this for conversion. Hence the marriage ceremony could be performed by the priests belonging to either faith. But this could come about only when the communities had shed mutual emnity and cultivated equal regard for all religions of the world."
[Q.] "Was not the institution of civil marriage a negation of religion and did it not tend to laxity in faith?"
[A.] "He did not believe in civil marriages, but he welcomed the institution of civil marriage as a much-needed reform to clear the way for inter-religious marriages." (*L*, I, 558; *C*, LXXXVII, 11f)

Animals

Hindus use the term *mata* ("mother") in their worship of the land (*Bhoo Mata*), the River Ganges (*Ganga Mata*) and cows (*Go Mata*). Their obligations include not only singing prayers of praise but also donating land or a cow on various occasions to a temple or, more often, to the personal estate of a priest. In Gandhi's day, the religious purification of a room polluted by a stray untouchable was achieved by sprinkling the room with cow's urine or a solution of cow-dung.

While most Brahmins and most members of Gandhi's varna are vegetarians, even those Hindus who are carnivores refrain normally from eating beef, and all Hindus tend to be more offended by Christians' and Moslems' consumption of beef than of other meats.

In Gandhi's adult years he was, though a vegetarian, less than orthodox in his attitude toward cows:

[208] *1908*: "I myself respect the cow, that is, I look upon her with affectionate reverence. The cow is the protector of India because, being an agricultural country, she is dependent on the cow. The cow is a most useful animal in a hundred ways. Our Moslem brethren will admit this." (*S*, IV, 138)

When he established Tolstoy Farm in South Africa as a communal home for the families of jailed satyagrahis, he considered it more important to prohibit smoking than beef-eating:

[209] *1910* (as recalled later): "There were Hindus, Moslems, Parsis and Christians among them.... The Moslem friends had already granted me permission to have a purely vegetarian kitchen; I had now to approach Christian sisters whose husbands or sons were in jail.... I assured them that even beef would be provided for them if they wanted it. The sisters kindly consented not to

have meat.... Drink, smoking, etc. were of course totally prohibited." (*S*, III, 321ff)

But in India he could be no more cosmopolitan than to advocate, as we have seen briefly in Reading 116, "the protection of the cow in its much larger sense than the popular." In the 1920s his elaborations of this concept were philosophical:

[210] *1921*: "Cow protection to me is one of the most wonderful phenomena in human evolution. It takes the human being beyond his species. The cow to me means the entire sub-human world. Man through the cow is enjoined to realize his identity with all that lives. Why the cow was selected for apotheosis is obvious to me. The cow was in India the best companion. She was the giver of plenty. Not only did she she give milk but she also made agriculture possible." (*C*, XXI, 248)

[211] *1925* (in a letter to Nehru): "The cow is merely a type for all that lives. Cow-protection means protection of the weak, the helpless, the dumb and the deaf. Man becomes then not the lord and master of all creation but he is its servant. The cow to me is a sermon in pity. As yet we are merely playing at cow-protection, but we shall soon have to grapple with the reality." (*C*, XXVI, 545)

[212] *1926*: "A Hindu who protects the cow should protect every animal. But taking all things into consideration, we may not cavil at his protecting the cow because he fails to protect the other animals." (*C*, XXXII, 27)

In the 1930s he developed the concept in practical terms:

[213] *1932*: "[At] the ashram... the word *goraksha* [cow protection] was replaced by *goseva* [cow service]. But as the experience of doing without milk or ghee [liquid butter] and

thus serving the cow without any selfish [human] considerations did not succeed, cattle were kept at the ashram. ...Mankind is not so benevolent that it will die to save the cow or allow it to live... as a parasite. The cattle population at present [in India] is so large that if it is well fed, the human population will not have enough food left for itself.... Hindu society must discard some superstitions masquerading as religion. Hindus do not utilize the bones etc. of dead cows.... Emaciated cattle are exported to Australia where their bones are converted into manure, their flesh into meat extract and their hides into boots and shoes. The meat extract, the manure and the shoes are then re-exported to India and used without any compunction. This stupidity makes for the destruction of the cow, and puts the country to huge economic losses. This is not religion but the very negation of it.... Hindu society should keep the cow, treat her and her progeny well so long as they are alive, cherish them in their old age, and fully utilize their carcasses when they are dead. Thus alone the cow can be saved, and in saving her we shall perhaps learn how to save the rest of sub-human creation. Thanks to our ignorance, laziness and [inter-religious] hatred, the cow today is hastening to her destruction. As for the other cattle, the less said about them the better.

"The ashram at present has a limited object in view: to conduct a model *goshala* [corral] at the ashram, to breed good cows and bullocks, to utilize their carcases fully when they are dead so as to show that cow-keeping is an economic proposition, [and] to train workers and provide for their employment upon the completion of their training. The work is going on at present. There are many difficulties, but we are fully confident of success." (*C*, L, 229ff)

[214] *1932*: "The ashram ideal is to do without milk, as it holds that the milk of animals, like meat, is no food for mankind. For a year and more no milk or ghee was used in the ashram, but as the health of the children... [and] adults suffered under this regime, first ghee and then milk had to be added to the ashram dietary." (*H*, 3/vi/50, 121)

[215] *1940*: "Mother cow is in many ways better than the mother who gave us birth. Our mother gives us milk for a couple of years and then expects us to serve her when we grow up. Mother cow expects from us nothing but grass and grain. Our mother often falls ill and expects service from us. Mother cow rarely falls ill.... Our mother when she dies means expenses of burial or cremation. Mother cow is as useful dead as when she is alive. We can make use of... her flesh, her bones, her intestines, her horns and her skin. Well, I say this not to disparage the mother who gives us birth, but in order to show you the substantial reasons for my worshipping the cow." (*H*, 15/ix, 28)

He was always concerned to prevent Hindus from reacting violently to Moslem practices:

[216] *1924*: "Though I regard cow protection as the central fact of Hinduism, I have never been able to understand the antipathy towards the Moslems on that score.... The only effective and honorable way to befriend the Moslems is to leave it to their honor to save the cow. Cow-protection societies must turn their attention to the feeding of cattle, prevention of cruelty, preservation of the fast-disappearing pasture land, [and] improving the breed of cattle...." (*C*, XXIV, 150f)

In the 1920s he subscribed explicitly, however, to the traditional Hindu view (though quite capable of adapting a Christian phrase to help explain it to a Westerner) of man's cosmic relation to all the other higher animals:

[217] *1922*: [Q.] "You think we come back again to this earth?"

[A.] "Yes. I think we all come back again if we are not pure enough to go to heaven.... 'Render unto Caesar the things which are Caesar's.' The body must give back to the earth the things that are of the earth before the soul can give itself absolutely to God; or rather, the soul must refuse to coöperate with the things of this earth; it must become quite free from any earthly desires and entanglements."

[Q.] "And do you believe animals have souls too?"

[A.] "Yes, we never kill them at our ashram. It is a high stage in the development of the soul to feel a love for all humanity, but it is a higher stage to have a heart of love for every living thing. I confess that I have not reached this stage. I still feel afraid when I actually see these creatures come near me. If we have no fear at all, I do not think they will harm us.

"I met an Englishman once. He was a veterinary surgeon and had a wonderful way with animals. We were visiting a house together, and suddenly a gigantic brute of a dog rushed toward us, fierce as a lion.... I was petrified with fear, but this Englishman went forward to meet it as it charged, and embraced it without a trace of fear. Its anger evaporated at once and it began wagging its tail. It impressed me very much. That is the true way of meeting animals by non-resistance."

[Q.] "But do you not think a man's life is worth more than an animal's? ...Supposing you were confronted by a crocodile and you could only escape by injuring it...."

[A.] "No, I should say — or at least I ought to say — to this crocodile, 'Your need is greater than mine,' and let it devour me. You see, our life does not finish with the death of the body. God knows all about it; we none of us know what will happen next. If I escaped the crocodile, I could not escape the flash of lightning that might come next minute."

[Q.] "But surely a man's soul is different from that of a crocodile — if it has one at all. You remember what Chesterton says about it: When a man is taking his sixth whisky and soda, and is beginning to lose control over himself, you come up to him and give him a friendly tap on the shoulder and say, 'Be a man.' But when the crocodile is finishing his sixth missionary, you do not step up to it and tap it on the back and say, 'Be a crocodile.' Doesn't this show [that] a man has an ideal in him to strive after in a way that no animal has?"

[A.] [Laughter.] "True, there is a difference between the souls of men and of animals. Animals live in a sort of perpetual trance, but man can wake up and become conscious of God. God says, as it were, to man, 'Look up and worship Me; you are made in My image.'"

[Q.] "And the souls of animals, where do they come from? Do you think the soul of a man can become the soul of an animal?"

[A.] "Yes, I think all these horrible and evil creatures are inhabited by the souls of men who have gone wrong — snakish men, greedy, unmerciful crocodile men, and so on." (*C*, XXIII, 107)

This view entailed moral difficulties:

[218] *ca.1912* (recalled later): "One day a snake was found... [at Tolstoy Farm] at such a place that it seemed impossible to drive it away or to catch it. One of the students... wanted my permission to kill it... and I permitted him." (*S*, III, 345)

In the late 1920s he made several remarkable statements about such moral shortcomings (in his opinion) in his own relation to animals:

[219] *1928*: "There is *himsa* [violence] in the use of antiseptics, yet I cannot bring myself to discard the use of disinfectants like kerosene etc. to rid myself of the mosquito pest and the like. I suffer snakes to be killed in the ashram when it is impossible to catch them and put them out of harm's way. I even tolerate the use of the stick to drive the bullocks in the ashram.... If, as a result of this humble confession of mine, friends choose to give me up as lost, I would be sorry, but nothing will induce me to try to conceal my imperfections in the practice of ahimsa [non-violence].... I know that I have a long distance yet to cover in this direction." (*C*, XXXVII, 409)

In the following statement he was explaining to a friend that the reason why he had not made Calcutta the center of his activities was that sheep are ritually sacrificed there in a temple to the goddess Kali (from whose name the word "Calcutta" is derived):[112]

[220] *1928*: "My soul rises in rebellion against the cold-blooded inhumanity that goes on there in the name of religion. If I had the [moral] strength I would plant myself before the gate of the temple and tell those in charge of it that before they sacrificed a single innocent animal they should have to cut my throat. But I know that for me to do so would be an unreal, a mechanical thing today because I

112. He had for the same reason asked his eldest son, Harilal, not to settle in Calcutta. (*C*, XIX, 290)

have not yet completely overcome the will to live. And till I can do that I must bear the cross of my imperfect existence." (*C*, XXXVIII, 244)

Another time he said, in regard to the same temple:

[221] *late 1920s*: "To my mind the life of a lamb is no less precious than that of a human being.... I hold that, the more helpless a creature, the more entitled it is to protection by men from the cruelty of man. But... I must go through more self-purification and [self-]sacrifice before I can hope to save these lambs from this unholy [religious] sacrifice. It is my constant prayer that there may be born on earth some great spirit, man or woman, fired with divine pity, who will deliver us from this heinous sin, save the lives of the innocent creatures, and purify the temple. How is it that Bengal, with all its knowledge, intelligence, sacrifice and emotion, tolerates this slaughter?" (*A*, III, ch. 18)

Later he changed his mind, however, as to whether animals dangerous to humans should be caught and set free rather than killed:

[222] *1943*: "If I were faced with the option of killing a tiger or a snake, or otherwise being killed by it, I would rather be killed than take its life. But that is a personal position, not to be put forward for adoption by others. If I had the fearless power to tame these dangerous creatures by the force of my love and my will, and could show others how to do likewise, then I should have the right to advise other people to follow my example. But I have not that power. I must, therefore, advise others to kill all creatures dangerous to human life, such as tigers, bears etc.,

snakes, scorpions etc., as well as rats and other crop-destroying vermin. It should be done in the most humane way possible.... With regard to vermin, which is often the outcome of carelessness and dirt, we should try to live in such a way as not to give rise to its occurrence."

[Q.] "Then this means that you are no longer satisfied with the catching of snakes, rats etc., and the turning of them loose elsewhere, as is done in Sevagram and other places."

[A.] "That is right. If one is not prepared to live in the company of these creatures oneself, one has no right to turn them loose on other peoples' land. For that is what it comes to." (*C*, LXXVII, 207f)

And his humanism became far stronger than his advocacy of vegetarianism:

[223] *1946*: "Fish abound in the seas around the coast of India. The war is over; there are innumerable small and medium-size vessels which were used for doing patrol and guard duties along our shores for the last five years. The R[oyal] I[ndian] N[avy] could arrange about staffing these, with the Department of Fisheries giving all assistance.... Dry fish does even now form part of the normal diet of a great number of people who are very poor — that is, when it is available and they can afford to buy it." (*C*, LXXXIII, 161)

Even more telling is the dramatic change which can be seen in Gandhi's attitude toward vivisection. For a long time he was, as one might expect, ardently opposed to it:

[224] *1925*: "I abhor vivisection with my whole soul, I detest the unpardonable slaughter of innocent life in the name

of science and humanity so-called, and all the scientific discoveries stained with innocent blood I count as of no consequence.

"If the circulation of blood theory could not have been discovered without vivisection, the human kind could well have done without it....

"Even as we are slowly but surely discovering that it is an error to suppose that Hindus can thrive upon the degradation of a fifth of themselves [the 'untouchables'] or that people of the West can rise or live upon the exploitation and degradation of the Eastern and African nations, so shall we realize in the fullness of time that our dominion over the lower order of creation is not for their slaughter, but for their benefit equally with ours. For I am as certain that they are endowed with a soul as that I am." (*C*, XXIX, 325f)

And yet when he had to decide in 1945 whether to allow the vivisection of a frog in order to demonstrate, in a nurses' class at Sevagram, the phenomenon of heartbeat, he said:

[225] *1945*: "Dissect the frog if that is the only way to explain the heartbeat." (*G*, 40)

CHAPTER 5

OTHER RELIGIONS

Here we will look at what might be called — though it would be an exaggeration — Gandhi's ecumenical tendencies, as well as his relations specifically to Jainism, Buddhism, Zoroastrianism (whose adherents in India are called Parsis), Theosophy, Ethical Culture, Christianity and Islam. We will distinguish between his attitudes to Jesus and to real Christianity,[113] and likewise between those to Mohammed and to real Islam.

Gandhi as a child was exposed to several cults:

[226] *Childhood* (recalled later): "I got an early grounding in toleration for all branches of ...sister religions.... Jain monks... would pay frequent visits to my father.... He had, besides, Moslem and Parsi friends who would talk to him about their own faiths, and he would listen to them always with respect, and often with interest. Being his nurse, I often had a chance to be present at these talks.... Christian missionaries used to stand in a corner near the high school and hold forth...." (*A*, I, ch. 10)

It should be noted that religious tolerance has been historically characteristic of India:

[227] **From the Gita**: "Whatever form one desires to worship in faith and devotion, in that very form I [Brahma, the supreme spirit] make that faith of his secure." (VII, 21)

---

113. The well-established term "real Marxism" means the way of life of avowedly Marxist people and nations. "Real Christianity" in the analogous sense includes but is broader than the churches. It is in contrast to the idea of "true Christianity" which some Christians use to sift out the distasteful lumps of real Christianity from the humanism embodied in the parable of the good Samaritan and in the saying, "Inasmuch as you have done it to the least of these, you have done it to me."

[228] **From the "Rock-Edict XII" of Asoka** (the first great Indian emperor, 3rd century BC): "The root [of spiritual strength] is to guard one's speech so as to avoid extolling one's own religion and decrying that of another or speaking of it without occasion or relevance." (K. L. S. Rao 1978: 108)

At a south Indian temple to Kesava, a royal edict refers to that deity as one whom "the Saivas worship as Siva, the Vedantins as Brahman, the Buddhists as Buddha" and so on."[114] And according to a famous religious poet some of whose works Gandhi is known to have read in prison in 1922 and again (in Tagore's translation) in 1923:[115]

[229] **Kabir,** *1400s*: "How can there be two lords of the universe? Who has confused your mind? The same Lord is named Allah and Kesab by Hazar [Moslem clergy] and Rama and Kesab by [the Hindu] high priest. Different ornaments made of gold are named differently, but the gold in them remains the same. The names you call them make no difference." (translation after G. N. Das 1996, 81)

Among the three "sister religions" referred to in the first three sentences of Reading 226, Zoroastrianism seems to have had the least effect on Gandhi. It is true that he would call Zoroaster the "first of the wise men,"[116] but Gandhi's writings refer only now and then to Parsis and only rarely and vaguely, as far as we have noticed, to their ideas:

---

114. *L*, II, 92.
115. K. L. S. Rao 1979: 109. (See also Reading 77.)
116. *C*, XXIII, 150 and 179.

[230] *1893* (recalled later): "I also read a book called *The Sayings of Zarathustra.*" (A, II, ch. 22)

We have seen (Readings 109-111) how Theosophy was a catalyst for the quickening of his interest in Hinduism. His rejection of modern Western civilization was also undoubtedly influenced to some extent by Theosophical sentiments:

[231] *1905*: "Madame Blavatsky [the inventor of Theosophy] came to India, told both the Hindus and the Moslems of the evils of Western civilization and asked them to beware of becoming enamoured of it." (*C*, IV, 408)

(She had described Western civilization as being like a "hideous leprosy... canting and deceitful, from its diplomats down to its custodians of religion... selfish, greedy and brutal beyond expression in its grabbing characteristics."[117])

The following excerpts from a letter of Gandhi's to a friend suggest how well acquainted Gandhi was with the cult and show his considered opinion of it:

[232] *1911*: "The Society's rule respecting brotherhood appealed to me, [but] I had no sympathy for its search for occult powers. I do not think that Mrs. Besant [head of the cult since 1907] is a hypocrite; she is credulous and is duped.... All the same, I have drawn from Theosophy the lessons which seemed to me worth drawing. Theosophy sent many Hindus inquiring into their own religion. [So] it has performed the same service as Christianity has. Moreover, Theosophists believe in the same ba-

117. Blavatsky 1891, cited in Iyer 1973: 28 and in Green 1993: 100.

> sic principles as we [Hindus] do and therefore it is easy enough to come across good persons among them.... Ritch... urged me to become a member. Not only did I not become one,[118] I helped him to be free from that humbug. Polak is a Theosophist, but he stays miles away from the practices and writings of Theosophists.... When I was in India, I sent Gokaldas to [Central Hindu] College [founded by Besant] at Benares. Then also I was disappointed. Cordes... is a staunch Theosophist. I have not yet been able to get him out of the hold of Theosophy.... Being honest, he will see the fraud that is there and turn his back on it, unless he is taken in. It is worth ascertaining what humbug prevails there safe under the cover of Mrs. Besant's goodness. Her desire to pass off as the 'Master' is understandable. One who runs after occult powers cannot but become so intoxicated." (*C*, XI, 64f)

Gandhi did very much admire Anna Kingsford and Edward Maitland, who after being active in the mid-1880s in the Theosophical Society broke away and founded the mystical, vegetarian and nature-loving Esoteric Christian Union, for which Gandhi became an agent — advertising, selling and lending out its books — during his early years in South Africa.[119] Some of its teachings were that one should take vows of abstinence, fearlessness and voluntary poverty; that the mystics of Egypt, Persia, India and the West had selected Osiris, Mithras, Buddha and Jesus as "names or persons" representing a "full manifestation of the qualities of spirit"; and:

118. In his student days in London, however, Gandhi on one occasion had enrolled as an associate member for six months. See Power 1960, 17.
119. *C*, I, 139ff, 168; *A*, II, ch. 15.

[233] **Anna Kingsford, Edward Maitland,** *1890*: "In order to be made in the image of God, the individual must... be spiritually both man and woman." (*E*, 324)

Anyone who knows Gandhi will know that this idea must have appealed to him — and no less the grace with which Kingsford and Maitland would say:

[234] **Anna Kingsford, Edward Maitland,** *1890*: "We disclaim alike authority and dogma, we appeal to the reason of humanity." (Preface)

Also profoundly appealing to him was Ethical Culture, a small but influential American movement, founded in 1876, eschewing creed and supporting practical social work. Gandhi published in 1907 a series of articles in Gujarati summarizing part of a book (in English) by the founder of the Chicago Society for Ethical Culture.[120] We are struck by the reference, in Gandhi's summary, to moral culture progressing like a science — since that is a fair description of Gandhi's own achievement — and by some remarks bringing out an aspect of Darwin's thought contrary to the dog-eat-dog "social Darwinism" of the late 19th and early 20th centuries:

[235] *1907*: "Moral culture is still in its infancy; it is as science was before the birth of a Bacon or a Darwin....

"With a mass of evidence... [Darwin] has shown how man came into being... [and] that moral strength is even superior [in promoting the survival of the species] to physical

120. (Salter 1889); see *C*, VI, 273, 280, 284, 298, 312, 316, 330, 340.

and intellectual strength.... A peaceful disposition is one aspect.... Freedom from bad habits forms another.... It is the duty of man to bear this truth in mind and to practice altruism, which is the highest form of morality." (*C*, VI, 316ff)

Jainism and Buddhism

Jainism and Buddhism were founded around 500 BC (very approximately speaking),[121] each by a non-Brahmin Hindu prince who, while accepting or adapting the concepts of inherited karma and moksha, and while teaching that the cause of all human suffering is human desire, attributed no authority at all to the vedas and disparaged the traditional rituals, especially ritual sacrifice.

The founder of Jainism, Mahavira, was clearly an atheist, clearly opposed to the concept and practice of caste, and an extreme ascetic believing that self-denial and even self-torture help one to attain moksha:

[236] **The Acharanga Sutra**: "He [Mahavira] wandered naked and homeless... never sought medical aid... took no medicaments... in winter meditated in the shade, in the heat of the summer in the scorching sun... drank no water for months.... sometimes took a meal only every 6th, 8th, 10th or 12th day... [and] pursued his meditations without craving."

Mahavira's behavioral precepts were simple and fairly clear:

---

121. See Schumann 1989, 10-13.

[237] **Mahavira,** *ca.500 BC*: "The right conduct of a human is found in the five commandments of the soul: [1] Do not kill any living thing or hurt any living thing by word, thought or deed. [2] Do not steal. [3] Do not lie. [4] Do not live an unchaste life and never become intoxicated. [5] Do not covet or desire anything."

The first of these five precepts entails such extreme non-violence — one must love and preserve even worms and insects — that Jainism is perforce an elitist religion, of potential interest to members of a merchant caste (such as Gandhi's family), and claiming even today well over a million practicing adherents from such castes, but unacceptable to peasants and to military or political people.

Gandhi's exposure to Jainism in his childhood and youth was quite substantial:

[238] *Childhood* (recalled later): "Jain monks... would pay frequent visits to my father [and] have talks with [him] on subjects religious and mundane.... Jainism was strong in Gujarat and its influence was felt everywhere and on all occasions." (*A*, I, chh. 10 and 16)

His strong self-discipline, his partiality to vows, and the actual content of many of the vows he took, were all Jain-influenced, as was his belief in the "manyness of reality" (see Reading 368). And, his familiarity with Jainism helped him consider deeply to what extent he could practice non-violence:

[239] *1946*: "The emphasis laid on the sacredness of sub-human life in Jainism is understandable. But that can never mean that one is to be kind to [sub-human] life in preference to human life....

"To benefit by others' killing [of sub-human creatures] and delude oneself into the belief that one is being very religious and non-violent, is sheer self-deception.... In life it is impossible to eschew violence completely. The question arises, where is one to draw the line?[122] ...To allow crops to be eaten up by animals in the name of ahimsa while there is a famine in the land is certainly a sin. Evil and good are relative terms. What is good under certain conditions can become an evil or a sin under a different set of conditions....

"[The brilliant young Jain, Rajchandra Mehta's] advice to me was that if I had courage, if I wanted to see God face to face, I should let myself be bitten by a snake instead of killing it.... My ideal is to be able to play with snakes and scorpions fearlessly; but it is merely a wish so far. ...I have let my people kill both. I could have prevented them if I had wished. But how could I? I did not have the courage to take them up with my own hands and teach my companions a lesson in fearlessness. I am ashamed of that. But my shame could not benefit them or me." (*C*, LXXXIV, 231f)

During the least successful phase of Gandhi's life, in the early 1890s (see Appendix), his friendship with Rajchandra (1868-1901) sustained his spirits. Years later he would explain:

[240] *1891-93* (recalled later): "My first meeting with him convinced me that he was a man of great character and

---

122. In E. M. Forster's novel, *A Passage to India*, there is a moment when an open-minded Anglican missionary accepts that cows have eternal souls like humans, and hence so also must other sentient beings like dogs and cats, and in that case also spiders and insects — but not the amoebae, because a line has to be drawn somewhere.

> learning.... I came to know afterwards... his spotless character and burning passion for self-realization.... No knotty business problem [dealing in jewelry] was too difficult for him. But... the center around which his life revolved... was the passion to see God face to face.... Amongst the things on his business table there were invariably to be found some religious book and his diary. ...Immediately on finishing his talk about weighty business transactions [he normally] began to write about hidden things of the spirit.... I never saw him lose his state of equipoise. There was no business or other selfish tie that bound him to me, and yet I enjoyed the closest association with him. I was but a briefless barrister then, and yet whenever I saw him he would engage me in conversation of a seriously religious nature.... His intellect compelled as great a regard from me as his moral earnestness, and deep down in me was the conviction that he would... always confide in me his innermost thoughts.... Three moderns have left a deep impress on my life and captivated me: Raychandbhai [Rajchandra] by his living contact; Tolstoy by his book, *The Kingdom of God is Within You*; and Ruskin by his *Unto This Last*." (*A*, II, ch. 1)

We have mentioned in Chapter 4 (Reading 110) how in 1894 in South Africa he took religious guidance from Rajchandra by correspondence. The most important of Rajchandra's three letters to Gandhi in South Africa answered a set of 27 questions which Gandhi had sent him, starting with "What is soul?". In reply to that question Rajchandra set out the traditional Jain teaching of a non-material, living, yet indestructible substance whose true nature (not attainable when soul is fused with matter) is complete consciousness, perfect knowledge, passionless bliss and freedom.[123] In answer to some of the other questions he said:

[241] **Rajchandra,** *1894*: "God is atman [soul] freed from all bonds of karma.... Both the atman and the [material] universe are eternal, without beginning and without end.... Passions... bind the soul to matter.... Moksha is complete freedom from [passions].... The miracles of Christ pale into insignificance before the omnipotence of the perfected atman." (*E*, I, 328; *C*, XXXII, 593ff)

Readings 93, 373 and 380 are among those which illustrate the pertinence of all this to Gandhi's religious thinking during the next three or four decades. And, he drew from Rajchandra's answers the following definition of religion (which may well have helped him resolve his "mental churning" due to "wavering between Hinduism and Christianity"[124]):

[242] *1935*: "Religion is not different sets of opinions... [but] the quality of one's soul. [It] exists among humans in visible or invisible form. Through religion we are able to know our duties as human beings... [and] our true relationship with other living things.... We should take this discipline from wherever it may be found." (Hay 1970: 35)

Unlike Jainism, Buddhism fields missionaries and so is, like Christianity, a would-be universal cult (particularly strong in Tibet, Sri Lanka, Burma, and East Asia). Terms like "equa-

123. Hay 1970: 33.

124. Ibid, 35. *Y*, 27/iv/1921, 136.

nimity," "benevolence" and "compassion" figure prominently in Buddhist thought. It was mainly because of his compassion for animals that Buddha — the "Enlightened One" — favored vegetarianism, according to the following passage from an ancient layer of Buddhist scriptures (in the Pali language):

[243] **Buddha,** *ca.500-450 BC,* **paraphrased:** "Meat is not to be accepted... if one has seen, heard or suspects [that the animal was killed specifically for one's consumption]. But if that is not the case, a monk may accept meat.... But [then]... he should eat the alms-food without being caught up in the pleasure of eating....

"Anyone who kills for my sake or for that of one of my disciples commits a [great] evil." (Schumann 1989: 102f)

This passage illustrates also how he advocated — and this was true in many respects — a "middle path of moderation" in one's worldly life.[125] He believed neither in a creator-god nor in an eternal soul,[126] and was generally rationalist:

[244] **Attributed to Buddha:** "Do not accept my teaching as true because it has been handed down from generation to generation, or because it is in accordance with your [own] past traditions, or because it seems probable, or logical, or is in accordance with practical justice, or because it seems very good, or because it strengthens your faith, or because I am a celebrated and respected sage; but accept

125. An analogous element in Western culture is the praise of moderation in Aristotle's *Nichomachean Ethics*, where each virtue is defined as a mean between two forms of excess, for instance courage between caution and rashness.

126. Lang 1985.

my teaching only if it appears right to your discriminating intelligence." (*H*, 6/i/1951, 397)

As one might expect of an exceptionally intelligent person who was brought up, like Gandhi, in a governing household, Buddha displayed great administrative skills in organizing his monastic order. He was, also like Gandhi, a respecter of law and order, instructing his monks to obey their kings and avoid any form of polemics against the state. When the first king to subscribe to Buddhism learned that some soldiers whom he wanted to send into action in a frontier dispute were trying to avoid the danger by becoming monks, he asked Buddha not to accept them, and the request was cordially honored.[127]

The caste system was probably simpler and less rigid at that time than it later became. According to Pali scriptures, Buddha taught — to the dismay of the Brahmins — that members of all four varnas were equally pure and equally capable of developing benevolence and loving-kindness.[128] Gandhi saw in such teaching an example for his own work to reform the caste system in the 20th century:

[245] *1920*: "Buddha would have died resisting the priesthood, if the majesty of his love had not proved to be equal to

127. Schumann 1989, 88-93 and 154f.

128. Ibid., 193. Tiwari 1988: 30. According to Pali scripture, Buddha also taught that since neither the Brahmins nor any sages of old claimed to know or have seen "whence or whither Brahma is," yet the Brahmins claim they can point out the way to union with "that which they know not, neither have seen," it follows that "the talk of the Brahmins versed in the three vedas is foolish." (See T. W. R. Davis 1899.)

the task of bending the priesthood. Christ died on the cross with a crown of thorns on his head defying the might of a whole empire. And if I raise resistance of a non-violent character, I simply and humbly follow in the footsteps of the great teachers." (*C*, XVII, 408)

A medieval Hindu reaction obliterated Buddha's monastic order in India well before 1000 AD, but he remained venerated as a great teacher. Gandhi's view was:

[246] *1913*: "It is difficult to say who was the greatest among Krishna, Rama, the Buddha, Jesus, etc.... They lived in different times and under different circumstances. In point of character alone, possibly the Buddha was the greatest; but who can say?" (*C*, XII, 126)

According to the esoteric doctrine of "Mahayana" scriptures (in Sanskrit and dating from about 100 to 500 AD), Buddha countenanced three basic attitudes toward *nirvana* (the Buddhist counterpart to moksha), more or less as follows: *(1)* finding one's own sublime extinction from the world of phenomena and rebirth, independently of everyone else and as expeditiously as may be; *(2)* finding liberation from desire and from life, yet still somehow thereafter helping to enlighten and benefit others (by being a *bodhisatva*); *(3)* overcoming all selfish desires and yet remaining in the world of phenomena in order to help the others there.[129] While Gandhi was, like us, no expert in esoteric doctrine, this last idea seems obviously to have

129. Stcherbatsky, 2 and, in both paginations, 29f. Warder, 355f. Mahajan, I, 105.

inspired his beautiful sentiment that if he must be reborn, it should be as an untouchable (Reading 68), and his even more beautiful statement (Reading 424), upon completing his last and most painful fast, that if only the religiously motivated ethnic cleansing would stop, he could wish to live many more years, "doing service of humanity till the last moment."

Gandhi attributed positive social activity to Buddhism and Jesus alike:

[247] *1939*: "The love that Jesus taught and practiced was not a mere personal virtue, but... was essentially a social and collective virtue. Buddhism taught and practiced the same thing six hundred years before Jesus." (*C*, LXVIII, 307)

That which scholars normally call Buddhist agnosticism or atheism he considered superior to Biblical theism:

[248] *1927*: "Buddha... rejected the notion that a being called God was actuated by malice, could repent of His actions, and like the kings of the earth could possibly be open to... bribes and could possibly have favorites.... [But he] re-declared the eternal and unalterable existence of the moral government of this universe. He unhesitatingly said that the Law was God Himself.[130] ...And hence the great confusion that Buddha disbelieved in God and simply believed in the moral law."[131] (*C*, XXXV, 246)

He was not much inclined, however, to a scholarly approach:

---

130. As far as we know, Buddha never subscribed to such use of a personal name or pronoun.

131. But see Reading 326.

[249] *1947*: "Though [Sri] Lanka might be the most suitable place for studying Pali... one does not get at the secret of Buddhism by getting to know its externals." (*C*, LXXXVII, 510)

—nor to contemporary Buddhist monasticism:

[250] *1932*: "Today we find Buddhist monks in Ceylon, Burma and Tibet sunk in ignorance and the veritable images of sloth. In India, too, the monks known as *sannyasis* are not found to be shining examples of humanity." (*C*, L, 410)

[251] *1947*, to the Dalai Lama: "I advised the friends who saw me on your behalf to give up secretiveness and superstition if Buddhism (which is but an attempt to reform Hinduism) is to live." (*C*, LXXXVII, 224)

The Bible and Jesus

When Gandhi was 21 years old he became acquainted with the Bible and was enchanted, enduringly, by the message of non-violence in the Sermon on the Mount:

[252] *1889* (recalled later): "I met a good Christian from Manchester in a vegetarian boarding house.... He said, 'Neither meat-eating nor drinking is enjoined [i.e. prescribed] by Scripture. Do please read the Bible.' I accepted his advice.... I read the Book of Genesis, and the chapters that followed invariably sent me to sleep.... But the New Testament produced a different impression, especially the Sermon on the Mount, which went straight to my heart. I compared it with the Gita. The verses, 'But I say unto you, that ye resist not evil: but whosoever shall smite thee on thy right cheek, turn to him the other also. And

if any man take away thy coat let him have thy cloak too,' delighted me beyond measure and put me in mind of Shamal Bhatt's 'For a bowl of water, give a goodly meal' etc." (*A*, I, ch. 20)

[253] *1927*: "Supposing I was deprived of the Gita and forgot all its contents but had a copy of the Sermon [on the Mount], I should derive the same joy from it as I do from the Gita." (*Y*, 22/xii, 426)

[254] *1931*: [Q.] "What is the difference between your message and the Christian [one]?" [A.] "...My message is as old as this earth and I do not know that it is at all different from the Christian message. If you mean by it non-violence, I should be sorry to discover that you have given up the teaching of the Sermon on the Mount." (*C*, XLVIII, 421)

He interpreted Jesus' death as an example of turning the other cheek:[132]

[255] *1939*: "Though I cannot claim to be a Christian in the sectarian sense, the example of Jesus' suffering is a factor in the composition of my undying faith in non-violence which rules all my actions, worldly and temporal." (*C*, XLVIII, 278)

He would even interpret it (in Reading 245) as an act of satyagraha against the Roman Empire. We consider more valid, in view of the parable of the good Samaritan, his opinion that Jesus taught love as a social rather than a "mere personal"

132. He would put on the wall a picture Jesus or a small crucifix, as a symbol of morally purposeful suffering. In South Africa, a "beautiful head of Christ... adorned the wall over his desk" (M. G. Polak 1931, ch 3). We noticed a crucifix in his hut at Sevagram.

virtue (Reading 247). It is most likely that when Gandhi sent to his nephew Maganlal the famous Christian eulogy (by St. Paul) of love, both Gandhi and Maganlal took it to express a good-Samaritan-like ideal rather than an our-family-first precept:

[256] *1917* (on the Hindu New Year's Day): "What shall I give you on this auspicious day?... I am trying to send to you what you and I and many others lack.... Let us pray for it together.

"'Though I speak with the tongues of men and of angels and have not charity, I am become as sounding brass or a tinkling cymbal.... And now abideth faith, hope, charity, these three; but the greatest of these is charity.'[133]

"Read this, ponder over it. Read it over again. Read the original English from the Bible and translate it into Hindi. Ruminate over it and strive to have even for one moment a large glimpse of charity that is love." (*C*, XIV, 90f)

In South Africa he had studied Christianity in depth (Reading 261) and concluded, in regard to Jesus:

[257] *1893* (recalled later): "It was more than I could believe that Jesus was the only incarnate son of God.... If God could have sons, all of us were His sons.... [Jesus'] death on the cross was a great example to the world, but that there was anything like a mysterious virtue in it my heart could not accept. (*A*, II, ch. 15)

---

133. Gandhi wrote out, in his own translation into Gujarati, this passage from I Corinthians, xiii.

He was too cosmopolitan to be swayed by stories of miracles:

[258] *1937*: "I do not need either the prophecies or the miracles to establish Jesus' greatness as a teacher. Nothing can be more miraculous than the three years of his ministry. There is no miracle in the story of the multitude being fed on a handful of loaves. A magician can create that illusion. But woe worth the day on which a magician would be hailed as the saviour of humanity. As for Jesus raising the dead to life, well, I doubt if the men he raised were really dead. I raised a relative's child from supposed death to life, but that was because the child was not [really] dead.... The laws of Nature are changeless, unchangeable, and there are no miracles in the sense of infringement or interruption of Nature's laws." (*H*, 17/iv, 87)

But he venerated Jesus as a teacher for all humanity:

[259] *1941*: "Man has within his breast an impulse for good and a compassion that is the spark of divinity, and which some day, I believe, will burst forth into full flower; that is the hope of all mankind. An example of this flowering may be found in the figure and in the life of Jesus.... The lives of all have, in some greater or lesser degree, been changed by His presence, His actions, and the words spoken by His divine voice.... And because the life of Jesus has the significance and the transcendency to which I have alluded, I believe that He belongs not solely to Christianity, but to the entire world: to all races and people, it matters little under what flag, name or doctrine they may work, profess a faith, or worship a God inherited from their ancestors." (*C*, LXXV, 70)

Real Christianity

Gandhi was first exposed to Christianity while still a child:

[260] *Late 1870s and early '80s* (recalled later): "Christian missionaries used to stand in a corner near the high school and hold forth, pouring abuse on Hindus and their gods.[134] ...[I felt that] a religion that compelled one to eat beef, drink liquor, and change one's own clothes did not deserve the name." (*A*, 47f)

He gained a better image of it in London in the late 1880s, and then became very well acquainted, during his South African years, with some kind and gentle Christian missionaries[135] and their teachings:

[261] *1894* (recalled later): "I said to [a Christian friend], 'I am a Hindu by birth and yet I do not know much of Hinduism, and I know less of other religions. In fact I do not know... what should be my belief. I intend to make a careful study of my own religion and, as far as I can, of other religions as well.'... I returned home, had my dinner, went to my room and lay there absorbed in deep

---

134. He never lost sight of this aspect of Christianity. When asked in 1938 what would be the place of its missions in the new India, he suggested that the missionaries come as "fellow-helpers and fellow-seekers rather than as preachers to a people allegedly wandering in darkness. "Does not Bishop Heber in his well-known hymn 'From Greenland's Icy Mountains' describe India as a country where 'every prospect pleases, and only man is vile'? To me this is a negation of the spirit of Christ." A year later he reiterated, "My quarrel with missionaries is that they think no religion other than Christianity is true." (*C*, LXVIII, 252f, 421)

135. For a detailed account see Hunt 1986.

thought: ...I should make a dispassionate study. ...God might guide me; I should not think of embracing another religion before I had fully understood my own.

"When we met on Sundays, I used to give [another such friend] my religious diary for the week, and discuss with him the books I had read.... The ladies used to narrate their sweet experiences and talk about the peace they had found.... He loaded me with books, as it were... and as I went on reading them, we discussed them.... He had great affection for me. [On one occasion] he saw, round my neck, the Vaishnava necklace.... 'This superstition does not become you. Come, let me break the necklace.' — 'No, you will not. It is a... gift from my mother.'...

"...I was delighted at their faith.... I saw that many were praying for me. I liked some of their hymns, they were very sweet.... But... it was impossible for me to believe that I could... attain salvation only by becoming a Christian.... According to Christianity, only human beings had souls... while I held a contrary belief.... Philosophically there was nothing extraordinary in Christian principles. From the point of view of sacrifice, it seemed to me that the Hindus greatly surpassed the Christians....

"Though I took a path my Christian friends had not intended for me, I have remained for ever indebted to them for the religious quest they awakened in me.

"I shall always cherish the memory of their contact." (*A*, II, ch. 10, ch. 11, ch. 15)

It is true that he was more tolerant than some of them were of their different viewpoints:

[262] *1893* (recalled later): "My connection with the family I used to visit every Sunday was abruptly broken.... My hostess was a good and simple [Christian] woman, but somewhat

> narrow-minded. We always discussed religious subjects. I was then re-reading Arnold's *Light of Asia*. Once we began to compare the life of Jesus with that of Buddha. 'Look at Gautama's compassion!', said I. 'It was not confined to mankind, it was extended to all living beings. Does not one's heart overflow with love to think of the lamb joyously perched on his shoulders? One fails to notice this love for all living things in the life of Jesus....' Her son, a cherub of five, was also with us... and this youngster and I had long been friends. I spoke derisively of the piece of meat on his plate and in high praise of the apple on mine....
>
> 'Mr. Gandhi,' [the lady] said, 'please don't take it ill if I feel obliged to tell you that my boy is none the better for your company. Every day he hesitates to eat meat. ...Your discussions should henceforth be only with us elders....' — 'I am sorry. I can understand your feelings as a parent, for I too have children.... What I eat and omit to eat is bound to have a greater effect on the child than what I say. The best way, therefore, is for me to stop these visits. That certainly need not affect our friendship.' — 'I thank you.'" (*A*, II, ch. 22)

(This account omits the fact, which he had recorded in his diary at the time, that "she questioned my sincerity. Said I should not go to their house if I was insincere and not seeking truth."[136])

He was deeply impressed by the character and way of life of the German Trappists (120 monks, 60 nuns) whom he visited at their agricultural settlement some twenty miles from Durban:

136. Hunt 1986: 44

[263] *1895*: "The settlement is a quiet little model village, owned on the truest republican principles.... The sisters' cloister is about a half a mile from the brothers'.... No brother or sister may speak except... [when they] have to go to town to make purchases or to look after visitors.... A model Trappist gets up at 2 a.m. and devotes four hours to prayer and contemplation.... The brothers eat no fish, flesh or fowl.... [They] take no intoxicating liquors except under medical advice. None may keep money for private use. All are equally rich or poor.

"We saw no wardrobes [or] chests of drawers... though we were allowed to see every inch of the place....

"They are... healthy and cheerful.... Their dining tables... are made, on the settlement, of wood, without any varnish. They use no tablecloths. The knives and spoons are the cheapest to be had in Durban.... For bedrooms they have a large hall (but none too large for the [number of] inmates).

"...Natives are accorded the same treatment as the Whites. They [the natives] are mostly children. They get the same food as the brothers, and are dressed as well as they themselves are....

"There are about 1200 natives in the mission, including children and adults. They have all exchanged a life of sloth, indolence and superstition, for one of industry, usefulness and devotion to one Supreme God.

"...There are various workshops — blacksmiths', tinsmiths', carpenters', shoemakers', tanners' etc., where the natives are taught all these useful industries, in addition to the English and Zulu languages.... All these natives work side by side with the Whites.

"At the sisters' cloisters, they have the ironing, sewing, straw-hat manufacturing and knitting departments....

"About two miles from the Abbey is situated the printing department, and the flour mill worked by a waterfall ...[and a machine] for pressing the oil from monkey nuts....

"...They grow many kinds of tropical fruits on the farm, and the settlement is almost self-supporting.

"They love and respect, and are in turn loved and respected by, the natives living in their neighborhood....

"Such are our vegetarians in Natal.... One cannot help but exclaiming, after a visit to the farm, 'If this is Roman Catholicism, everything said against it is a lie.' It proves conclusively, to my mind, that a religion appears divine or devilish, according as its professors choose to make it appear." (*C*, I, 182-86)

The impact on his later advocacy of simple living, chastity, and village autonomy seems obvious.

Tolstoy was a Christian, and Gandhi owed much to him in the early phases of the development of satyagraha:

[264] *1909*: "Tolstoy... may be looked upon as the greatest of the satyagrahis." (*C*, IX, 447)

And there were some other good moral influences from Christianity upon Gandhi:

[265] *1931*: "My fierce hatred of child-marriage is due to Christian influence." (*C*, XLVIII, 122)

[266] *1931*: "Before I knew anything of Christianity I was an enemy of untouchability. I could not understand my mother, whom I adored, withdrawing the hem of her garment from the untouchables. My feelings gained momentum owing to the fierce attack from Christian sources on this evil." (*loc. cit.*)

A certain disillusionment began to set in, however, when the Indian businessman (a Moslem) who brought him to South Africa as a lawyer explained to him that the "white clergymen" and their Indian converts were politically obsequious:

[267] *1893* (recalled later): "The case having been concluded [successfully],... Abdulla Sheth... gave a farewell party in my honor at [his home in] Sydenham. It was proposed to spend the whole day there. Whilst I was turning over the sheets of some of the newspapers that I found there, I chanced to see a paragraph in a corner of one of them under the caption 'Indian Franchise.' It was with reference to a bill then before the House of Legislature, which sought to deprive the Indians of their right to elect members of the Natal Legislative Assembly.... I inquired of Abdulla Sheth about it. He said, '...We generally take in newspapers simply to ascertain the daily market rates, etc. What can we know of legislation? Our eyes and ears are the European attorneys here.'

"'But,' said I, 'there are so many young Indians born and educated here. Do they not help you?'

"'They!', exclaimed Abdulla Sheth in despair. 'They never care to come to us.... Being Christians, they are under the thumb of the white clergymen, who in their turn are subject to the Government.'

This opened my eyes.... Was this the meaning of Christianity?" (*A*, II, ch. 16)

In later years he would distinguish clearly between an ideal of good Christianity on the one hand and, on the other hand, the "nominal Christianity" of "many Christians." The first of the following excerpts is from a report of a meeting in a church in Switzerland:

[268] *1931*: [Q.] "What do you think of Christianity?" [A.] "A delicate question. Christianity is very good; many Christians are very bad.... I would like very much, being in the House of God, to say, 'Cast out the beam from your eye before you dare to see a mote in your neighbor's eye.' If we would but be good enough to take care of ourselves, I have very little doubt that the world would take care of itself." (*C*, XLVIII, 407)

[269] *1931*: "I have never been able to reconcile myself to the gaities of the Christmas season. They have appeared to me to be so inconsistent with the life and teaching of Jesus.

"How I wish America could lead the way by devoting the season to a real moral stocktaking and emphasizing consecration to the service of mankind for which Jesus lived and died on the Cross." (*C*, XLVIII, 437)

[270] *1941*: "There certainly is reason for scepticism [about real Christianity] when one observes the bloody butchery that European aggressors have unloosed, and when one thinks about the misery and suffering [due to Christian war-making] prevalent in every corner of the world, as well as the pestilence and famine that always follow, terribly and inevitably, upon war." (*C*, LXXV, 70)

[271] *1946*: "Perhaps most of the evils that are at the back of the prejudice against Negroes are the result of nominal Christianity.... They have learnt [from Christianity] to drink, dance immoral dances and so on." (*H*, 24/ii, 18)

[272] *1947*: "I see from the papers that the Government [of India] proposes to stop the grants made to [the Christian churches]. The money they receive from America and England will also stop coming. It is feared that 75 percent of the churches in India will have to be closed down. But a religion does not prosper with the help of money. Most Chris-

> tians in India are poor people.... The human body is the real church. It is there that God dwells. Then we have the sky for the roof and the earth for the floor. We can utter God's name anywhere. I shall therefore say that the Christians need not feel worried. They do not really need assistance from the Government or anyone. They should follow the teachings of their religion. If they but persevere in the path of sacrifice shown by Christ, no one can take their religion away from them."[137] (*C*, XC, 293)

His negative image of real Christianity was always liable to be strengthened by fresh encounters. The following conversation ensued when a Christian asked him whether Denmark had not carried out his ideal of non-violence by surrendering to Germany at the outset of the Second World War:

[273] *1940*: "Not a bit.... What I have asked for is not surrender but non-violent resistance...." — "Well, well, what's the good of it?" — "What was the good of Jesus Christ laying down his life?" — "Oh, that was a different matter! He was the son of God." — "And so are we!" — "No. He was the *only* son of God.... He is our salvation." — "So those who accept the Christ are all saved, they need do nothing more?" — "We are sinners all, and we have but to accept Him to be saved." — "...You talk like some of the Plymouth Brothers I met long ago in South Africa." — "Yes, I am afraid you were so unfortunate in the Christian contacts you formed in South Africa. You did not meet the right kind of people." —

137. For other such passages, see *C*, LXXXVII, 192; LXXXVIII, 471; LXXXIX, 112; and *H*, 7/xii/1947, 453.

"Surely you will not say that. I met a number of estimable people; they were all honest and sincere." — "But they were not *true* Christians." — "...Why all this quarrel about labels?" (*C*, LXXII, 296f)

The everyday behavior of some Indian converts to Christianity annoyed him:

[274] *1925*: "The aping of Europeans... by Indian converts is a violence done to their country and, shall I say, even to their new religion. There is a verse in the New Testament to bid Christians to avoid meat if it would offend their neighbors.[138] Meat here, I presume, includes [alcoholic] drink.... Is it not truly deplorable [also] that many Christian Indians discard their own mother-tongue and bring up their children only to speak in English? Do they not thereby completely cut themselves adrift from the nation in whose midst they have to live?" (*C*, XXVIII, 92)

And so did the missionaries' characteristic manipulativeness:

[275] *1931*: "I hold that proselytizing under the cloak of humanitarian work is, to say the least, unhealthy.... The methods of conversion must be like Caesar's wife above suspicion.... [And] yes, I do maintain that India's great faiths are all-sufficing for her.... Conversion in the sense of self-purification, self-realization is the crying need of the times. That, however, is not what is ever meant by proselytizing." (*C*, XLVI, 28)

[276] *1940* (speaking with some Christian missionaries): "There should be less of theology and more of truth in all that you say and do.... If you go on questioning and cross-questioning

138. I Corinthians, viii, 13.

me, I dare say you will floor me without being any the wiser for having done so." (*C*, LXXI, 329)

[277] *1942*: "The missionaries have of course the right to preach the gospel of Christ and to invite non-Christians to embrace Christianity. But every attempt to press material benefits or attractions in the aid of conversion should be freely opposed, and the Harijans should be educated to resist these temptations." (*C*, LXXV, 207)

[278] *1947*: "[It has been said] that if Moslems asked Hindus to accept Islam if they wanted to save themselves or their property, and if the latter responded, there was no compulsion.... I am reminded of the days when Christian missionaries so-called used to buy **children in days of** famine and bring them up as Christians." (*C*, LXXXVI, 338)

Indeed he considered them socially destructive:

[279] *1927*: "While I am strengthening the faith of the [Indian] people, you [missionaries] are undermining it." (*C*, XXXIV, 260)

[280] *1935*: "In Hindu households, the advent of a missionary has meant the disruption of the family in the wake of change of dress, manners, languages, food and drink." (*C*, LXI, 46)

[281] *1935*: "It is a conviction daily growing upon me that the great and rich Christian missions will render true service to India, if they can persuade themselves to confine their activities to humanitarian service without the ulterior motive of converting India or at least her unsophisticated villagers to Christianity, and destroying their social superstructure, which, notwithstanding its many defects, has stood now from time immemorial." (*C*, LXI, 457f)

Yet he always respected those who modestly upheld justice. A missionary whom he singled out for praise on this account —

[282] *1931*: "[Verrier] Elwin is planning to... establish Christian ashrams among the untouchables, with a church in a mud hut for his own and his colleagues' use. He wants simply to live among them as God may guide his life." (*C*, XLVIII, 125)

— was excommumicated because of his unusually modest approach.[139] The following exchange was with another missionary, Holmes Smith, who had been dismissed from his job for expressing support for Indian independence:

[283] **Smith,** *1940*: "I am now on my way to America where so far as it lies in our power we propose to start a twofold campaign by opening the eyes of missions against continuing an unholy alliance with imperialism, [and] starting a movement to be organized by friends of Indian freedom...."

Gandhi: "...I would like you to retain your spiritual and purely American character. You are interested in our movement, I understand, because it is claimed to be strictly non-violent.... You should study the movement through and through, criticize it, find flaws in it.... Thousands of [Christians] believe that the message of Christ was that of peace on Earth, goodwill to men.... The message of Jesus has been before the world for 1900 years; but what are 1900 years in the life of a religion or in the life of a message fraught with great consequence

---

139. *C*, L, 367. For a comprhensive account of Father Elwin, see Guha 1998.

for mankind? I therefore want you to be my fellow-workers, testing everything I say on the anvil of cold reason." (*C*, LXXI, 168f)

Islam

We have seen how Gandhi in his childhood would be present as his father listened, "always with respect and often with interest," when Moslem friends talked about their faith (Reading 226). His mother had been raised in the eclectic "Kabir-Panthi" sect which at one time, Gandhi later said, had been "looked upon as crypto-Moslems."[140]

In his teens his best friend was an exhuberant Moslem lad, who persuaded him to experiment surreptitiously with meat-eating[141] and then with going to a brothel (Reading 14).

In London a few years later, he began to read about Mohammed:

[284] *1890* (recalled later): "A friend recommended Carlyle's *Heros and Hero-Worship*. I read the chapter on the hero as a prophet and learned of the Prophet's greatness and bravery and austere living." (*A*, I, ch. 20)

His employer in South Africa was a Moslem from Porbandar (the town where Gandhi was born) and their discussions of religion inspired him to read the Koran and various books about Islam:

140. *E*, 214. See Reading 228.

141. *A*, I, chh. 6-8. *E*, 208-11, 222f, 492f. Green 1993: 65ff.

[285] *1893-94* (recalled later): "Abdulla Sheth was there to receive me [when the ship arrived]. His firm was... one of the biggest of the Indian firms.... He was proud of Islam and loved to discourse on Islamic philosophy. Though he did not know Arabic, his acquaintance with the holy Koran and Islamic literature in general was fairly good.... Contact with him gave me a fair amount of practical knowledge of Islam. When we came closer to each other, we had long discussions of religious topics....

"I purchased a translation of the Koran and began reading it. I also obtained other books on Islam....

"I read Washington Irving's *Life of Mahomet and His Successors* and Carlyle's panegyric on the Prophet. These books raised Mohammed in my estimation." (*A*, II, chh. 7, 15 and 22)

The weekly journal edited by Gandhi in South Africa, *Indian Opinion*, was at first devoted exclusively to secular issues, but then some religious articles began to appear as his interest in religion was aroused by the Christian missionaries' efforts to convert him. A talk by Annie Besant in Madras on "the value of Theosophy in the raising of India" was published in the first two issues of March 1904. In the 16 July issue, an article by an American missionary (J. P. Jones), reprinted from another journal, discussed Indian religion, with remarks like "To the student of comparative religion there appear many striking consonances between Hinduism and Christianity." In November and December, religion was discussed in a series of articles recounting the "impressions of India" gleaned by an ex-commandant of the Boers (J. L. P. Erasmus). Then, in

March 1905 Gandhi himself delivered to the Theosophical Society in Johannesburg four lectures on religion in India, which were duly summarized (in Gujarati) in *Indian Opinion*. His account of Islam included the following:

[286] *1905*: "Zeal or passion... is a great speciality, a mighty force, of Islam. It has been the cause of many good deeds, and sometimes of bad ones too.... The Islamic principle that all those who embraced Islam were equals made such a favorable impression on the lower classes that hundreds of thousands of Hindus accepted that faith." (*C*, IV, 406f)

— and soon he was obliged to declare publicly, "I had no intention of offending" and to apologize in a letter to a group of Islamic trustees ("I am sorry about this and beg to be forgiven").[142]

In 1909 he argued, in regard to some Hindu-Moslem riots in Calcutta, that overseas Indians "must not support either side":[143]

[287] *1909*: "None of us can judge how far these reports are true. It is apparent, however, that the cause of the riots was a White officer.... We should feel sorry that a third party has provoked quarrels among us and pray to *Khuda-Ishwar* in mosques and in temples to grant that there might be an end to the disputes that frequently arise between our two communities." (*C*, IX, 134)

---

142. *C*, IV, 431 and 454.
143. See also *C*, X, 387f and, for other references to Khuda-Ishwar, IX, 41, 152, 196 and 243, and X, 2.

After his definitive return to India, his first main way of coping with the separateness of the religious communities there — and very effective it was in the short run — was to declare in 1920, with the consent of his Moslem political colleagues, that his program of mass satyagraha in India had two goals: *(1)* her independence from the British Empire (which he predicted would be achieved within a year) and *(2)* a revision of the terms and conditions imposed upon Turkey at the end of the First World War — which the Ottoman sultan of Turkey had, in hopes of strengthening his claim to be Mohammed's "successor" (*caliph*), declared to be a "holy war" (*jihad*).[144]

[288] *1920*, recalled later: "I had a hand in the agitation for the release of the Ali brothers [who were vigorous political leaders]. So when they came out, they and [some other Indian Moslem leaders] and I met together.... I discussed with them the implications of non-violence and told them that if they could not accept non-violence as true Moslems, I should be out of the picture. Their reason was satisfied, but they said they could not act without endorsement from Moslem divines, and so there was a conference.... They [the Moslem divines] held that belief in non-violence was not only not inconsistent with Islam, but it was obligatory in the sense that Islam always preferred it to violence. It is noteworthy that this took place before the acceptance of non-violence by the [Indian National] Congress in 1920. Many were the discourses given by learned

144. We have seen (Reading 61) how and why Gandhi had urged Hindus to fight *against* Turkey. His support for the Khilafat Movement was likewise politically expedient.

Moslems on non-violence before crowded Moslem meetings.... Religions are meant to tame our savage nature, not to let it loose." (*C*, LXXI, 178f)

Gandhi would say to his fellow Hindus:

[289] *1921*: "Does Hinduism sanction killing of Moslems for [the sake of] saving cows? No.... I am positive [also] that Islam does not sanction the use of force [to achieve religious conversions].... Victory on the Khilafat [caliphate] issue will certainly increase the strength of Moslems and enhance their courage, but to think that they will use these against Hindus is to suggest that Moslems have no sense of honor, that it is in their nature to return evil for good, that, in other words, they have no true religion in them! All my experience is to the contrary."[145] (*C*, XXI, 203)

He would assure his worried American friends that Islam was not a menace like Bolshevism:

[290] *1924*: "Two American friends have written to me a passionately-worded letter saying that... the alliance between Moslems and myself is an unholy alliance and a menace to the world, for, they argue, Moslems are today aiming at supremacy in the East with the help of Bolshevik Russia.... My movement is not atheistic... [and] Islam is not a denial of God [but] a passionate avowal of one supreme deity." (*C*, XXV, 18f)

Meanwhile he would say to his Islamic constituency:

---

145. See for instance Gandhi's obituary (*C*, XII, 231-35) of Haji Hussain Dawad Mahomed.

[291] *1921*: "There is nothing in the Koran to warrant the use of force for conversion. The Holy Book says in the clearest language possible, 'There is no compulsion in religion.' The Prophet's whole life is a repudiation of compulsion in religion." (*Y*, 29/ix, 307)

[292] *1925*: "Regarding the stoning to death in Afghanistan of two members of [a certain] sect, ...I understand that the stoning method is enjoined in the Koran only in certain circumstances which do not cover the cases under observation. But as a human being living in the fear of God I should question the morality of the method under any circumstances whatsoever. Whatever may have been necessary or permissible during the Prophet's lifetime and in that age, this particular form of penalty cannot be defended on the mere ground of its mention in the Koran. Every formula of every religion has, in this age of reason, to submit to the acid tests of reason and universal justice if it is to ask for universal assent. Error can claim no exemption even if it can be supported by the scriptures of the world. I extend my sympathy to the sect in its distress. Needless to say I can express no opinion on the merits of the case. I do not think the public has any data for forming an opinion on [the] merits. It is the form of penalty that wounds the human conscience. Both reason and heart refuse to reconcile themselves to torture for any crime, no matter how vile the crime may be." (*C*, XXVI, 202)

[293] *1925*: "Every true scripture only gains by criticism. After all we have no other guide but our reason to tell us what may be regarded as revealed and what may not be. The early Moslems accepted Islam not because they knew it to be revealed but because it appealed to their virgin reason." (*C*, XXVI, 226)

A salient difference between Hinduism and Islam is that Hindu temples are full of idols but Islam tends to heed the second of the Ten Commandments: not to make any engraved image or other likeness of anything "in heaven above, on the earth or in the water under the earth." When Moslems would on this account desecrate Hindu temples, Gandhi would urge them instead to oppose "idolatry in the form of fanaticism":

[294] *1924*: "I am both an idolater and an iconoclast in what I conceive to be the true sense of the terms. I value the spirit behind idol-worship. It plays a most important part in the uplift of the human race, and I would like to possess the ability to defend with my life the thousands of holy temples which sanctify this land of ours. My alliance with the Moslems presupposes their perfect tolerance for my idols and my temples.

"I am [also] an iconoclast, in the sense that I break down the subtle form of idolatry in the shape of fanaticism that refuses to see any virtue in any other form of worshipping the deity save one's own. This form of idolatry is more deadly for being more fine and evasive than the tangible and gross form of worship that identifies the deity with a little bit of a stone or a golden image.

"Remember that his own religion is the truest to every man even if it stands low in the scales of philosophic comparison." (*C*, xxv, 46f)

He would tend to blame the Hindu-Moslem tensions on the British:

[295] *1925*: "A Bengal zamindar sends me a long letter... [saying]: 'For over 500 years the relation between Hindus

and Moslems was that of foes.... The present cordial relations are due to British rule and not to the catholicity of modern Hinduism.' I regard this statement as pure superstition.... Many Hindus embraced Islam before the advent of Moslem rule in India.... There is nothing to prove that Hindus and Moslems lived at war with one another before the British rule. My belief is that the British policy of 'divide and rule' has accentuated our differences and will continue to do so, till we recognize that we must unite in spite of the policy." (*C*, XXVI, 203f)

The "Khilafat Movement" failed to save the caliphate, and Gandhi never found another such expedient to win strong political consensus with vast numbers of Moslems. There is wistfulness in the following statements:

[296] *1929*: "[Islam's distinctive contribution to India's national culture has been] its unadulterated belief in the oneness of God and a practical application of the truth of the brotherhood of man for those who are nominally within its fold." (*Y*, 21/iii, 95)

[297] *1938*: "Islam, it is said, believes in the brotherhood of man. But you will permit me to point out that it is not the brotherhood of Moslems only but it is universal brotherhood.... [Thus] we must not believe in non-violence as a matter of policy, but as a matter of faith. The Allah of Islam is the same as the God of the Christians and the Ishwara of Hindus.... Living faith in this God means acceptance of the brotherhood of mankind. It also means equal respect for all religions. If Islam is dear to you, Hinduism is dear to me and Christianity is dear to the Christians." (*C*, LXVII, 64)

[298] *1940*: "'Islam' means 'peace.' It does not mean peace to the Moslems only; it means peace to all communities and to the entire world." (*C*, LXXIII, 26)

One can see in historical retrospect that the year 1940 was a disastrous watershed in this regard. For many years the British had followed a divide-and-rule strategy in India:[146] dividing Bengal along religious lines in 1905, encouraging the foundation of the Moslem League, and so on. Now as the outbreak of the Second World War made it likely that Britain would lose most of her empire, the president of the Moslem League, Mohammed Ali Jinnah (*ca.*1870-1948), declared:

[299] **Jinnah**, *1940*: "The Hindus and the Moslems... neither intermarry nor dine together, and indeed they belong to two different civilizations which are based mainly on conflicting ideas and conceptions.... To yoke together two such nations under a single State... must lead to growing discontent." (cited in *C*, LXXI, 389)

The Moslem League passed a resolution demanding that "with such territorial readjustments as may be necessary... the areas in which the Moslems are numerically in a majority... be grouped to constitute independent states."[147] In vain did Gandhi protest:

[300] *1940*: "I feel deeply hurt over what is now going on in the name of the Moslem League. I would be failing in my

---

146. See Pando 1995.

147. Sarkar 1983, 379. In 1941 Jinnah said, "Pakistan is not only a practicable goal but the only goal if you want to save Islam from complete annihilation in this country" (Chandra *et al.* 1989, 435).

duty if I did not warn the Moslems of India against the untruth that is being propagated amongst them. This warning is a duty because I have faithfully served them in their hour of need and because Hindu-Moslem unity has been and is my life's mission." (*C*, LXXI, 389)

[301] *1940*: "Nowadays I read as many Moslem papers as I can... and as I find them so full of poison and conscious or unconscious untruths, I feel it necessary to redeclare ...[that] I certainly regard Islam as one of the inspired religions and, therefore, the Holy Koran as an inspired book and Mohammed as one of the prophets." (*C*, LXXII, 253)

The "poison and untruths" were due by no means only to Jinnah's ambition, but also to the anxiety with which many Moslems witnessed the spectacle of the vast and vigorous movement that Gandhi had built up for Indian self-rule. Gandhi's willing use of Hindu religious sentiment aroused a fear that Indian self-rule would become Hindu rule over Moslems:

[302] **Jinnah**, *1940*: "Mr. Gandhi's hope is to subjugate and vassalize the Moslems under a Hindu *raj*." (Jinnah 1960-64, I, 127)

Two forms of "communalism" were now, especially after the elections of 1937, feeding upon each other: *(1)* the Hindu communalism — which Gandhi opposed — according to which the Hindus were the only natives in India (Moslems and others being aliens), and *(2)* the "two-separate-nations" Moslem communalism to which Jinnah had began to subscribe in the late 1930s[148] even though he had in the '20s taken a far more moderate line, calling for Moslems to "press every reasonable claim for the protection of their community," while privately making remarks like: "My boy, no, you are an Indian first and then a Moslem."[149]

Moslems of good will would now tell Gandhi that they could not follow him and remain good Moslems:

[303] **Correspondent,** *1940*: "We Moslems believe that the Prophet's life was wholly directed by God and truly non-violent, though not in your sense of the term. He never waged an offensive war, and he had the tenderest regard for the feeling of others, but when he was driven to a defensive war he drew his sword for a holy war, and he permits the use of the sword under conditions he has laid down. But your non-violence is different. You prescribe it under all conditions and circumstances. I do not think the Prophet would permit this. Whom are we to follow? If we follow you, we cease to be Moslems. If we follow the Prophet, we cannot join the Congress with its creed of extreme non-violence. Will you solve this dilemma?"
Gandhi: "I can only answer that, since you notice the difference, you should unhesitatingly follow the Prophet, not me. Only, I would like to say that I claim to have studied the life of the Prophet and the Koran as a detached student of religions, and I have come to the conclusion that the teaching of the Koran is essentially in favor of non-violence. Non-violence is better than violence, it is said in the Koran. Non-violence is enjoined as a duty, violence is permitted as a necessity.

---

148. Chandra 1987, 207. Jinnah's Moslem League did poorly in the 1937 elections, and many Congress leaders, including Nehru, thought he could be written off.

149. Chandra 1988, 433.

"I must refuse to sit in judgement of what the Prophet did.... If I handled a motor car, I would surely run it and me into the danger zone and probably into the jaws of death. How much more dangerous would it be, then, for me to imitate a prophet! When the Prophet was asked why, if he could fast more than the prescribed times, the companions also could not, he promptly replied, 'God gives me spiritual food which satisfies even the bodily wants; for you He has ordained the Ramadan [an annual fast analogous to Lent]. You may not copy me.' I quote from memory." (*C*, LXXII, 224)

And there were, as so often when religion and politics are mixed, the intellectuals who would turn demagogue:

[304] **Correspondent**, *1940*: "For some time you seem to have made it a point to strengthen your arguments in favor of non-violence by frequent but invariably vague references to the Holy Koran and the teachings of Islam.... But can't you realize that nothing can offend the religious sensibilities of a Moslem more than to see a non-Moslem citing the scripture for his own purpose? ...You are a non-Moslem. Hence the Koran cannot be the source of your ideas or ideals...."

Gandhi: "This letter is from... a research scholar in the Moslem university [at Aligarh].... I have sweet memories of Aligarh. I have more than once visited the great university. I have still associations with it.... As for the Holy Koran, it was my Moslem clients and friends in South Africa who invited me to read it. They furnished me with Islamic literature. On my return to India, Moslem friends sent me copies of translations of the holy book.... Have I changed or have the times so changed that it has beome a crime for a non-Moslem to read and even dare to put his own interpretation upon the Koran? Many pious Moslems have remarked that I am a better Moslem than most Moslems in that I act in the spirit of the Koran and know more of the life of the Prophet than most Moslems....

"The research scholar is right in imputing to me the desire to read my meaning into the Koran. Surely there is no harm in it so long as I remain absolutely faithful to the text and approach my task with a prayerful and open mind. My correspondent should know as a scholar that an interpretation of a life or a book is not necessarily correct because it has been handed down for generations. ...It is just possible that the research scholar's views about the qualifications for reading and interpreting the Koran and his own interpretation are wrong, and that my being a non-Moslem is no bar to my reading of the Koran or interpreting it. And it is not at all impossible that my interpretation may be found right. It will be an evil day if the reading and interpreting of religious books are to be confined only to those who wear particular religious labels. I ask my correspondent and his companions, as their friend, to shed what in my opinion is their gross intolerance and give the same credit to others for seeking truth as they claim for themselves." (*C*, LXXIII, 50f)

The extent to which the Moslems' palpable anxiety came to limit Gandhi's freedom to address sensitive moral issues is shown in the following statements about *purdah* (the custom, observed in Gandhi's day by more than 90% of Moslem women and by a majority of the Hindu women in north India, of hiding their faces behind a veil). The first of these statements was addressed to Hindus, the second to Hindus and Moslems alike:

[305] *1924*: "How can a woman who remains in purdah, suppressed, teach a man purity? ...The very fact of keeping a woman behind purdah has the effect of creating moral weakness in her. I believe that purdah helps not the maintenance but the destruction of morality." (*C*, XXIV, 278)

[306] *1927*: "Whenever I have gone to Bengal, Bihar or the United Provinces, I have observed the purdah system more strictly followed than in the other provinces.... Why do not our women enjoy the same freedom as men do? Why should they not be able to walk out and have fresh air?

"Chastity is not a hot-house growth. It cannot be superimposed.... It must grow from within.... Let us then tear down the purdah with one mighty effort." (*C*, XXXIII, 45)

Thus he would, in the 1920s, speak out clearly (albeit not very often). But by 1947, Moslem sensitivity to critical remarks from a Hindu was such that on one occasion he evidently said — though he cannot really have meant it — that he was glad to see Hindu women observing purdah:[150]

[307] *1947* (as reported): "Then he dealt with the questions that were addressed to him.... He [had been] warned by some Moslem critics against speaking on the purdah; he had therefore some hesitation in speaking about it. But he took heart when he turned round and saw that many Hindu women observed it and that... many distinguished Moslem women of India... did not observe it. Lastly the real purdah is of the heart. A woman who peeped

150. See also *C*, LXXXVI, 412 and 418.

through the purdah and contemplated a male on whom her gaze fell violated the spirit behind it. If a woman observed it in spirit, she was truly carrying out what the great Prophet had said." (*H*, 23/iii, 78)

[308] *1947* (as reported): "Two telegrams... said that he, an unbeliever, had no right to interfere in the Islamic Law. [But] he had not interfered at all in the practice of religion. He had neither the right nor the wish to do so. All he had done was to tender advice and that based on his reading of the Prophet's sayings.... It was open to the Moslem hearers to reject his advice if they felt it was in conflict with the tenets of Islam." (*C*, LXXXVI, 342)

Throughout the last ten years Gandhi had taken care to make known, as in Readings 301 and 303, his regard for basic Islamic scripture:

[309] *1938*: "I have read the Koran with as much care and reverence as I have the Gita. I have read other important books on Islam too. I claim to have as much regard in my heart for Islam and other religions as for my own." (*C*, LXVIII, 2)

[310] *1939*: "I have more than once read the Koran." (*C*, LXX, 282)

But he would not yet move distinctly closer to Islam than he would to Christianity:

[311] *1940*: "A writer in a Moslem paper has suggested that, if I regard Islam as an inspired religion and Mohammed as the Prophet of God, I should declare my belief, so that Moslems' doubts may be dispelled and Hindu-Moslem unity may possibly be more easily achieved...."

"I certainly regard Islam as one of the inspired religions, and therefore the Holy Koran as an inspired book, and Mohammed as one of the prophets. But even so I regard Hinduism, Christianity, Zoroastrianism as inspired religions." (*C*, LXXII, 253)

In the last year and a half of his life, he would say outright that he was more faithful to the original message of Islam than were "many" of the real Moslems:

[312] *1946*: "If Mohammed came to India today, he would disown many of his so-called followers and own me as a true Moslem." (*H*, 17/xi, 405)

All the while he was pleading with everyone — and at the end virtually despairing — to stop their religiously motivated violence:[151]

[313] *1946*, from a report of a meeting with some Moslem-League leaders: "[A Moslem] agreeing with Gandhiji quoted a verse from the Koran to the effect that there could be no compulsion in religion." (*C*, LXXXVI, 95)

[314] *1946*: "So far as I now, Islam does not permit forcible conversion and atrocities on women.... I have come to stay in East Bengal [the territory which is now Bangladesh] till there is reconciliation." (*C*, LXXXVI, 124)

[315] *1946* (as reported): "If Hindus and Moslems in India gathered courage and cast from their heart the fear of loss of possessions and life, the face of India would change in no time, Gandhiji said. But the reformed social relations

---

151. See also *C*, LXXXVI, 98f, 338f, 348 and 355.

must be based upon character built on the rock of fearlessness; only thus could true mutual trust be generated." (*C*, LXXXVI, 213)

[316] *1946*, to Hindus in Bihar: "I regard myself as a part of you. Your affection has compelled that loyalty in me. And since I claim to have better appreciation than you seem to have shown of what Bihari Hindus should do, I cannot rest till I have done some measure of penance... [for] the Bihar tragedy. [My current] low diet will become a fast unto death if the erring Biharis have not turned over a new leaf." (*C*, LXXXVI, 82)

[317] *1947*, to Hindus: "In Bihar the Moslems form only 13 or 14 percent of the population. But we ought to cover them all.... The work of the peace committee is easy enough. It has to compensate for the damage caused by us and repair the houses which have been burnt. If it succeeds in doing this much, the rest will be easy to accomplish." (*C*, LXXXVII, 519)

[318] *November 1947*, to the All-India Congress Committee: "I repeat to you that it is your prime duty to treat Moslems as your brothers, whatever may happen in Pakistan." (*C*, XC, 41)

[319] *December 1947*, to Moslems: "You will never hear Gandhi utter the words that you should leave India. Gandhi can only tell you that you should stay, for India is your home. And if your brethren should kill you, you should bravely meet death. That is the way I am made. That is the way I would have people behave.

"In Pakistan many Hindu girls have been forcibly converted and subjected to extreme barbarities. Hindus too have done similar things. But I am telling you how you should behave like true Moslems. You should seek help from the Pakistan government and persuade your brethren there to console the young [Hindu] women.... You should tell them, 'Sisters, you have been cruelly treated. We forgot that we were human. From now on you are our mothers, our sisters, our daughters.' ...[If you] dedicate yourselves wholly to service, then I assure you, Hindus will worship you and you will be able to serve not only Pakistan but also the Moslems living in India.

"The [Indian Government] ministers have assured you that they will protect you even at the risk of their own lives. Still if you are resolved to go and do not place any trust in their word, there is nothing further I can say to you. ...You have to decide for yourselves after considering what your duty is towards the... land that gave you birth, where you grew up.... This will not be because Gandhi says it. There was a time when I wished to live 125 years. Today I do not have that wish any more. I do not consider our present freedom as freedom.... If even now you take up the work of service without asking where and by whom the present tide of violence was started, you can still taste the nectar of freedom.... I do not believe in shedding tears. But today, having heard you and seen you, my heart weeps.

"Do as God guides you. I have said what I had to say. I can only pray to God to grant us good sense." (*C*, xc, 254f)

To understand the final stage in this development — using the name "Allah" in a traditional Hindu prayer and invoking, perhaps even in his very last utterance, Rahim on a par with his beloved Rama — we must first survey some of Gandhi's views of religion in a broader sense than that of any traditional cults.

Religion in general

Gandhi loved religion, but not indiscriminately:

[320] *1927*: "I believe that all the great religions of the world are true more or less.... Everything that the human hand touches, by reason of the very fact that human beings are imperfect, becomes imperfect." (*C*, xxxiv, 550)

[321] *1928*: "I came to the conclusion long ago, after prayerful search and study and discussion with as many people as I could meet, that all religions were true and also that all had some error in them." (*C*, xxxv, 461)

He declared:

[322] *1925*: "Every formula of every religion has, in this age of reason, to submit to the acid test of reason and universal justice if it is to ask for universal assent." (*C*, xxvi, 202)

Once when he referred to his own "humble" or "disciplined" faith and someone asked what he meant by this, his reply showed also, to some extent, what he meant by the test of reason:

[323] *1932*: "Faith should not be undiscriminating or blind. For instance as regards some question which can be solved by human intelligence, someone may say, 'I do not care what the intellect has got to say in the matter; I will hold a particular belief from faith'; his faith is not characterized by humility. It is for the human intellect to decide whether the earth is round or flat.... If someone says he has full faith that it is flat, his faith is not coupled with humility." (Desai 1953, I, 184; for a different translation, with "disciplined" instead of "humble," see *C*, L, 80)

"Humble" or "disciplined" did not mean (as we have seen already in several readings) yielding authority to religious scripture:

[324] *1936*: **[Q.]** "Where do you find the seat of [religious] authority?" **[A.]** "It lies here [pointing to his breast]. I exercise my judgement about every scripture.... Nothing in them comes from God directly." (*H*, 5/xii, 345)

Notwithstanding his regard for reason, Gandhi would tolerate, in other people's religions, unreason more readily than immorality:

[325] *1920*: "I reject any religious doctrine that does not appeal to reason and is in conflict with morality. I tolerate unreasonable religious sentiment when it is not immoral." (*C*, XVIII, 73)

And sometimes when he said "religion" he meant only belief in a general moral order:[152]

[326] *1940*: **[Q.]** In your autobiography [written in the 1920s] you have said that you cannot think of politics apart from religion. Do you still hold that view?...." **[A.]** "Yes [but] here religion does not mean sectarianism. It means a belief in ordered moral government of the universe." (*C*, LXXI, 177)

We think his "universe" was a human world and not an astronomical one. He would associate "struggle for Truth" with "human nature struggling to find itself":

152. But see Reading 248.

153. For a related earlier statement see *C*, XVII, 406.

[327] *1924* "Let me explain what I mean by religion. It is not Hinduism, which I prize most highly, but the religion which transcends Hinduism — the basic Truth which underderlies all the religions of the world. It is the struggle for Truth... the permanent element in human nature, constantly struggling to find itself, to know its Maker. This is religion." (*C*, XXIII, 196)[153]

He longed for a broad "heart-unity" based on the "religion of humanity":

[328] *1924*: "I believe that the time is fast coming when politicians will cease to fear the religion of humanity.... Hence it is that I am inviting all India... to promote the establishment of heart-unity between Hindus, Moslems, Parsis, Christians, Jews and others who vainly consider that the God of each is different from the God of the rest." (*C*, XXV, 53)

This would entail regarding all religions as equal, which he considered a new idea:

[329] *1932*: "Probably this view of mine about equality of all religions is a new idea. If other people also have thought about the matter along similar lines, I am not aware of the fact. For me at any rate, the idea is original and it has given me the purest joy." (*C*, LI, 317)

For this he would even sacrifice his principle that every religious formula has to submit to the test of reason (Reading 322):

[330] *1941*: "I believe that it is impossible to estimate the merits of the various religions of the world, and moreover I believe that it is unnecessary and harmful even to attempt it.

But each one of them, in my judgement, embodies a common motivating force: the desire to uplift man's life and give it purpose." (*The Modern Review*, October, 406)

To evoke his concept of an ideal society, he would use whichever religious term was most palatable to the audience before him:

[331] *1946*: "*Rama-Rajya* [the Kingdom of Rama]... is a convenient and expressive phrase, the meaning of which no alternative can so fully express to [the Hindu] millions.[154] When I... address predominantly Moslem audiences I would express my meaning to them by calling it *Khudai Raj*, while to a Christian audience I would describe it as the Kingdom of God on earth. Any other mode would, for me, be self-suppression and hypocrisy." (*C*, LXXXV, 135)

[332] *1929*: "By Ramarajya I do not mean [a] Hindu *raj* [kingdom],... [but] the kingdom of God. For me Rama and Rahim[155] are one and the same deity." (*C*, XLI, 374)

The underlying problem is that it is painful to shed the various unreasonable ideas which our parents (or whoever has parented us) have instilled in us, along with other, more reason-

---

154. Partly because of this kind of rationalization, the Indian Supreme Court has allowed Hindu politicans to use the slogan "Ramraj!" even though the Constitution of the Republic of India prohibits the political exploitation of religion.

155. Manalel 1991: 109 shows how "Rahim" comes from an ancient Hebraic word for "womb" (*Genesis*, XX, 18 and XLIX, 25; *Hosea*, IX, 14; *Jeremiah*, I, 5 and XX, 17, etc.) and its plural form means "mercy" or "compassion" (*Exodus*, XXXIII, 19; *Deuteronomy*, XIII, 17-18; *Isaiah*, IX, 17, XIV, 1 and LXIII, 7-15; *Psalms*, LXXVII, 9, LXXIX, 8 and CXIX, 77; etc.). In Islam it was transformed from an alleged attribute to a synonym of "Allah."

able ideas, during our weakest and most susceptible years; so, we tend to shed only those outworn beliefs which are obviously interfering with our proper functioning. For many of us, at least some of the religious ideas instilled in us as children are not in that category, so even if we doubt their validity, it seems the better part of wisdom not to bring the opprobrium, real or imagined, that would be involved in disowning our "inherited" religion — especially if the opprobrium is real or if our love for our parents is tender and we know that they would feel hurt. Gandhi was perfectly sensitive to all this and therefore felt that rather than changing one's religious identity, one should only try to draw morally better implications from it:[156]

[333] *1928*: "You have used the word 'viewpoint' as synonymous with 'religion.' I do not. Whilst I would not press my religion upon others, I would press my viewpoint upon others, as every one of us must. Religion is a matter of feeling or the heart and, therefore, not a matter for argument, and I would hold everybody's feeling as dear as my own, because I expect him to do so with reference to my feeling. Viewpoint is a matter of reasoning, the mind, the intellect. It may shift from time to time without touching the heart. Change of religion is a change of status. Change of viewpoint is an accident often due to external causes. My feeling about the existence of God cannot be easily altered. My viewpoint regarding the connotation of the term may vary from time to time and expand with the expansion of my reason. Religion is beyond explanation and it seems to me to be impertinent

156. See also C, XLVI, 28f.

for anyone to touch another's religion. A viewpoint must always be capable of explanation. I have entered upon this distinction because it enables me to explain my position about religion more clearly than by any other means. I do not want you to become a Hindu. But I do want you to become a better Christian by assimilating all that may be good in Hinduism and that you may not find in [the] same measure or at all in the Christian teaching. I can't explain why I delight in calling myself and remaining a Hindu, but my remaining does not prevent me from assimilating all that is good and noble in Christianity, Islam and other faiths of the world." (*C*, XXXVII, 224)

[334] *1933*: "Just as a husband does not remain faithful to his wife, or wife to her husband, because either is conscious of some exclusive superiority of the other over the rest of his or her sex but because of some indefinable but irresistible attraction, so does one remain irresistibly faithful to one's religion and find full satisfaction in such adhesion. And just as a faithful husband does not need, in order to sustain his faithfulness, to consider other women as inferior to his wife, so does not a person belonging to one religion need to consider other religions as inferior to his own. To pursue the analogy still further, even as faithfulness to one's wife does not presuppose blindness to her shortcomings, so does not faithfulness to one's religion presuppose blindness to the shortcomings of that religion." (*C*, LV, 352f)

Yet in 1947 he was quite aware of having moved so far away from orthodox Hinduism that he could no longer claim such an identity as he had done in the 1920s:

[335] *1947* (as reported): [Q.] "If there was only one God, why should there not be only one religion?" [A.] "That was

a strange question. Just as a tree had a million leaves, ...there were as many religions as there were men and women, though they were rooted in one God. They did not see this plain truth because they were followers of different prophets and claimed as many religions as there were prophets. As a matter of fact, whilst he believed himself to be a Hindu, he knew that he did not worship God in the same manner as one or all of them." (*C*, LXXXVI, 484)[157]

In this last phase of his life, his ideas about religion evolved more dynamically than at any other time since the mid-1890s. Sometimes he expressed his dismay that other people were not also changing in this regard:

[336] *1947* (as reported): [Q.] "You have said castes should go. But then will Hinduism survive? Why do you mix up Hinduism with the progressive religions like Christianity?" [A.] "He maintained that caste as it was understood must go if Hinduism was to survive.... As a matter of fact he noticed no definite progress in any religion. The world would not be the shambles it had become if the religions of the world were progressive." (*C*, LXXXVI, 484)

His most famous change in this regard took place in November 1946, early in the course of his four-month tour of violence-torn villages in Bengal. For quite a few years his observances had included some prayers and hymns from other reli-

157. *Ashram Observances in Action* (p. 54): "Everyone has his own conception of God. I believe myself to be a Hindu but I know I do not worship God in the same manner as many of the Hindus do."

gions besides Hinduism.[158] Now he went a step further and adopted an unusual variant of a venerated Hindu prayer (*Ramdhun*), whereby the phrase *Ishwar Allah tere nam*, meaning "Your name is 'Ishwar'[159] [and is] 'Allah'," replaced the more traditional second line (*Patita pavana Sita Ram*, meaning "The sinner's purifier, Sita's [husband] Rama"). (The first line of the prayer is *Raghupati Raghava Raja Ram*, meaning "Almighty Lord, King Rama"; its meaning to Gandhi at that time is explained to some extent in Reading 415.)

We have seen in Reading 287 how Gandhi had already, in South Africa in 1909, upon learning of some Hindu-Moslem riots in India, spoken of a need to "pray to Khuda-Ishwar in mosques and in temples." That it is acceptable to worship an allegedly supreme spirit of the universe in any of various forms is an idea set out in the Gita (Reading 227). In India in the 1940s, however, religion had intruded so far into politics that to adopt the unorthodox form of the Ramdhun prayer was hardly a matter of soft talk in a safe haven. Again and again

---

158. Lavanam and Mythri observed this at Sevagram in 1944. Mme. Pandit recalled in the 1970s that when she visited the ashram around 1920, "Gandhiji's prayers included readings from the Gita and the Koran. To these were later added verses from the Bible and recitations from Parsi, Sikh, and Buddhist prayers, as well as the singing of hymns from various religions." (V. L. Pandit 1979, 66) For two of Gandhi's typical references (from the early 1930s) to this practice, see *C*, L, 34 and *T*, III, 206.

159. "Ishwar" is the traditional Hindu term for a supreme divinity including all the Hindu gods and goddesses (Brahma, Vishnu, Shiva, Kali, etc.). Gandhi's grand-niece, Manu, had heard this variant of the prayer in her childhood and it was her idea to use it now.

there were strenuous objections to it and to the inclusion of readings from the Koran in Gandhi's inter-religious praying. The following extracts are from his remarks to Hindus on three among several such occasions:

[337] *1947*: "If my words can reach the policemen I would request them to release the man and allow him to come over here.... I would again stop the prayer if he wants me to do so tomorrow. But victory to Hinduism cannot be won in this manner [i.e. by shouting "Stop it! Victory to Hinduism!"]....

"...I would have brought him round. He would have been convinced, if not today then tomorrow, if not tomorrow then the day after.... Force cannot be employed in furtherance of religion...." (*C*, LXXXVII, 398f)

[338] *1947*: "If tomorrow also, anyone raises an objection... maybe your violence will be provoked and my non-violence will be put to the test. It will also show how far you can go with me.... If the Moslems here have gone astray it does not mean that the Koran is at fault. The Koran written in Arabic is sublime and eternal. I do not think anyone can be more ignorant than one who shows contempt for the Koran. You must convince the man who objects in this manner.... But I cannot tolerate it that you should beat up anybody.... If I am left alone and five persons come up to me wanting to kill me, I would say that my head is ready for them. Even a single man could cut my throat. But still I would hold the prayer.... Now please go home quietly without arguing among yourselves. Think over this at home." (*C*, LXXXIX, 437-40)

[339] *1947*: "Anyone who says that I cannot go and offer my prayer before the Moslems does not know Gandhi.... I

am ashamed of this gentleman who... is so terribly ignorant. When the ocean catches fire, who can extinguish it?" (*C*, LXXXVII, 431)

In Chapter 6 we will see how Gandhi's personal opening to Islam represented a deepening of his opening to all truth-seeking beliefs, including those contrary to theism as well as to the doctrine of inherited karma.

Gandhi's last words

A few days after Gandhi was shot dead, his secretary wrote a detailed account, including the following:

[340] **Pyarelal**, *1948*: "At the first shot, the foot that was in motion, when he was hit, came down. He still stood on his legs when the second shot rang out, and then collapsed. The last words he uttered were 'Rama Rama'." **(*H* 15/i, 31)**

A different exclamation, "Hey, Ram!", is normally attributed to him[160] (and is inscribed on his tombstone and posted in his bedroom at Sevagram). According to his grand-niece, Manu, he said, "Hey Ram, Hey Ram."[161] According to one of the conspirators (though not the one who came out of the throng to shoot him), he produced only an inarticulate guttural sound.[162] All these contradictions make us wonder if he was heard clearly. (He was a frail old man and some bullets had

160. Green 1993, 386, names Gurbadu Singh as his source for this version.
161. Manubehn Gandhi 1964, II, 428.

just entered his chest.) Almost all the witnesses were Hindus. Did they hear what they expected or wanted to hear rather than another, similar-sounding invocation? The alternative we have in mind is the one which Gandhi himself, nine months earlier, had said unequivocally would be his last words. Was it only a passing remark?

[341] *1947*: "Even if I am killed, I will not give up repeating the names of Rama and Rahim, which mean to me the same God. With these names on my lips, I will die cheerfully." (*H*, 20/iv, 118)

To equate Rama and Rahim was hardly a new idea. Gandhi himself had previously done so (Reading 332). The idea goes back at least as far as his beloved Kabir (cited in Reading 229 and mentioned again on page 203):

[342] **Kabir,** *1400s*: "Rama and Rahim are one and the same." (G. N. Das, 18)

A Moslem religious leader had recently made it known that he "resented coupling of the name of Rama, a mere young king, with Rahim, name of God; similarly of Krishna with Karim"; but Gandhi said that this was a narrow view of Islam and that "this erroneous view had emanated from his wrong notion that Rama and Krishna were names of ordinary human beings. Man worshipped the same God under different names and the Koran was not opposed to it."[163] However, such oppo-

---

162. Green, *loc.cit.* Payne, 1969 632ff (on the other conspirator's presence).

163. *C*, LXXXVI, 418.

sition might have prompted Gandhi to keep mainly to himself his idea of dying with the name "Rahim" as well as "Rama" on his lips. The good effect would come only at that moment, rather than from apparently provocative discussions of the idea in the meantime.

If *Rama, Rahim* really were his last words, he probably had, it seems to us, two reasons thus to complement what he had done by praising *Ishwar Allah* in his daily prayers. One reason was to ensure that his death would have the social and political effect which it did in fact have: to bring virtually to a halt the appalling extremes of religious strife in India and Pakistan and to lay the foundations for a less hostile relation between those two nations than any ordinary person in 1948 could have expected. The other reason would be the broader one — a mathematician might call it a generalization of the first reason — suggested in Reading 328: to promote the eventual development of a "religion of humanity" derived from a "heart-unity" among Hindus, Moslems, Parsis, Christians, Jews and others.

Our reason for imagining this is that Gandhi in 1945 and '46 had gone so far (see Chapter 6) as to make remarks privately in the following vein to an outspoken atheist: "I can neither say my theism is right nor your atheism wrong" — "Do you think I am superstitious? I am a super-atheist" — "It looks as if you will carry this old man into your camp." And in 1948 he went even further by declaring for publication, when he broke his last fast: "In the name of God we have indulged in lies, massacres.... I am not aware if anybody has done these things in the name of Truth. With the same name on my lips I have broken the fast." We think that a man who could open himself so much to atheism would not be satisfied to die merely a Hindu-Moslem, but would die instead a universal humanist.[164]

164. A professional Roman-Catholic theologian, Backanianadan, reaches the following conclusion in his book-length study (1991, 266): "In conclusion, it may not be out of place to mention Paul. F. Knitter's contention that we [Christians] have experienced a Copernican Revolution in turning from a long standing Ecclesiocentrism to Christocentrism. ...What Gandhi advocated could be described as Cosmocentrism, but in an Indian sense, where the line between Theocentrism and Cosmocentrism is blurred *but not destroyed*. This provides an excellent basis for the theists, atheists, agnostics and the religiously indifferent. What do we mean by this? It means an assertion that Reality is basically one despite its 'manyness'. You may call this One Reality (*Sat*) as God, Rama, Rahim, Baghavan or Allah. For Gandhi it did not matter what name one used, the Reality is the same. He himself would prefer to call 'It' as Truth. It did not even matter whether one spoke of this One Reality as personal or impersonal...." We atheists believe that this last distinction does matter, since a person has a will and therefore can be meaningfully petitioned — for instance (in the hypothetical case of a divine person) to rescue mankind by supernatural intervention from macro-ecological catastophe due to human recklessness.

CHAPTER 6

THEISM, ATHEISM, SECULARISM

In his early teens Gandhi became "an agnostic" inclined "somewhat towards atheism." This was when he first looked into the *Ordinances of Manu*, a famous code of Hindu moral law:[165]

[343] *1921*: "I was once an agnostic." (*Y*, 27/iv, 472)

[344] *Early 1880s* (recalled later): "The fact that I had learnt to be tolerant to other religions [besides Hinduism] did not mean that I had any living faith in God. I happened, about this time, to come across *Manusmriti*... [in] my father's collection. The story of the creation and similar things in it did not impress me very much, but on the contrary made me incline somewhat towards atheism." (*A*, I, ch. 10)

An elder cousin advised him not to think such thoughts:

[345] *Early 1880s* (recalled later): "A cousin of mine, for whose intellect I had great regard, ...[said] 'When you grow up, you will be able to solve these doubts yourself. These questions ought not to be raised at your age.'... [Therefore I told myself], 'With intellect more developed and with more reading I shall understand it better.'" (*A*, I, ch. 10)

So the issue faded. In England a few years later when his budding friendship with an attractive young woman obliged

---

165. A brief sample (albeit not necessarily of precepts that repelled Gandhi at that age): "Hear now the laws for women. No act is to be done according to her own free will by a young girl, by a young woman, nor yet by an old woman, not even in [their own] houses. In her childhood she should be under the will of her father; in youth, of her husband; her husband being dead, of her sons.... Though of bad conduct or debauched, or even devoid of [good] qualities, a husband must always be served like a god by a good wife." (Part V, 146-8, 154)

him to tell the lady who had brought them together that he was a married man, he felt that God had given him "the courage to speak out the truth" (*A*, I, ch. 19), and later he looked back on this and reflected:

[346] *1890* (recalled later): "For me, this was an occasion when I first became aware of the existence of God." (*C*, XXVII, 110)

Around that same time:

[347] *1890* (recalled later): "I read some book about [atheism], the name of which I forget. It had no effect on me, for I had already crossed the Sahara of atheism. Mrs. Besant, who was then very much in the limelight, had turned to theism from atheism, and that fact... strengthened my aversion to atheism." (*A*, I, ch. 20)

From the following undated remark, however, one might infer that a trace of atheist rationality lingered on until Rajchandra taught him (Reading 241) that "God is soul":

[348] (undated recollection): "I started accepting the existence of God when I accepted the existence of soul. Prior to that my condition was similar to that of an atheist if not exactly of an atheist." (*C*, XCV, 180)

Yet any such tendency must have disappeared by the time Gandhi remarked in *Indian Opinion*, in regard to a fire in the underground electric railway in Paris which killed 84 people in 1903, that such untoward happenings were "divine visitations" revealing the grim tragedy of modern civilization:

[349] *1903*: "The only consolation one can derive from such visitations has to come from a firm faith not in the theory, but in the fact, of the existence of a future life and real godhead." (*C*, III, 415)

Without some such conviction — so wierd to us[166] — Gandhi and his followers in South Africa would not have developed satyagraha. The pivotal issue for him in 1906 was that of taking a theistic oath:

[350] *1906* (recalled later): "The old Empire Theatre was packed from floor to ceiling.... Sheth Haji Habib... declare[d] in the name of God that he would never submit to that [unjust] law, and advised all present to do likewise.... I was taken aback.... I asked... to explain... the implications. ...'We all believe in one and the same god.... An oath in the name of that god or with Him as witness is not something to be trifled with.'..." (*S*, III, 140-43)

Again and again in the 1920s and '30s, Gandhi would argue that his theism was invulnerable to reason:

[351] *1924*: "There cannot be any proof for the existence of God which is acceptable to human reason.... The soul and God are not objects of knowledge. They are knowers themselves and therefore cannot be apprehended by the intellect. There are two stages in the knowledge of God: (1) faith and (2) experience arising from faith." (cited in *H*, 2/ix/1950, 226)

166. In our view a correct, corresponding atheist precept is the one set out in Reading 427.

[352] *1925*: "To me God is truth and love... ethics and morality ...fearlessness... conscience... even the atheism of the atheist.... He transcends speech and reason.... He is all things to all men." (*C*, XXVI, 222f)

[353] *1926*: "An atheist might floor me in a debate, but my faith runs so very much faster than my reason that I can challenge the whole world and say, 'God is, was, and ever shall be.' ...Reason is powerless to know Him." (*C*, XXIX, 411f)

[354] **Correspondent**, *1928*: "I read... where you wrote, 'I think it is wrong to expect certainties in this world, where all else but God that is Truth is an uncertainty'... [and]... 'God is long-suffering and patient... only issuing grave warnings at stated intervals.' I humbly beg to say that God is not a certainty. His goal ought to be to spread Truth all round. Why does He allow the world to be populated by bad people...? Should not God, omniscient and omnipotent as He is, know where wickedness is by his omniscience and kill wickedness by his omnipotence...? I wish to believe in God but there is no foundation for my faith. Kindly enlighten me....'

Gandhi: "The argument is as old as Adam. I have no original answer.... There is an indefinable mysterious Power that pervades everything. I feel It, though I do not see It.... I see It as purely benevolent... the supreme Good.

"But the foregoing does not answer the correspondent's argument. I confess to him that I have no argument to convince him through reason.... I know that He has no evil in Him and yet if there is evil, He is the author of it and yet untouched by it." (*C*, XXXVII, 347ff)

[355] *1928*: "To whom should you pray then [if not to God]? Therefore hold fast to your belief in God, never mind the reasoning." (*C*, XXXVI, 209)

[356] *1930*: [Q.] "You use the word 'god.' May I know its meaning and how far the meaning is consistent with the practice of life?"

[A.] "God is beyond human comprehension." (*G*, 26)

[357] *1931*: "It is beyond my power to induce in you a belief in God. There are certain things which are self-proved, and certain which are not proved at all.... I would have you brush aside all rational explanations and begin with a simple childlike faith in God. If I exist, God exists. With me it is a necessity of my being as it is with millions.... But I have no argument to address to those who have no faith." (*C*, XLVII, 399)

[358] *1936*: I believe in faith... in things where reason has no place, e.g. the existence of God." (*H*, 5/xii, 345)

Virtually throughout his life he found very useful his acceptance of a belief in divinity:

[359] *1921*: "Optimism indicates faith; only an atheist can be a pessimist. The optimist... believes that God ordains everything for the best....

"[So] I hope that no one will believe that I ever told anyone I would commit suicide if swaraj [national self-rule] was not won this year." (*C*, XXI, 330f)

[360] *1924*: "Did I not place my worries at the feet of God I should have gone mad by this time." (*C*, XXIII, 267)

[361] *1935*: "God always saves the world from the consequences of unintended errors of men who live in fear of Him."[167] (*H*, 11/v, 99)

167. Thus Gandhi would not subscribe to the proverb, "The road to hell is paved with good intentions."

[362] *1939*: "So long as the satyagrahi is not convinced that there is some great Power that would give him strength in all situations, he cannot face tyranny, strife and humiliations and sustain his non-violence.... This power that thus sustains us is God. Not to bear any malice towards the tyrant even on such occasions [as torture] is another name of faith in God." (*C*, LXIX, 231f)

[363] *1947*: "My walking pilgrimage [in Bengal][168] gives me immense peace of mind. The upshot I do not know nor do I care to know. Man has no control over results. That is the sole prerogative of God. Hence I can sing[169] with Cardinal Newman: 'I do not ask to see / The distant scene: one step enough for me.'" (*L*, I, 567)

He told Romain Rolland:

[364] *1931*: "I have no power except what God has given me. Look at me. A boy of fifteen could fell me with a blow. I am nothing. But I have become detached from fear and desire, so that I know something of God's power. I tell you, if all the world were to deny God, I should be His sole witness. It is a continual miracle to me." (Chandrashanker 1949, 146)

He told an English girl who had sent him a letter saying he was a father to her:

[365] *1933* "My dear daughter, I was very pleased to get your letter. You are quite right in addressing me as you have done. I enjoy the happiness of having thousands

168. See note 199 (page 292).
169. The words are from his favorite Christian hymn, Cardinal Newman's "Lead, Kindly Light."

of daughters. You are a welcome addition to the ever-growing family; and since I, a puny mortal, cannot cope with such a large family, I entrust you all to the safe keeping of the All-powerful and Eternal Father, and so I never feel the burden of having a large family; on the contrary, only the joy of possessing the truth remains." (*C*, LII, 368)

To those who argued that "if faith is beyond reason, it can only be blind," he would reply:

[366] *1929*: "My view is just the opposite.... That which is blind cannot be faith. If someone asserts with full conviction [that] there are flowers in the sky, the assertion cannot be considered valid. For the experience of the vast masses of people contradicts it. Belief in the existence of flowers in the sky is not faith; it is crass ignorance. Whether there are flowers in the sky is something that is amenable to rational inquiry and such an inquiry will prove the falsity of the assertion.

"On the contrary, when we say, 'God is,' no one can prove that the proposition is false.... [Indeed] the experience of millions proves the existence of God. In every matter, faith must be supported by empirical knowledge. For ultimately experience is the basis of faith and everyone who has faith must at some time pass through experience.

"He who has faith, however, does not desire experience, for true faith does not admit of doubt.... One man with faith will ford a river, while another who blindly follows him will surely be drowned." (*C*, XLI, 435f)

His religion even helped him maintain his vital love of truth:

[367] *1939*: "I am never too old to learn. One is ever young in the felt presence of the God of Truth or Truth which is God." (*C*, LXIX, 86)

Divine attributes

From the perspective of Westerners brought up more or less in the Christian tradition, Gandhi's theism[170] can be seen most clearly by looking at it in the light of some basic tenets of Christian theism. Most of the following are taken from the two ancient statements of belief — the Apostle's Creed and the Nicene Creed — one or the other of which Christians still today normally recite by heart in the most widely familiar of all Christian rituals (the "mass" or "communion"), or else from the "Lord's Prayer" (prescribed by Jesus to be said in private) which is normally recited by heart in every service of worship:

— that God is comprised of three persons (the "trinity");

— that God the Father is a person who created Heaven and Earth;

— that he has since acted in other ways, for instance by promulgating moral law (as in the Ten Commandments);

— that he rewards and punishes;

— that he is in Heaven;

— that, in addition to praising God and enjoining the divine

170. A brief anthology, entitled *My God*, was published at Ahmedabad in 1962. For a recent analytical discussion by a thoughtful Roman Catholic, see Backianadan 1991, 9-13, 43-50, 119-133 and 218ff.

father's will to be done on Earth as in Heaven, we should ask him to give us our daily bread and deliver us from evil.

We have seen (Readings 257-58) how Gandhi declined to convert to Christianity partly because he could not believe the doctrine of Jesus' unique divinity. He never took seriously the concept of the Trinity.

He was ambivalent as to whether God had created anything:

[368] *1926*: "I believe God to be creative as well as non-creative. This... is the result of my acceptance of the doctrine of the manyness of reality. From the platform of the Jains I prove the non-creative aspect of God, and from that of Ramanuja the creative aspect. As a matter of fact, we are all thinking of the Unthinkable, describing the Indescribable, seeking to know the Unknown, and that is why our speech falters, is inadequate and even often contradictory.... The vedas describe Brahma as 'not this, not this' [i.e. indescribable]. But [even] if He or It is not this, He or It is." (*C*, XXIX, 411)

(He need not have evoked Jainism here.[171] There is a traditional Hindu concept of a physical and moral order maintained, but not ordained, by the greatest of the gods, Varuna.[172] And according to the "Hymn of Creation" in the Rig Veda,[173] "The gods are later than this world's production. Who knows, then, whence it first came into being?")

He would often say unequivocally that God "is not a person." The first of the following excerpts is from a conversation

171. It is regarded as altogether atheist.

172. Embree 1966, 8-15.

173. See note 59 (page 93).

with Romain Rolland, the second from an article in *Harijan*:

[369] *1931*: "God is not a person. God is an eternal principle. That is why I say that Truth is God. Even the atheists do not doubt the necessity of truth."[174] (*T*, III, 147)

[370] *1947*: "God is not a person.... He dwells within every human being and all may, therefore, be said to be incarnations of Him. But this leads us nowhere. Rama, Krishna, etc. are called incarnations of God because we attribute divine qualities to them. In truth they are creations of man's imagination. Whether they actually lived or not does not affect the picture of them in men's minds....

"God is the force. He is the essence of life. He is pure and undefiled consciousness. He is eternal. And yet, strangely enough, all are not able to derive either benefit from or shelter in the all-pervading living presence.

"Electricity is a powerful force. Not all can benefit from it. It can only be produced by following certain laws. It is a lifeless force. Man can utilize it if he labors hard enough to acquire the knowledge of its laws. The living force which we call God can similarly be found if we know and follow His law leading to the discovery of Him in us." (*C*, LXXXVIII, 148f)

He might sometimes hedge:

[371] *1930*: "Nothing is or exists in reality except Truth. That is why... it is more correct to say Truth is God than to say God is Truth. But as we cannot do without a ruler or general, the name God is and will remain more current." (*C*, XLIV, 40)

174. But see note 187 (page 263).

[372] *1944*: "I do not believe in a personal deity, but I believe in the Eternal Law of Truth and Love which I have translated as non-violence. This Law is... a living thing — the Law and the Law-Giver are one. For those who realize this truth, the Law-Giver becomes a personal deity." (*C*, LXXVII, 399)

Yet it remained clear to him that God neither rewards nor punishes individuals (albeit committing indiscriminate, mass "visitations" as referred to in Readings 155 and 349):

[373] *1913*: "God is no dispenser of rewards and punishments, nor is He an active agent ...but pure consciousness.... In no circumstances do we need a kinglike God. By thinking that we do, we put a limit to the power of the atman, which is infinite."[175] (*C*, XII, 92)

It was clear to him that God has promulgated no laws:

[374] *1934*: "He and His Law are one. The Law is God. Anything attributed to Him is not a mere attribute. He is the attribute. He is Truth, Love and Law and a million other things that human ingenuity can name." (*H*, 16/ii)

[375] *1928*: "Law and Law-Giver are one." (*C*, XXXVII, 348)

[376] *1940*: "Truth for me is God, and God's Law and God are not different things or facts, in the sense that an earthly king and his law are different, because God is an Idea, Law Himself." (*C*, LXXI, 321)

---

175. On the other hand, Gandhi felt that "Those who deny the existence of God will end up on the wrong path, for they will be obliged to deny the existence of the atman [i.e. the world soul in us]." (*C*, XII, 126)

We may find anthropomorphism in his suggestion that God is a matter of unswerving will-power:

[377] *1931*: "To do at any cost something that one ought to do constitutes a vow. It becomes a bulwark of strength.... To do something 'as far as possible' is to succomb to... temptation....

"God is the very image of the vow. God would cease to be God if He swerved from His own laws even by a hair's breadth." (*S*, IV, 249f)

His humanitarianism entailed a belief, however, that God is not in Heaven:

[378] *1946*: "The execution of the constructive program in its entirety means more than swaraj [self-rule]. It means Ramarajya, Khudai Sultanate or the divine kingdom. I am thirsting after such Ramarajya. My God does not reside up above. He has to be realized on Earth. He is here, within you, within me." (*C*, LXXXII, 334)

Finally, even though he had accepted image-worship so long as it was not "idolatry... encrusted with false beliefs," he would never condone praying for one's personal desires to be met:

[379] *1929*: "I am both a supporter and opponent of image worship. When image worship degenerates into idolatry and becomes encrusted with false beliefs and doctrines, it becomes a necessity to combat it as a gross social evil. On the other hand in the sense of investing one's ideal with a concrete shape it is inherent in man's nature, and even valuable as an aid to devotion.... We worship an image when we visit a temple or a mosque with a feeling of sanctity or reverence. Nor do I see any harm in all

> this. On the contrary, endowed as man is with a finite, limited understanding, he can hardly do otherwise.
>
> "Even so, far from seeing anything inherently evil or harmful in tree worship, I find in it a thing instinct with a deep pathos and poetic beauty. It symbolizes true reverence for the entire vegetable kingdom, which with its endless panorama of beautiful shapes and forms, declares to us as it were with a million tongues the greatness and glory of God. Without vegetation our planet would not be able to support [animal] life even for a moment. In such a country [as India] especially, tree worship assumes a profound economic significance.
>
> "...It is true that the poor simple-minded women who offer worship to trees have no reasoned understanding of the[se] implications of their act.... They act in the purity and utter simplicity of their faith. Such faith is not a thing to be despised; it is a great and powerful force that we should treasure.
>
> "Far different, however, is the case of vows and prayers which votaries offer before trees. The offering of vows and prayers for selfish ends, whether offered in churches, mosques, temples or before trees and shrines, is a thing not to be encouraged.... A personal selfish prayer is bad whether made before an image or an unseen God." (*C*, XLI, 292f)

Thus he rejected the basic elements of Western theism, even though he was, unquestionably, a religious man and loved to praise Rama, Vishnu, Ishwar, Allah and God. What then did he mean by these names?

We have seen (Chapter 4) that in his youth he learned to believe in a universal soul, an ocean of which the individual soul, the atman, is but a drop whose final self-realization will consist of its rejoining the ocean when it attains salvation (moksha) by being released from the cycle of rebirths. In this context Gandhi's theism would be, first of all, a belief that the atman by finding or realizing itself in union with the world-soul becomes "God":

[380] *1913*: "God exists, and yet does not. He does not, in any literal sense. The atman that has attained moksha is God and therefore omniscient. The true meaning of *bhakti* [religious devotion] is search for the atman." (*C*, XII, 126)

This exalted but quite traditional Hindu concept of the human soul supported in turn his belief that God is a force dwelling in each of us (Reading 370), which does not reside "up above" but has to be realized within us on Earth (Reading 378), and if we exist then God exists (Readings 357 and 383); and also his injunction not to "limit" the infinite power of the soul (Reading 373).

For Gandhi it was not idle talk, but the pivot by which he leveraged the voluntary suffering of a few disciplined souls into substantial political and social achievements:

[381] *1939*: "If there are some Jains or Buddhists who do not believe in the atman, they cannot join satyagraha." (*C*, LXIX, 227)

The "infinite power" was not only in the satyagrahis' souls but also in those of their antagonists — in *their* capacity to realize, when their moral shame and humanistic pity were deeply and publicly aroused, that in the depths of their souls they really wanted to do the humane thing more than they wanted to satisfy whatever desire it was of their merely carnal shell that was interfering with that deeper yearning.[176] So the civil disobedience and the fasting were never to make people do anything against their will, but only to help them realize the deepest yearnings of their divine souls to become less selfish and more humane:

[382] *1932*: "Nothing can or should be done by compulsion. Fasting and the like are not designed to compel people to act against their wills, they are designed to make people think and act." (*C*, LI, 195 and again 199)

[383] *1932*: "If we exist, God exists as well; for the totality of life is God even as the totality of solar rays is the sun. In order to have faith in this God, you must have faith in yourself. Faith in oneself can be won by the selfless service of humanity." (*S*, v, 353)

However, when experience gradually taught him, after his return from South Africa to India, that the language of atman and reincarnation could just as well be used to maintain as to do away with the inhuman treatment of the "untouchables" (Reading 151), he tended to equate God less often with the (realized) atman than with Truth. (Perhaps he was hoping that even a conservative Brahmin might, if he had heart, see that it was inhumane, and therefore *against Truth*, to treat the un-

176. Kim 1983, 3-7, explains this in more detail.

touchables as even more miserably impure specimens of atman than stray dogs and the like.)

[384] *1908*: "Truth is God, or God is nothing but Truth." (*C*, VIII, 61)

[385] *1918*: "There is no God but Truth." (*C*, XIV, 385)

[386] *1927*: "If God who is indefinable can be at all defined, then I should say that God is Truth. It is impossible to reach Him, that is, Truth, except through Love." (*C*, XXXIII, 452)

[387] *1931*: "For myself I came to the conclusion that God is Truth. But two years ago I went a step further and said Truth is God.... And I came to that conclusion after a continuous and relentless search after Truth which began nearly fifty years ago. I found that the nearest approach to Truth is through love. But I found also that 'love' has many meanings, in the English language at least, and human love in the sense of passion becomes a degrading thing also. I found, too, that love in the sense of ahimsa has only a limited number of votaries in the world.... But I never found a double meaning in connection with truth and not even the atheists had demurred to the necessity or power of truth. Yet... when you want to find Truth as God, the only inevitable means is love... and since I believe that ultimately, means and ends are convertible terms, I should not hesitate to say that God is love." (*C*, XLVIII, 404f)

A hidden philosophical advantage of this equation between God and Truth was that it implicitly supported what a Westerner might informally call a "quasi-ontological argument" for its own validity. The traditional Western ontological proof is along the following lines: "*(1)* God is by definition the perfect being. *(2)* A being with the attribute of existence is more perfect than one without that attribute. *(3)* Therefore God exists."[177] The counterpart would be along the lines of: "*(1)* I define God as Truth. *(2)* Truth cannot be false. *(3)* So my idea of God cannot be false." Unconcerned with this kind of analysis and unschooled in the Marxist doctrine that truth is class-bound, Gandhi would equivocate as to whether his theism was now derived from atheism:

[388] *1931*: "I never found a double meaning in connection with Truth and not even atheists have denied the necessity or power of Truth. Not only so. In their passion for discovering Truth, they have not hesitated even to deny the very existence of God — from their point of view rightly. And it was because of their reasoning that I saw that I was not going to say 'God is Truth', but 'Truth is God'." (*C*, XLVIII, 404)

[389] *1932*: "That God has many names, a thousand, is quite true. But remembering God as the possessor of many names is fraught with the possibility of a diminution in the significance of the entity to which we wish to offer total surrender. But all other attributes fade away when we proclaim that Truth alone is God; only the attribute of Truth remains in mind and this is more prevalent in

---

177. The answer to this argument is that existence is not an attribute. In modern logic, one may write "(x | x is a god)" for the long-winded expression: "the set of all x's such that x is a god," and may then go on to discuss whether this set is "empty" or not.

monism [than in polytheism]. Atheism has no place here as even an atheist accepts existence which is a development of *sat*. Here Truth does not imply merely truthfulness of speech; its meaning here is unity of thought, word and deed and yet more. Whatever is in reality here, what existed in the past and will remain in the future is the substance, Truth, *Parameshwar* [universal God], and nothing [else] but that [is God]." (*C*, LI, 76)

Gandhi's theism may seem idiosyncratic, but he did not see it that way. A sophisticated Oxonian (A. D. Lindsay, subsequently vice-chancellor of the university) whom he visited in 1931 recalled later that Gandhi "did not believe anything could be the will of God which could not be understood by simple unlettered people."[178] And Gandhi would often likewise justify his ultra-rational belief in divinity with an appeal to common sense:

[390] *1932*: "We may believe in God because all the world believes in Him." (*S*, V, 353)

[391] *1929*: "However hard we might try through reason to disprove the existence of God, some doubt would still remain in the mind of everyone." (*C*, XLI, 435f)

Gandhi's theism would remain serene so long as he did not become intimately acquainted with an outspoken atheist whose integrity and dedicated humanitarianism he found equal to his own.

178. Chandrashanker Shukla 1949, 150.

Atheism

Charles Bradlaugh (1833-1891) was an atheist of great integrity and a dedicated humanitarian in Victorian England. He founded the National Secular Society in 1866 and with Annie Besant's collaboration in the late 1870s and '80s made it an influential organization.[179] In 1880 he was elected to the House of Commons, but was denied the right to participate without taking a religious oath; after years of litigation he secured the right in 1886, and thereupon became a distinguished member of parliament[180]— establishing the government's responsibility to collect and publish comprehensive labor statistics, speaking out on British justice and injustice abroad, introducing a bill to set up a democratic form of government in India, and so on.[181] Shortly before his death he visited Bombay to address the Indian National Congress, where the reception of his speech was "cheer-drenched":[182]

[392] **Bradlaugh,** *1889*: "For whom should I work, if not for the people? ...And I know no geographical or race limitations...." (K. I. Dutt, 42)

---

179. Royle 1985. (In the 1870s Bradlaugh and Besant established in England the right to read about birth control.)
180. Majumdar 1971, 367 and 428. (See also Chand 1974, 563.)
181. When he died, a leader of the coal miners and fellow member of parliament said of him, "No man ever did his parliamentary work more thoroughly and conscientiously; no member ever in so short a period made such a mark on the statute book by passing useful measures, or so beneficially influenced the public administrations."
182. Tribe 1971, 280.

Gandhi never met Bradlaugh. But he knew vaguely about him:

[393] *1890* (recalled later): "And how could I help knowing something of atheism too? Every Indian [in England] knew Bradlaugh's name and his so-called atheism." (*A*, I ch. 20)

A distasteful conversation which he witnessed on the day of Bradlaugh's funeral demonstrated to Gandhi that atheism is arrogant and unsavory:

[394] *1891* (recalled later): "I attended the funeral, as I believe every Indian residing in London did. A few clergymen also were present to do him the last honors. On our way back from the funeral we had to wait at the station for our train. A champion atheist from the crowd heckled one of these clergymen. 'Well, sir, you believe in the existence of God?'

"'I do,' said the good man in [a] low tone.

"'You also agree that the circumference of the Earth is 28,000 miles, don't you?' said the atheist with a smile of self-assurance.

"'Indeed.'

"'Pray tell me then the size of your God and where he may be?'

"'Well, if we but knew, He resides in the hearts of us both.'

"'Now, now, don't take me to be a child,' said the champion with a triumphant look at us.

"The clergyman assumed a humble silence.

"This talk still further increased my prejudice against atheism." (*A*, I, ch. 20)

So it seemed to him that Bradlaugh must really have been, unbeknownst to himself, a religious, God-fearing man whose joy sprang from a communion with the divine and whom God had sustained throughout all his trials:

[395] *1925*: "Bradlaugh described himself as an atheist no doubt, but many a Christian declined to regard him as such [and] recognized in Bradlaugh a greater kinship with himself than many a lip Christian. I had the privilege of attending the funeral of that good friend of India. I noticed several clergymen at the function. There were certainly several Moslems and many Hindus in the procession. They all believed in God. Bradlaugh's denial of God was a denial of Him as He was known to Bradlaugh to have been described. His [Bradlaugh's] was an eloquent and indignant protest against the then current theology and the terrible contrast between precept and practice." (*C*, XXVI, 224)

[396] *1925*: "I must... adhere to my opinion that neither Jainism nor Buddhism are atheistic. I present [my correspondent] with these definitions of God:[183] The sum total of karma is God. That which impels man to do the right is God. The sum total of all that lives is God. That which makes man the mere plaything of fate is God. That which sustained Bradlaugh throughout all his trials was God." (*C*, XXVI, 571)

[397] *1930*: "Bradlaugh, whose atheism is well known, always insisted on proclaiming his innermost conviction. He had to suffer a lot for thus speaking the truth, but he delighted in it and said that truth is its own reward. Not that he was quite insensible to the joy resulting from the observance of truth. This joy however is not at all world-

183. According to Western logic, one definition is all that is wanted for each term.

ly, but springs out of a communion with the divine. That is why I have said that even a man who disowns religion cannot and does not live without religion." (*C*, XLII, 411)

[398] *1931*: "I would never consider him an atheist. I would call him a God-fearing man although I know he would reject the claim and his face would redden. I would say, 'No, Mr. Bradlaugh, you are a truth-fearing man and not a god-fearing man,' and I would disarm his criticisms by saying 'Truth is God,' as I have disarmed the criticisms of many a young man. Add to this the great difficulty that millions have taken the name of God and in His name committed nameless atrocities. (Not that scientists do not very often commit cruelties in the name of Truth ...[such as] vivisection....) So I know that there are these difficulties in one's way no matter how you describe God." (*C*, XLVIII, 404f)

An outspoken atheist whom Gandhi did know personally in the 1920s was Periyar (1879-1973), the "Vaikom hero" whom we have mentioned in Chapter 4:

[399] **Gandhi**, *1927*: "Many great men have expressed many of their ideas in the name of religion.... Can't all of us join together at this time and, acting from within the religious fold, remove all that you consider to be defects in Hinduism?"

Periyar: "It is my humble view that you can't do it. Even if you succeed in doing it, after you another great man will come up, reverse all the changes you have made, and leave religion as we find it today."

Gandhi: "How can he do that?"

Periyar: "Just now you said that people can be made to accept and follow whatever we say in the name of religion. Can't a great man of the future do anything in the name of religion?" (Periyar 1994, 69)

Notwithstanding Periyar's use here of the word "humble," he was hardly ever humble in the everyday sense. He would, it is true, routinely end his speeches by declaring:

[400] **Periyar,** *1930s-1970s*: "Whatever I have said, do not blindly accept it. Think! Use your reasoning! Only accept what I have said if you find it correct; otherwise discard it."

But he would routinely begin by declaring:

[401] **Periyar,** *1930s-1970s*: "There is no god, there is no god, there is no god at all! He who invented God is a fool, he who propagates God is a scoundrel, he who worships God is a barbarian!"

The atheism of his "Self-Respect Movement" was humanitarian:

[402] **Periyar** *1935*: "Economic inequalities and social hardships derive support from religion... [but] the members of the Self-Respect Movement have come forward to find fault with the god concept... because they have realized the acute suffering faced by poor people and the reasons for their suffering." (Periyar 1994: 7f)

But the whole style of Periyar's movement would, to Gandhi's way of thinking and feeling, reflect no credit on atheism:

[403] **V. S. Naipaul,** *1990*: "In Madras... a garlanded black statue of Periyar [stands] in the middle of [a] big sandy plot, with this inscription on the plinth: '(1) PERIYAR THE PROPHET OF THE

NEW AGE, (2) THE SOCRATES OF SOUTH EAST ASIA, (3) FATHER OF THE SOCIAL MOVEMENT, (4) ARCH ENEMY OF IGNORANCE, SUPERSTITIONS, MEANINGLESS CUSTOMS AND BASELESS MANNERS.'" (Naipaul 1990: 217)

So it could hardly induce him to take atheism seriously:

[404] *1930*: "Ahimsa teaches us to entertain the same respect for the religious faiths of others as we accord to our own.... [But] we should never tolerate irreligion." (*C*, XLIV, 166f)

[405] *1932*: "Atheism is merely a pose.... My definition of God must always be kept in mind. For me there is no other God than Truth." (*C*, XLIX, 284)

[406] *1934*: "During my visit to the South I met Harijans and others who pretended not to believe in God. At one place where a conference of Harijans was being held, the chairman[185] delivered a harangue on atheism under the very shadow of a temple which Harijans had built for themselves with their own money....

"Ever since its commencement, the world [of people] — the wise and the foolish included — has proceeded upon the assumption that if we are, God is, and that if God is not, we are not.... Even the atheists who have pretended to disbelieve in God have believed in Truth. The trick they have performed is that of giving God another... name. His names are legion. Truth is the crown of them all." (*C*, LIX, 43f)

[407] *1936*: "A man without faith is like a drop thrown out of the ocean, bound to perish." (*C*, LXII, 349)

---

185. This may well have been Swami Narayana Guru's distinguished disciple, the atheist (and Buddhist) social-worker, Sadhoran Ayyappan. See Sreenivasan 1989, 78f and 117.

[408] *1939*: **[Q.]** "Should the path of satyagraha be considered closed to... atheists?"

[A.] "I am sorry, but I shall have to say, 'Yes.'..."

[Q.] "What is the criterion for judging whether a person does or does not believe in God? If an individual accepts God as a metaphysical possibility but not as a mysterious power, will he be called an atheist?"

[A.] "This is a subtle question.... I do not insist that everybody should have the same idea of God as I have." (*C*, LXIX, 226f)

Nehru was free of any religious faith or concept of a god,[185] but was so little outspoken about this aspect of his views — though he did not hide it — that it was practically never a topic of conversation with Gandhi.[186] He nudged Gandhi toward secularism, but never toward atheism. That role was reserved for Gora.

We have seen (in Chapter 2) how a young friend of Gora's, Dasu Ramaswamy, aroused Gandhi's interest in Gora's social work in the early 1940s, and how Gandhi became acquainted to some extent with Gora's character and beliefs after the two of them came out of detention in 1944. At the outset of this development, their views were as follows:

[409] **Gora**, *1941*: "For one year I have tackled the problem of untouchability with the atheistic outlook... [which] mainly consists in the non-recognition of sectarian labels like Hindus, Muslims and Christians. We take man as man. Thus by discarding the labels and mixing up people in the general stream of humanity, we hope to remove un-

---

185. Nehru, *Discovery of India*, p. 11. 186. But see note 88 (page 135).

touchability also.... The results of one year's work encourage us to proceed [further] along the same lines. Before we do so, we desire to seek your advice.... We are prepared to revise our outlook and program. If you like, I will go to Sevagram for a personal talk with you."

Gandhi: "Dear Friend, Atheism is a denial of self. No one has succeeded in its propagation. Such success as you have attained is due to your sincere work among the people around you. I am sorry I cannot invite you to come here. I have no time to spare for talks." (*G*, 27; *C*, LXXIV, 311)

That which Gora here presented as the main element of his atheistic outlook was the same as that which Gandhi in 1946 would describe as "far superior" to his own thought and practice (Readings 197-98).

It was after a conversation with Ramaswamy that Gandhi changed his mind about meeting Gora. The following extracts are from an account by Gandhi's secretary at the time (Pyarelal):

[410] **Gandhi**, *1944*: "A cosmopolitan outlook is a necessity, but... unless you have a living faith in God to sustain you, when failure strikes you in the face... you may develop a revulsion for the [good] work that you have taken up.... This ashram [Sevagram]... may enable you to know God to the extent that you may able to say 'God is', just as you can say 'Truth is'."

Ramaswamy: "I can say that ['Truth is'] in the sense that truth is the antithesis of falsehood."

Gandhi: "That is good enough. The seers have described God as 'Not this; not that.' Truth will elude you: the sum total of all that is true is Truth, but you can't sum up all that is true. Like most of those who have had Western education, you have got an analytical mind. But there are things that cannot be analyzed. God who can be analyzed by my poor mind won't satisfy me.... I go behind the relative and I get my peace of mind."

Ramaswamy: "...Your way of life appeals to me very much; it offers scope for the exercise of individual will. [But] the idea of God introduces a determinism that limits man. It interferes with his free will."

Gandhi: "Is there such a thing as free will? Where is it? We are mere playthings in the hands of Providence."

Ramaswamy: "What is the relationship between God and man, between Truth and God?"

Gandhi: "I used to say 'God is Truth'; that did not completely satisfy me; so I said 'Truth is God.' He and His laws are not different: God's law is God Himself. To interpret it man has to resort to intense prayer and merge himself in God. Each one will interpret the same in his or her own way. As for the relationship between man and God, man does not become man by virtue of having two hands; he becomes man by becoming a tabernacle of God.... You will concede that we are not tabernacles of untruth: we are of Truth. [Now] everyone who wants to live a true life has to face difficulties in life, some of which appear insurmountable. At that time it is faith in God-that-is-Truth alone that will sustain you. The fellow-feeling which makes you feel miserable because of your brother's misery is godliness. You may call yourself an atheist, but so long as you feel akin with mankind you accept God in practice. I remember the clergymen who came to the funeral of the great atheist Bradlaugh. They said they had come to pay their homage because he was a godly man." (*G*, 29ff; *C*, LXXVII, 6ff)

Upon first meeting Gora, Gandhi was ready with a diplomatic jest that made them both laugh and brought the conversation directly to Gora's concept of "positive atheism":

[411] **Gandhi**, *1944*: "What shall I talk [say] to a godless man?"
Gora: "Bapuji, I am not a godless man, I am an atheist."
Gandhi: "How do you differentiate between godlessness and atheism?"
Gora: "Godlessness is negative. It merely denies the existence of [any] god. Atheism is positive. It asserts the condition that results from the denial of [any] god.... In general, theism is the manifestation of the feeling of slavishness in man. Conversely, atheism is the manifestation of the feeling of freedom in man...." (*G*, 32f)

Gandhi was inclined to dismiss this as a merely academic philosophy:

[412] **Gandhi**: "You are too theoretical. I am not so intellectual. Go to professors and discuss."
Gora: "If atheism were only theoretical, I would not have cared for it, nor wasted your time. We have practical programs based upon the atheistic outlook."
Gandhi: "Ah, ah, I know that; so I am talking to you. Tell me what you are doing among the villagers." (*G*, 33)

Gora obliged with a substantial account of what he had been doing. As the meeting ended (apart from some additional cordial jokes and an undertaking to continue with another appointment "very soon"), Gandhi became alarmed at Gora's views, and this caused Gora to say two things which, we may suppose, no other atheist ever said to Gandhi:

[413] **Gora**: "...Man... created god to make society moral.... Of course god was useful ...but like all falsehoods, belief in god also gave rise to many evils in the course of time, and today it is not only useless but harmful to human progress. So I take the propagation of atheism as an aid to my [social] work. The results justify my choice."

Gandhi: "I should fast even because atheism is spreading."

Gora: "I will fast against your fast."

Gandhi: "You will fast?"

Gora: "Yes, Bapuji. But why should you fast? Tell me how atheism is wrong and I will change."

Gandhi: "I see, your conviction in atheism is deep. The present conduct of people is giving room for the spread of atheism." (*G*, 34f)

"I will fast against your fast" meant that Gora understood satyagraha and that his "positive atheism" represented his deepest, most humanitarian impulses. The other statement ("...I will change") displayed a degree of courtesy which seemed to exclude fanaticism.

Within a year Gandhi would assume, privately to Gora, an agnostic stance:

[414] **Gora**, *1945*: "I could not remove god, if god were the truth. But it is not so. God is a falsehood conceived by man... [and hence] polluted life in the long run. So belief in god... must go now in order to wash off [the] corruption [due to falsehood].... I want atheism to make man self-confident and to establish social and economic equalities non-violently. Tell me, Bapu, where I am wrong."

Gandhi: "I can neither say my theism is right nor your atheism wrong. We are [both] seekers after truth.... There

> is no harm [in your atheism] as long as you are not fanatical. Whether you are in the right or I am in the right, results will prove.... So ...I will help you though your method is against mine." (*G*, 44)

A year later he would, at least in jest, yield further. The following extracts are from conversations occasioned by Gandhi's wish to preside at the wedding of Gora's daughter and Arjun Rao, and for Arjun Rao in the meantime to live at Sevagram:

[415] **Gandhi,** *1946*: "In the case of your daughter's marriage, I will say 'in the name of Truth' instead of 'in the name of God'.... [Our] concepts of truth may differ,[187] but all admit and respect Truth. That Truth I call God. For some time I was saying, 'God is Truth', but that did not satisfy me, so now I say 'Truth is God.'"

Gora: "If truth is god, then why don't you say 'Satyam' instead of 'Raghupati Raghava'? 'Raghupati Raghava' conveys to others a meaning very different from what it conveys to you."

Gandhi: "Do you think I am superstitious? I am a super-atheist." (*G*, 48)

---

187. Gora had remarked, "I think truth is only relative to human experience. The concept of absolute truth beyond human experience is but a hypothesis formed by man for the convenience of his thought process. Any absolute, like the infinite, is only an imaginary something." A comparable Western statement is the following, translated from Mauthner 1901 (p. 66): "Even the most certain truth is only more or less true. Real Truth is a metaphysical concept. Men attained to the concept of Truth just as they did the concept of God — without any experience [of the object]. In this sense one may certainly assert: God is Truth." Gandhi would say: "God is Truth. All else is unreal and false. Other things, therefore, can be true only in a relative sense." (*C*, XXI, 473).

[416] **Gora**, *1946*: "Arjun Rao will be in the ashram for two years. There must be clear understanding about the discipline. What shall be his position in relation to attendance at the prayers, Bapu?"

Gandhi: "Let him attend the prayers as a matter of discipline of the ashram, but let him not recite the verses if he does not believe in them."

[Gora bows to indicate consent.]

Gandhi: "Suppose in the two years that Arjun Rao sits regularly at the prayers, he turns towards theism?"

Gora: "I will be very happy, Bapu. I do not want anyone to be an atheist with closed mind; he should be an atheist out of conviction. If he takes to theism out of conviction, I welcome such a change in him."

Gandhi: "Oh, yes, I know you are not a fanatic. Instead of Arjun Rao taking to theism, it looks as if both of you will carry this old man into your camp!" (*G*, 49)

He would sometimes turn back:

[417] *1946*: "There is a fundamental difference between... your thought and mine. For you consciously ignore God. Equally consciously, probably more progressively, I rely upon God." (*G*, 52; *C*, LXXXIII, 390)

But far from dismissing atheism as he had done for so many years, he wished now to learn more about it:

[418] **Gandhi**, *1946* "You have tried atheism sufficiently long. Now you [should] give up the term 'atheism.' It does not help your work."

Gora: "I am well aware that the term 'atheism' is a condemned word.... Yet I have taken it up deliberately, because it is the only word that inspires full self-confidence[188] and complete social outlook in man.... So far I have not laid before you the several aspects of atheism as I see them. I am waiting for you to give me time. I want also to put my thoughts in a book form."

Gandhi: "I will go through the manuscript of your book. Come to me when I go to Sevagram next." (*G*, 54f)

One wonders how the dialogue would have worked out if Gandhi had returned home to Sevagram as he planned to do on February 1st, 1948. While both men were open-minded, their interactions during the previous three and a half years had led always to a strengthening of Gora's views and to Gandhi's evolving, fairly consistently, in that direction.

Secularism

In one of their last meetings, Gandhi told Gora that he had in mind a particular task which he wanted him to undertake and which he would explain at Sevagram.[189] We may suppose that it was not a philosophical book but something in the way of constructive social work.

---

188. By "self-confidence" he meant confidence in *swasakthi*, the earthly human individual, rather than confidence in the power of a yearning atman.

189. Gora told this to Lavanam. To judge by how Gandhi had, after reading J. C. Kumarappa's early writings and observing carefully his character (for instance during the earthquake-relief work in 1934), founded the All-India Village Industries Association with Kumarappa as executive secretary, one could speculate that Gandhi might in 1948 have asked Gora to help lead an organization promoting arranged intermarriages. (A few years after Gandhi's death Kumarappa and Gora co-founded an organization striving to mitigate India's gross economic inequalities.)

Now that India's independence was won, Gandhi himself was, at least for the time being, engaged very little in politics in the normal sense — except in one big way. Having failed to prevent the splitting off of Pakistan from India, he undertook to ensure that the Republic of India would be a secular and not a religious state.

[419] *1947* (as reported): "[Gandhi said that] religion was a personal matter and if we succeeded in confining it to the personal plane, all would be well with our political life. The manifestation of brotherhood which was being witnessed today would prove but a passing show if we did not consolidate it by suitable acts in the social and political spheres. If officers of the Government as well as members of the public undertook the reponsibility and worked whole-heartedly for the creation of a secular state, then only could we build a new India that would be the glory of the world." (*H*, 31/viii, 303)

[420] *1947*: "If I were a dictator, religion and state would be separate. I swear by my religion; I will die for it; but it is my personal affair, the state has nothing to do with it. The state should look after secular welfare, health, communications, foreign relations, currency and so on, but not your or my religion. That is everybody's personal concern." (*T*, VII, 264)

[421] *1947* (as reported): "He was also opposed to state aid, partly or wholly, to religious bodies." (*C*, LXXXV, 328)

After the appalling religious strife which he had struggled so long to contain (and which would soon include his own death), Gandhi was particularly concerned that there must be no religious indoctrination in the public schools:

[422] *1947*: [Q.] "What about the place of religious instruction in basic education [in independent India]?"
[A.] "I do not believe that a secular state should concern itself with religious education as such.... Those who want to give religious education may do so on their own, so long as it is not subversive of law and order and morality. The Government can only teach ethics on the main lines common to all religions and agreed to by all parties." (*L*, II, 116)

His reference to "all parties" represents a distinct change from the stance he had taken nearly 40 years earlier when he had imagined from abroad how things should be in an independent India:

[423] *1909*: "What education shall we give?... We should abandon the pretension of learning many sciences. Religious, that is, ethical, education will occupy the first place.... The question of religious education is very difficult... yet we cannot do without it. India will never be godless. Rank atheism cannot flourish in this land." (*C*, X, 56f)

1948

We have referred often to the fact that Gandhi's views evolved in response to the social conditions around him. This is obviously true of the remark, which he made privately to a Hindu friend when they met at Delhi in 1947, that he wished the communities would turn atheist if that would serve to stop the communal hatred and riots (Reading 39). It is true as well of the last statement that he had time to compose at leisure in regard to his equation between God and Truth. His six days of relative leisure between January 13th and 18th were one of the most difficult times of his life, as he fasted to put an end to religious violence against Moslems in Delhi. He had felt helpless in the face of that violence and of its implicit endorsement by the militant Hindu "RSS" (*Rashtriya Swayamsevak Sangh*: "National Volunteer Corps"). He said, "I have never put up with helplessness in all my life," and fasted until the leaders of the RSS and other organizations and communities in Delhi came to him with a pledge that "The incidents which have taken place in Delhi will not happen again" and "We shall protect the life, property and faith of the Moslems." To understand the written statement which Gandhi issued as he broke the fast, the reader should bear in mind the following points:

—His mature concept of God was not of a person "up above" but of a principle that could only be realized on Earth, "within you, within me" (Reading 378).

—Although he knew that cruelty against animals is committed in the name of truth (Reading 223), he was evidently unaware — perhaps it merely slipped his mind — that the Stalinist newspaper in Moscow was called "Truth" (*Pravda*).

—He may not have expected the religious leaders to keep their pledge.[190]

—In case the pledge were kept, his own "wish and prayer" would then be "before God," not "to God"; that is, he would still not petition God (see Reading 379).

---

190. Late in November he had written to a friend, "Now we are daily growing more and more barbarous.... That is why I am praying within, 'O Rama, now take me away soon.'" (*C*, XC, 83).

—On several occasions he suggested that the "full span of life" was 125 years.[191]

[424] *1948*: "I embarked on the fast in the name of Truth whose familiar name is God. Without [a] living Truth, God is nowhere. In the name of God we have indulged in lies, massacres of people, without caring whether they were innocent or guilty, men or women, children or infants.... I am not aware if anybody has done these things in the name of Truth. With the same name ['Truth'] on my lips I have broken the fast.... If the solemn pledge made today is fulfilled, I assure you that it will revive with redoubled force my intense wish and prayer before God that I should be enabled to live the full span of life, doing service of humanity till the last moment." (*C*, XC, 452f)

Thus he made his beloved theism contingent upon other people's humanistic behavior.

191. See for instance *C*, LXXXV, 205, 370 and 455, and LXXXVII, 522.

CHAPTER 7

CONCLUSIONS

We have argued that Gandhi continued to grow throughout his life, and have shown that the great humanist who was assassinated in 1948 differed significantly in his views of caste, intermarriage, religion and theism from the mahatma of the First World War era. In this light it seems a paradox that his greatest political invention, non-violent political satyagraha, took place during a phase of his life when he was still more concerned with the fate of his soul after death (Reading 93) than with the degrading effects, upon people in this life, of extreme, involuntary poverty.

We have seen how Gandhi relied, from the outset of his public life in India, on a religious approach to provide remedies to the various social and political problems he addressed, and how in the 1920s he described himself as an orthodox Hindu (Readings 115-16) and felt that some kind of theism was indispensable to the solution of the most difficult human problems (Readings 360, 362, 364 and 366). But later, as he saw more clearly the consequences of superstitious inertia (with regard to "karma" and "untouchability") and religious sectarianism acting like poison in the veins of Indian society, he began, though tentatively, to separate Truth and humanism from God. In 1945 he modified the last sentence of the Independence-Day pledge to accomodate atheism:

[425] *1945*: "I seek, for the fulfillment of my pledge, the assistance of that which we may or may not call divine but which we all feel within us." (*L*, I, 63)

When the question of Manorama's wedding came up in 1946, Gandhi decided to celebrate the marriage in the name of Truth alone with no mention of God (Reading 415), and in 1948 he fasted explicitly in the name of Truth and not of God (Reading 424). In this last and greatest phase of his spiritual development, he would privately make remarks along the lines of "I can neither say my theism is right nor your atheism wrong" (Reading 414), "I wish they would all turn atheist if that would stop their rioting" (Reading 39), "It looks as though you atheists will carry this old man into your camp" (Reading 416), "I am a super-atheist" (Reading 415), and:

[426] *1947*: "The first thing is that politics have divided India today into Hindus and Moslems. I want to rescue people from this quagmire and make them work on solid ground where people are people. Therefore my appeal... is not to the Moslems as Moslems, nor to Hindus as Hindus, but to ordinary human beings who have to keep their villages clean, to build schools for their children and take many other steps so that they can make life better." (Bose and Patwardhan 1967, 7)

On the other hand, we have seen how adept he was at giving new meanings to old words. He favored "the protection of the cow in its much larger sense than the popular" (Reading 116). Having described his faith as "humble," he said that this only meant he would not ignore the intellect so much as to believe something patently absurd like "the earth is flat" (Reading 323). He said almost in one breath that caste does not connote superiority or inferiority *and* that a hierarchy among the castes is inevitable because they cannot all realize the ideal in equal degree (Reading 121). The British complained that his habit of reinterpreting made it easy for him to quote himself in apparent contradiction to any view attributed to him.[192] But to harp on this would be to ignore his real growth, which he said (in 1932) went "unnoticed like the growth of hair on our heads" (Reading 10). And indeed, terms have to be redefined from time to time when one is working within a tradition, as Gandhi unquestionably was, and yet circumstances change. In this light we can see that Gandhi's most crucial, redefining shifts were from "God" to "Truth" and, in effect, from Rama to *Purushothama*, the personification of all good human qualities.

What is it that "we all feel within us"? The atheist Ludwig Feuerbach in the 1840s called it a consciousness of one's nature or species:

[427] **Feuerbach,** *1841*: "Consciousness in the strictest sense is present only in a being to whom his species, his essential nature, is an object of thought....

"The brute has only a simple life, but man a twofold life: ...inner and outer.... The inner life of man is his life which has relation to its species, to his [general] nature....

"Religion is the relation of man to his own nature — therein lies its truth — but to his nature not recognized as his own, but regarded as another nature, separate, indeed contra-distinguished from his own: herein lies its untruth.... [For] religion is not conscious that its elements

192. *T*, VII, 230.

are human; on the contrary, it rather places itself in opposition to the human.... The necessary turning-point of history is therefore the open confession and avowal that the consciousness of God is nothing else than the consciousness of the species, that man can and should raise himself only above the limits of his individuality, and not above the laws, the essential conditions, of his species." (translated from Feuerbach 1841, 28, 29, 316 and 443f)

A typical Gandhian formulation was:

[428] *1939*: "I recognize no God except the God that is to be found in the hearts of the dumb millions. They do not recognize his presence; I do. And I worship the God that is Truth, or Truth which is God, through the service of [to] these millions." (*C*, LXIX, 33)

Gandhi was so adept at filling old containers with new contents that most people would see only the container and neglect the contents. The religious and patriotic Gandhi was adored; the revolutionary Gandhi, calling us to a dedicated and disciplined humanism, was conveniently set aside. Yet once India's political independence was achieved, his leadership of the anti-colonial movement in India was, like his claim of being an orthodox Hindu, a thing of the past, and so his role as social reformer would surely have become ever more important, had he not been assassinated.

We Indians like to regard great people as incarnations of a god and worship them. This has to some extent prevented us from realizing Gandhi's value for the post-Gandhi era. Now we should rediscover and develop those aspects of his work and thought that are most relevant to our social needs. For India is still a land with vast social problems.

She needs today the vital spirit of the ever-growing Gandhi — the one that is still sacrificed, alas, at the altar of the religious and patriotic idol. We say "alas," not only because we are atheists, but also — and more important — because if India had heeded more carefully Gandhi's advice to make religion a purely personal matter and to carry on her social life in an explicitly secular way, she could have solved her worst social problems years ago. But instead, some of her politicians, disregarding this great lesson of Gandhi's, have exploited caste, religion and nationalism for politically selfish purposes, and in the process have corrupted India's cultural fabric and aggravated her social tensions.

Our non-Indian readers may be curious to know to what extent the caste system has crumbled today. A brief answer can be framed in terms of the four basic traditional rules of the caste system: to follow your inherited vocation; to marry within your caste; not to eat together with anyone of lower caste than yourself; and to avoid touching or looking at an "untouchable" if you were not one yourself.

It should be mentioned first that the abolition of caste (including varna and untouchability) was among the reforms advocated in principle by such 19th-century movements as *Brahmo Samaj* and *Arya Samaj* and by Jotiba Gobind Phule (1827-1890, said to have been the first modern person accorded the title "Mahatma"). Indeed, Phule's *Satya Sodhak*

Samaj ("Truth-Seeking Society"), which had a distinct cultural impact in Poona (not far south of Bombay), admitted men and women of all castes and religions. But whether "admission" entailed interdining etc. was another matter, and as far as Indian society in general was concerned, the most that Phule could urge was that untouchables "should have separate schools for them, as they are not allowed to attend the other schools owing to caste prejudices."[193] The time was simply not yet ripe for real progress in bringing down the caste system, and in most instances, for an upper-caste Hindu to be against it was like George Washington (who owned slaves) concurring that "all men are equal." The best that could really be hoped for was to diminish the religious authority of the Brahmins, to promote education for non-Brahmins, and to eliminate certain gross abuses of women such as *sati* (the religiously enforced self-immolation of widows).

The social work of people like Gandhi, Periyar, Ambedkar, Gora and their successors has had, in the context of the general trend toward urbanization and industrialization, a far more penetrating effect on the caste system. Interdining in public places is today the norm throughout India except in a few backwaters, and it is no longer abnormal, not even in a village, to invite someone from a lower caste to dine in your home. Most vocations today can be entered by people from any caste if they have the necessary ability and training. And, to treat

---

193. Keer 1964, 170f.

anyone explicitly as "untouchable" is illegal, and this law has been enforced. However, the old housing patterns remain in the villages, where 70% of the people live. Partly for this reason, and partly because everyone in a village knows everyone else's caste, intercaste marriage is rare in a village. And even in cities, less than 10% of marriages contracted nowadays are intercaste, the exact rate depending on how cosmopolitan the city is.

The Constitution of India specifies that one function of the government is "to promote with special care the educational and economic interests of the weaker sections of the people, and, in particular, of the Scheduled Castes and the Scheduled Tribes" — "scheduled castes" meaning former "untouchables" and their descendents who have remained Hindu and therefore in the same caste. To serve this function, government jobs and university places are apportioned between scheduled and non-scheduled so as to match their current shares of the population at large (which is about 20% "scheduled"). Also, people who were formerly in a scheduled caste or tribe but got out by converting to Buddhism or Christianity (or whose parents or grandparents did so) are among those covered in an apportionment for non-scheduled "weaker sections." (An American would call them disadvantaged.) However, the exact quota for each "weak section" depends not only on its relative size in the general population, but also on how weak (i.e. to what extent disadvantaged) it has officially been found to be. And meanwhile a court ruling has limited the total portion of reservations to 50% of all the university places and government jobs. So now the non-scheduled "weak sections" are vying with one another for allocations within the 30% (= 50% – 20%) which they can together get. This elaborate medicine has been instrumental in destroying the traditional vocational functions of caste, but has meanwhile created a vested interest, among half of the population, in maintaining their cult and caste identity.

The best way to eliminate this noxious vested interest would be to wind down the reservations system gradually over two generations — and meanwhile introduce reservations for *(1)* people who marry intercaste and *(2)* their children.

Apart from this peculiarly Indian problem, many parts of the world are suffering today from a demagogic resurgence of more or less rabid religious fundamentalism. So we have ever more reason to appreciate Gandhi's secularism. And here we may recall the little-known fact that one of Gandhi's closest and most deeply religious followers, Vinoba Bhave, decided in 1955 never again to indulge in any form of public prayer other than the silent, group contemplation of truth, non-violence and compassion.[194]

We would like to mention also the virtue, which Gandhi shared with Gora (and with J. C. Kumarappa, the founder of Gandhian economics), of keeping in mind the need to address

---

194. Lavanam 1995, p. 7. The fact that Vinoba made and kept to this decision has been suppressed in all the accounts (that we have seen) by his religious followers. Nor do most Christians heed Jesus' explicit prohibition of praying in public (Matthew, vi, 5).

at once the social structure and the individual within it. Gandhi wanted to inculcate a sense of self-respect, self-confidence and self-reliance to promote the power of decision-making among the people. He abhored blind following. He wanted that every individual would acquire the capacity to resist the abuse of power. And he regarded village self-sufficiency as an indispensable aspect (along with Hindu-Muslim unity and the eradication of gross social inequalities) of Indian self-rule.

Finally, we would like to call attention to Gandhi's deep yearning, in his maturity, for economic justice. He saw exploitation as the essence of violence, so he insisted on the sharing not only of political power and social respect, but also of economic benefits. He said that in a free India the poor must enjoy the same power as the rich, who must understand that their desires above and beyond the bare necessities were to be accommodated only after the essential needs of the poor were satisfied; a violent and bloody revolution would be a certainty one day unless there was a voluntary abdication — sharing for the common good—of riches and the power that riches gave.

To downplay these important ideas of Gandhi's and to project him instead through soft talk and public prayers and flag-waving will not invite the attention of today's youth. Mahatma Gandhi was a universal human and a social revolutionary. Now that he is beyond nationalism and religion and all the other traditions that he inherited and the fads he cherished, we should take a lesson from his universal secular morality. We should, as he did, actively work for cultural, social and economic reforms, to build better individuals and a more humanistic interaction among them.

APPENDIX

AN OUTLINE OF GANDHI'S LIFE

Northwest India, (Gujarat), 1869-88:

DATE	AGE	
1869		October 2nd: born in Porbandar, a town of *ca.* 70,000 on the northwest coast of India; the youngest child of the prime minister of a small and fairly prosperous Indian state.
1876	7	For the sake of his father's career the family moves 120 miles east to Rajkot.
(sometime)		Impressed by a the drama, *Harishchandra*, extolling truthfulness.
1881		Enters secondary school (English-language).
early 1880s		Is routinely present as his father conducts the bureaucratic and diplomatic work of governing.
1882	12	May 12th: Married to Kasturba; continues to attend school.
1883		With encouragement from a friend, furtively becomes carnivorous, but then resolves to be faithful to his parents' vegetarianism while they live. The family's income is much reduced as his father resigns his post and becomes bed-ridden with an illness.
1885		Experiments with smoking, pilfers some money and a piece of gold jewelry, repents, and is tearfully forgiven by his father.
	15 or 16	Upon his father's death (at 63), feels remorse for having left the bedside a few minutes beforehand in order to lie down with his wife.

(1886) (A few weeks later, their first child is born and dies.)

1888 18 Attends a nearby branch of the University of Bombay, but cannot follow the lectures as they are in advanced English.

(First surviving child, Harilal, born.)

Sails for England (unaccompanied) to study law and thus become qualified by modern standards for a government post such as his father and grandfather had held. (His caste excommunicates him for going abroad.)

England (mainly London), 1888-91:

1888 19 Enrolled as a law student, begins to adapt to British culture (e.g. by taking music and dance lessons) and to waste money, while keeping a vow—made to assuage his mother's anxiety—not to touch wine, woman or meat.

1888-90 Finds a vegetarian restaurant; joins the London Vegetarian Society. Curbs his spending.

Describes England as "the land of philosophers and poets, the very center of civilization."

Reads the Gita (in English), *The Light of Asia*, some books on Theosophy, and much of the Bible. Attends Bradlaugh's funeral.

1891 Licensed to practice British law, sails for Bombay.

India (mainly Bombay and Rajkot), 1891-93:

1891 Learns that his mother has died the year before.

Is introduced to Rajchandra.

(The caste elders at Rajkot, but not those in Bombay, end his excommunication.)

1892 22 In Bombay, fails as a courtroom lawyer; applies unsuccessfully to work as a part-time schoolteacher; quarrels with his wife and sends her back to her parents for a while.

(Second son, Manilal, born.)

Moves to Rajkot and finds work drafting legal documents, but in calling upon the local British political agent, offends him and is forcibly ejected — thus dashing his hopes of a bureaucratic career.

1893 Receives and immediately accepts an offer of employment assisting an Indian-owned business firm in South Africa in some litigation with another Indian-owned firm.

South Africa (mostly), 1893-1914:

1893 23 Sails to South Africa, is subjected to the color-bar in various ways (such as being thrown off a train because he would not leave the first-class seat for which he had a ticket), and resolves to stay and fight it.

1893-94 Studies the Bible, the Koran, Tolstoy's *The Kingdom of God is Within You* and some 80 other books on religion and mysticism; attends Bible classes.

1894 Founds an Indian cultural-political association. Becomes the first Indian allowed to argue legal cases before the local high court.

Persuades the litigants in his big case to submit their case to an arbitrator, who decides in favor of Gandhi's client (thereby initiating his prosperous career as a lawyer in South Africa).

Founds the Natal Indian Congress to struggle for civil rights.

1895 Impressed by the simple life of Trappist monks and nuns.

Writes and publishes *The Indian Franchise: An Appeal to Every Briton in South Africa.*

1896 Sails to India to agitate in behalf of his South African cause; returns to South Africa with his wife and sons.

1897 Upon his return to South Africa is lynched and nearly killed at shore by non-Indians influenced by a false newspaper account of a pamphlet he wrote in India. Declines to prosecute the attackers, but writes about the incident to the appropriate Cabinet secretary in London.

(Third son, Ramdas, born.)

1897 or 98 Quarrels with his wife on account of her opposition to their cleaning the chamber-pot of an "untouchable"-born Christian guest.

1899-1901 In the Boer War, raises and leads an ambulance corps (on the British side) of more than 1000 Indian volunteers; is awarded a war medal.

1900 (Fourth and last son, Devadas, born.)

1901 Returns to India to practice law there and to win support for the cause of Indians in South Africa, e.g. by proposing (successfully) a resolution at a meeting of the Indian National Congress.

1902 Meets Gokhale (his political mentor).

Receives a telegram from Indians in South Africa and returns there.

1903 Founds a political weekly in South Africa, *Indian Opinion* (in four languages).

Begins to learn the Gita by heart.

1904 Reads Ruskin's *Unto This Last* and, deeply impressed, founds Phoenix Settlement — 100 acres in a rural area — with facilities to produce *Indian Opinion* and with a home for the staff and their families.

1905 Delivers four lectures on Hindu religion; is obliged to deny that these were critical of Islam.

1906 Leads the Indian Ambulance Stretcher-Bearing Corps (assisting the British) during the Zulu Rebellion.

36 Vows chastity (with his wife's consent) and introduces rule of chastity at Phoenix Settlement.

September: organizes in Johannesburg a protest meeting where everyone vows to God to fight to death, if necessary, with "passive resistance" against a proposed South African law unjust to Indians.

(This undertaking will prove to be very complex, with many phases, broken promises, beatings, jail terms etc., but with a negotiated compromise settlement in 1914.)

1907 Dissatisfied with the phrase "passive resistance," conducts a contest for a better term: *satyagraha* ("holding on to Truth").

Organizes the first satyagraha campaign.

1908 Jailed; released upon negotiating a verbal compromise with Smuts. Attacked and wounded (for this compromise) by an Indian extremist.

(Smuts does not keep the agreement.)

Organizes another satyagraha campaign.

No longer accepts employment as a lawyer.

Jailed for two months (with hard labor).

1909 Jailed for three months (alone in a narrow cell); visits England for negotiations, which are unsuccessful.

Reads Edward Carpenter's *Civilization, Its Cause and Cure*. On shipboard returning to South Africa, writes *Hind Swaraj* ("Indian Home Rule"), condemning modern Western civilization.

1909-10 Corresponds with Tolstoy.

1910 Establishes (near Johannesburg) "Tolstoy Farm," a self-supporting commune for the families of jailed resisters.

1913 Closes Tolstoy Farm. Fasts (taking only one meal daily) for four months against someone's lapse from the rule of chastity at Phoenix Settlement.

(1913) Satyagraha; jailed; released for negotiations.

1914 Fasts for two weeks against another lapse from chastity at Phoenix Settlement.

Negotiates a written compromise with Smuts; leaves South Africa for England, thence India.

(First World War begins.)

India (mostly), 1915-48:

1915 Establishes Satyagraha Ashram in Gujarat; admits "untouchables."

Travels throughout India (at Gokhale's suggestion), finds extreme poverty.

1916 Declines to participate in Home Rule League, hoping that loyalty during the Great War will induce Britain to grant home rule.

1917 Helps bring an end to the recruiting of Indians to become indentured laborers in South Africa.

47 Campaigns successfully for a modicum of economic justice for peasants on indigo plantations in a remote district of north India. (Arrested and tried, explains in court his role, whereupon the government withdraws its case for the sake of moral decency.)

Indians generally take to addressing him as *Mahatma* ("Great Soul").

1918 Advises striking cotton-mill workers at Ahmedabad (the leading industrial city of Gujarat); arbitrates voluntary settlement.

(1918) Campaigns for peasants in a poor district of Gujarat.

Urges Indians to fight for England in the First World War.

Falls gravely ill; learns spinning during his convalescence.

1919 (Britain grants very little to India in the way of home rule, instead curtailing civil rights even more than during the war.)

Organizes a brief national satyagraha. Fasts against the ensuing violent anti-British protests (saying he made a "Himalayan miscalculation").

Becomes editor of *Young India* and of a similar Indian-language weekly, *Navajivan*.

(British perpetrate massacre at Amritsar and other brutalities.)

1920 Elected president of All-India Home Rule League. Plans and initiates mass Hindu-Moslem satyagraha campaign for Indian independence (predicting success within one year) and for restoration in Turkey of the caliphate.

Founds a university at Ahmedabad.

1921 Launches campaign for everyone to make homespun cotton daily; presides at a bonfire of British-made clothing; resolves to wear henceforth only a loincloth; has his head shaven.

Fasts against anti-British violence in Bombay.

(Mass civil disobiedence; thousands in jail.)

(1921) Invested by Congress with "sole executive authority."

1922 Suspends the satyagraha campaign altogether as he cannot maintain non-violence among some of his millions of ostensible supporters.

Arrested for writing seditious articles in *Young India*; eloquently pleads guilty; sentenced to six years in jail.

52 (Writers in Europe and India (Romain Rolland, Sarojini Naidu) begin to describe his moral stature as comparable with that of Jesus.)

1923 Starts writing *Satyagraha in South Africa*.

1924 Hospitalized; released from jail.

Fasts for three weeks against religious violence.

Chosen president of the Indian National Congress.[195]

1925 Undertakes a year of political silence (yet still urging that everyone spin cotton daily).

Fasts against a lapse from chastity at the ashram.

Starts writing autobiography.

1928 Moves Indian-National-Congress resolution calling for a satyagraha campaign if independence is not granted within a year.

Fasts against a moral lapse at the ashram.

195. For a normal one-year term; but he remained pivotal in its deliberations even after his resignation altogether from the Congress in 1934.

1929		December 31st: moves Congress resolution declaring complete independence as national goal.
1930	60	March: begins anti-salt-tax march to the sea. April: illegally picks up some salt at seashore. May: jailed without trial. (Some 90,000 other satyagrahis are jailed in this year. British methods of torture are described in *Y*, 12/vi.)
1931		Released from jail, reaches hopeful agreement with the viceroy; participates in an unsuccessful "Round Table Conference" in London (where he claims that he and not Ambedkar represents the untouchables). *En route* home, visits continental Europe, meets Romain Rolland.
1932		(Because of Gandhi's consciousness-raising in India, only 1/4 of British cotton exports are now to India, instead of 1/2 as before the war.) January: jailed until 1933. September: fasts to obtain the "Poona Pact" whereby *(1)* a British proposal (supported by Ambedkar) to establish separate electorates for "untouchables" is revised and *(2)* conservative religious leaders say that untouchability will no longer be practiced.
1933		February: founds a new periodical, *Harijan*, to succeed *Young India*. May: released from jail, fasts for three weeks for self-purification. July: disbands Satyagraha Ashram.

(1933) August: jailed but soon released after fasting against a ruling not to grant him the facilities he had previously had in jail for his Harijan work.

64 November: begins an eight-month "Harijan-uplift" tour.

1934 August: fasts for a week to atone for arousing hatred toward religious conservatives.

October: resigns from Congress,[196] launches All-India Village Industries Association.

1935 (In the wake of the "Poona Pact" and with a new administration in London, the British accept a degree of Indian self-rule with provincial elections to be held in 1937.)

Rejects an appeal from Margaret Sanger to sanction birth control.

1936 Makes his home (later named "Sevagram Ashram") in a poor village near Wardha, a town where the Madras-Delhi and Bombay-Calcutta rail lines cross in central India.

1937 (Indian National Congress candidates win most of the provincial elections.)

1938 Upset when his wife attends a temple closed to Harijans.

1939 (Britain declares India to be at war with Germany. The provincial government ministers from the Congress resign *en masse*.)

---

196. The resignation is precipitated when a drafting committee replaces his terms "truthful" and "non-violent" with "legitimate" and "peaceful."

1941 May and again June: fasts against religious strife.

November: devises a campaign of "individual satyagraha" by selected representatives walking unaccompanied to villages and shouting, "It is wrong to help the British war effort with men and money. The only worthy effort is to oppose war with non-violent resistance."

1942 (Japan conquers Burma. Britain proposes that India — after the war if Britain wins — may devise a constitution, provided that every province and princely state may have "full status" of independence from India.)

72 At Gandhi's urging, the Indian National Congress adopts a "Quit India" resolution. The leaders are immediately detained and prohibited from communicating with their followers.

1943 Fasts to protest British allegations that Congress is responsible for the current widespread anti-British violence in India.

1944 (February: his wife dies in detention.)

May: very ill, released from detention.

(June: D-day. August: Paris liberated)

(July: Churchill sends the viceroy "a peevish telegram to ask why Gandhi had not died yet.")[197]

---

197. Wavell 1973, 79. The main point of the telegram was to deny, on grounds of military security, a request from the viceroy to permit famine-relief measures in Bengal.

1945 (Germany and Japan defeated. Churchill voted out of office. The new British administration seeks "an early realization of self-government in India.")

(The leader of the Moslem League, Jinnah, proposes an independent nation with a state religion and with 1/4 of the territory then comprising India.)

1946 Urges "every Brahmin girl" to marry a Harijan; vows to attend only weddings between a Harijan and non-Harijan.

(August, September, October, November: a storm of religious violence, launched by Jinnah, makes inevitable the establishment of Pakistan.)

Fasts for four days to atone for a having caused a misunderstanding in negotiations with the Moslem League.

Undertakes private, super-chastity experiments with young women. ("If I can master this, I can still beat Jinnah.")[198]

November: begins four-month walking tour of violence-torn districts of Bengal to mitigate religious violence there. Praises "Ishwar-Allah" in his daily prayer meetings.

1947 August: on Independence Day, fasts to lament the separation of Pakistan.

September: fasts against religious violence in Calcutta.[199]

198. Green 1993, 375.

1948 78 January 13-18: fasts, in the name of Truth but not of God, to obtain pledges from Hindu leaders to stop the violence against Moslems in Delhi.

January 30: assassinated by a member of a Hindu group opposed to his "pro-Islamic" activities.

---

199. The British viceroy: "In the Punjab we have 55 thousand soldiers and large-scale rioting on our hands. In Bengal our forces consist of one man, and there is no rioting." (*L*, II, 382)

GLOSSARY

Allah "The One." Islamic monotheistic name.

Ashram A more or less secluded place for a community of Hindus leading a life of simplicity and religious practices.

Atman Self. "[Individual] soul."

Avatar "Incarnation." Hindu term for human incarnations of divinity.

Bhakti Relgious devotion.

Bhangi Scavenger. (Collector and disposer of human feces.)

Bramacharya Strong self-discipline. Celibacy.

Brahma "Supreme Spirit." "God the Creator."

Brahmin Member of a priestly caste. Priest.

Dharma Duty.

Gita The *Bhagavad Gita*, a especially venerated Hindu scripture (700 verses long).

Hari Another name for Vishnu.

Harijan "Child of God." Gandhi's term (from 1932) for "untouchables."

Ishwar "[Spiritual] Power." "Supreme God."

Karma "Deed[s]." "Consequences of deeds from one's former life."

Khudai-Raj "God's Kingdom." (Islamic term.)

Mahatma	"Great soul."
Moksha	"Salvation."
Mukti	"Release."
Rahim	"Supreme Compassion" [personified], an Islamic synonym for Allah.
Rama	The name of an ancient Indian king, regarded as a divine avatar.
Ramanama	"The name of Rama" (when recited over and over).
Rama-Raj	"The Rule of Rama." "God's Kingdom" (Hindu term).
Sanatani	Orthodox Hindu.
Sat, Satya	"That which exists." "Truth."
Satyagraha	"Insisting upon Truth."
Swaraj	"Self-rule."
Upanishads	Ancient Hindu scriptures of instruction in the philosophy of the vedas.
Vaishnava	"Vishnu-devotee."
Varnas	"Four [castes]." Four groups of castes.
Varnashrama	The varna-system; and, a theoretical division of life into four stages of development.
Veda	"Knowledge." Very ancient Hindu book.
Vishnu	"God the Sustainer."

WORKS CITED

By abbreviation:

A M. K. Gandhi 1927-29 *An Autobiography, or The Story of My Experiments with Truth* (Ahmedabad)

B B. R. Ambedkar 1979-93 *Writings and Speeches* (12 vols., Bombay)

C [Gandhi] 1958-94 *The Collected Works of Mahatma Gandhi* (100 vols., Delhi)

D C. B. Dalal 1971 *Gandhi: 1915-1948. A Detailed Chronology* (Delhi)

E Pyarelal 1965 *Mahatma Gandhi, the Early Phase* (Ahmedabad)

G Gora 1951 *An Atheist with Gandhi* (Ahmedabad)

H M. K. Gandhi *et al.*, 1933-50 (with interruptions) *Harijan* (Ahmedabad)

I M. K. Gandhi, ed. (in effect) 1903-14 *Indian Opinion* (South Africa)

L Pyarelal 1956-58 *Mahatma Gandhi, the Last Phase* (Ahmedabad)

R *Romain Rolland and Gandhi Correspondence*, tr. R. A. Francis 1976 (Delhi)

S [Gandhi] 1968 *The Selected Works of Mahatma Gandhi*, ed. S. Narayan (6 vols., Ahmedabad)

T D. G. Tendulkar 1962 *Mahatma. Life of Mohandas Karamchand Gandhi* (8 vols., Delhi; 2nd ed.)

Y M. K. Gandhi *et al.*, ed. 1919-32 *Young India* (weekly, Ahmedabad)

Other works:

Horace Alexander 1984 *Gandhi Through Western Eyes* (Philadelphia; 2nd ed.)

Geoffrey Ashe, 1968 *Gandhi* (New York)

Joseph F. Backianadan 1991 *Love in the Life and Works of Mahatma Gandhi* (Delhi)

Balvantsinha 1962 *Under the Shelter of Bapu* (Ahmedabad)

Blavatsky, H.P. 1891 "Civilization and the Death of Art and Beauty," in her periodical, *Lucifer* (May issue)

Nirmal Kumar Bose 1953 *My Days With Gandhi* (Calcutta)

—— 1957 *Selections from Gandhi* (Ahmedabad; 2nd ed.)

—— and P. H. Patwardhan 1967 *Gandhi in Indian Politics* (Bombay)

Judith M. Brown 1990 *Gandhi, Prisoner of Hope* (Delhi)

S. N. Busi 1997 *Mahatma Gandhi and Babasaheb Ambedkar* (Hyderabad)

Tara Chand 1974 *History of the Freedom Movement in India*, Vol. II (Delhi)

Bipan Chandra 1987 *Communalism in Modern India* (Delhi; 2nd ed.)

—— *et al.* 1988 *India's Struggle for Independence* (Delhi)

Chandrashanker: see Shukla

G. N. Das 1996 *Mystic Songs of Kabir* (Delhi)

T. W. R. Davis, tr., 1899 *Dialogues of the Buddha Translated from the Pali*, vol. ii of Max Müller, ed., *Sacred Books of the Buddhists* (Oxford)

Govind N. Deodhekar 1985 "Gora," in Gordon Stein, ed., *The Encyclopedia of Unbelief* (Buffalo), i, 301f

Mahadev Desai 1953 *The Dairy of Mahadev Desai* (Ahmedabad)

—— 1968 *Day-to-day with Gandhi* (Delhi)

R. R. Diwakar, N. M. Ketkar *et al.* 1970 *Mohandas Karamchand Gandhi: A Bibliography* (Delhi)

H. P. Diwedi 1950 *Kabir* (3rd edition, Bombay)

Joseph J. Doke 1909 *M. K. Gandhi* (London)

K. Iswara Dutt [undated] *Congress Cyclopaedia. The Indian National Congress: 1885-1920. Vol. 1. The Pre-Gandhian era* (Delhi)

Albert Einstein, 1944 "Einstein on Gandhi", preface to *Gandhiji: His Life and Work. Published on his 75th birthday, October 2, 1944* (n.p.)

A. T. Embree 1966 *The Hindu Tradition* (New York)

Ludwig Feuerbach 1841 *Das Wesen des Christentums* (Leipzig; edition cited: vol. 5 of Feuerbach's *Gesammelte Werke*, Berlin 1973)

Louis Fischer 1942 *A Week with Gandhi* (New York)

—— 1950 *The Life of Mahatma Gandhi* (New York)

Manubehn Gandhi 1964 *Gandhiji at Delhi* (in Gujarati; Ahmedabad)

M. K. Gandhi 1922 *Ethical Religion*, 2nd ed. (Ahmedabad)

—— 1948-49 *Non-violence in Peace and War* (2 vols., Ahmedabad)

—— 1956 *The Gita According to Gandhi* (Ahmedabad)

—— 1962 *My God* (Ahmedabad)

M. D. Gopalakrishnan 1991 *Periyar: Father of the Tamil Race* (Madras)

Gora, ed., 1949-54, *Sangham* (Vijayawada)

K. P. Goswami 1971 *Mahatma Gandhi: A Chronology* (Delhi)

Martin Green 1993 *Gandhi: Voice of a New Age Revolution* (New York)

Ramachandra Guha 1998 *Verrier Elwin: An Englishman for India* (Delhi)

Stephen N. Hay 1970 "Jain Influences on Gandhi's Early thought," in Sibnarayan Ray, ed., *Gandhi, India, and the World* (Melbourne), 29-38

James D. Hunt 1978 *Gandhi in London* (Delhi)

—— 1986 *Gandhi and the Nonconformists* (Delhi)

M. A. Jinnah 1960-64 *Speeches and Writings* ed. Jamil-ud-Din (Lahore)

C. B. Khairmoday 1972 "Ambedkar, Bhimrao Ramji (Dr.)," in S. P. Sen, ed., *Dictionary of National Biography* (Calcutta), i, 46-49

Dhananjay Keer 1964 *Mahatma Jotirao Phooley: Father of Our Social Revolution* (Bombay)

—— 1971 *Dr. Ambedkar: Life and Mission* (Bombay; 3rd ed.)

S. B. Kher, ed., 1962 *The Law and Lawyers. By M. K. Gandhi* (Ahmedabad)

N. G. S. Kim 1983 "Gandhian Contribution to the Theory of Politics," in V. T. Patil, ed., *Studies in Gandhi* (Delhi), 3-16

Anna Kingsford and Edward Maitland 1890 *The Perfect Way or the Finding of Christ* (London)

K. C. Lang 1985 "Buddhism, Unbelief within," in Gordon Stein, ed., *The Encyclopedia of Unbelief* (Buffalo), i, 74-77

Lavanam, ed. M. Lindley, 1995 *An Autobiographical Account of Lavanam* (Cambridge MA)

Philip McManus and Gerald Schlabach, eds. 1991 *Relentless Persistence. Nonviolent Action in Latin America* (Santa Cruz CA)

R. C. Majumdar 1971 *History of the Freedom Movement in India*, Vol. I (Calcutta)

P. L. Malhotra, ed., 1984 *Nehru: An Anthology for Young Readers* (Delhi)

Joseph C. Manalel 1991 "Bible and Women's Liberation," Vol. xxi, No. 122 of *Jeevadhara* (Kottayam)

Fritz Mauthner 1901 *Beiträge zu einer Kritik der Sprache*, vol. I (Stuttgart)

Mirabehn 1964 *New and Old Gleanings* (Ahmedabad)

Arne Naess 1965 *Gandhi and the Nuclear Age* (Towata NJ)

Mirabehn 1960 *The Spirit's Pilgiimage* (London; 2nd ed., 1984, Arlington VA)

V. S. Naipaul 1990 *India: A Million Mutinies Now* (London)

Bal Ram Nanda 1958 *Mahatma Gandhi: A Biography* (London and Boston)

—— 1973 *Gokhale, Gandhi and the Nehrus: Studies in Indian Nationalism* (New York)

—— 1980 *Jawaharlal Nehru: A Pictorial Biography* (Delhi)

—— 1985 *Gandhi and his Critics* (Delhi)

Anil Nauriya 1995 "Unfolding of Gandhi's Thought: the Undermining of Varna," *Janata* (Bombay), 8/x

—— 1996 "Criticising Gandhi," *Mainstream*, vol. xxxiv, no 8 (27/i)

Jawaharlal Nehru 1950 *An Autobiography*

—— 1948 *Nehru on Gandhi*, ed. Richard J. Walsh (New York; 5th ed.)

—— 1958 *A Bunch of Old Letters* (Bombay)

—— 1960 *The Discovery of India* (Bombay)

—— 1950-64 *Speeches* (four vols., Delhi)

Geoffrey Ostergaard and Melville Currell 1971 *The Gentle Anarchists: A Study of the Leaders of the Sarvodaya Movement for Non-violent Revolution in India* (Oxford)

Bhikhu Parekh 1989 *Gandhi's Political Philosophy: A Critical Examination* (London)

B. N. Pande 1995 *The Hindu-Muslim Problem* (Delhi)

C. N. Patel 1981 *Mahatma Gandhi in his Gujarati Writings* (Delhi)

Robert Payne 1969 *The Life and Death of Mahatma Gandhi* (London)

Periyar 1994 *Religion and Society: Selections from Periyar's Speeches and Writings* (Madras)

H. S. L. Polak *et al* 1949 *Mahatma Gandhi* (London)

M. G. Polak 1931 *Mr. Gandhi the Man* (London)

P. F. Power 1960 *Gandhi on World Affairs* (Washington and London)

R. K. Prabhu 1954 *This Was Bapu* (Ahmedabad)

—— and U. R. Rao 1967 *The Mind of Mahatma Gandhi* (Ahmebadad, 3rd ed.)

B. S. Rao et al. 1968 *The Framing of India's Constitution: A Study* (Delhi)

K. L. Seshagiri Rao 1978 *Mahatma Gandhi and Comparative Religion* (Delhi)

R. V. Rao 1969 *Sevagram: Gandhiji's Ashram and Other Institutions in Wardha* (Sevagram; 3rd ed.)

Baren Ray, ed. 1996 *Gandhi's Campaign Against Untouchability, 1933-34: An Account from the Raj's Secret Official Reports* (Delhi)

Romain Rolland, tr. C. Groth 1924 *Mahatma Gandhi* (London)

E. Royle 1985 "Bradlaugh, Charles," in Gordon Stein, ed., *The Encyclopedia of Unbelief* (Buffalo), i, 65-68

W. M. Salter 1889 *Ethical Religion* (Chicago)

Sumit Sarkar 1983 *Modern India 1885-1947* (Macmillan)

H. W. Schumann 1989 *The Historical Buddha* (Boston)

A. B. Shah, ed. 1965 *Jawaharal Nehru: A Critical Tribute* (Bombay)

J. S. Sharma 1968 *Mahatma Gandhi: A Descriptive Bibliography* (Delhi; 2nd ed.)

Chandrashanker Shukla, ed., 1949 *Incidents of Gandhiji's Life* (Bombay)

Donald Eugene Smith 1963 *India as a Secular State* (Princeton)

K. Sreenivasan 1989 *Sree Narayana Guru* (Trivandrum)

Th. Stcherbatsky 1977 *The Conception of Buddhist Nirvana* (Delhi; 2nd ed.)

K. Swaminathan and C. N. Patel, ed. 1983 *A Gandhi Reader* (Orient Longman)

Govind Talwakar 1997 "Spokesman of the Dumb Millions," forthcoming in a Siddartha College 50th-anniversary commemorative volume (Bombay)

K. N. Tiwari 1988 *World Religions and Gandhi* (Delhi)

D. H. Tribe 1971 *President Charles Bradlaugh, M.P.* (London)

A. K. Warder 1980 *Indian Buddhism* (Delhi; 2nd ed.)

Lord Wavell 1973 *Viceroy's Journal* (Oxford)

E. Zelliot 1972 "Gandhi and Ambedkar—A Study in Leadership," in J. Michael Maher, ed., *The Untouchables in Contemporary India* (Tucson AZ)

INDEX